Decolonial Queering in Palestine

This book provides a vivid account of the political valence of weaving queer into native positionality and the struggle for decolonisation in the settler colonial context of Palestine, referred to as decolonial queering. It discusses how processes of gender and sexuality that privilege hetero-colonising authority shaped and continue to define both the Israeli-Zionist conquest of Palestine and the Palestinian struggle for liberation, thus future imaginings of free Palestine. This account emerges directly from the voices and experiences of Palestinian activists and artists; particularly, it draws on fieldwork with Palestine's most established queer grassroots movement, alQaws for Sexual and Gender Diversity in Palestinian Society, and a variety of artistic Palestinian productions (photography, fashion, music, performance, and video art). Offering a comprehensive and in-depth engagement with the situated context, history, and local practices of Palestinian queerness, scholars, students, and activists across (de)colonial, race, and gender/sexuality studies would appreciate its unique insights; its empirical focus also reaches to those academics in the wider fields of Middle Eastern, anthropological, and political studies.

Walaa Alqaisiya is a Marie Curie Global Fellow working between Ca' Foscari University of Venice, Italy, Columbia University in the City of New York, United States, and the London School of Economics and Political Science, United Kingdom.

Theorizing Ethnography
Series Editors: Elisabeth L. Engebretsen,
EJ Gonzalez-Polledo, and Silvia Posocco

The 'Theorizing Ethnography' book series seeks to reorient ethnographic engagements across disciplines, methods and ways of knowing. By focusing on ethnography as a point of tension between abstract thinking and situated life-worlds, the series promotes ethnographic method and writing as an analytical form that is always partial, open-ended and epistemologically querying.

Against this background, 'Theorizing Ethnography' employs 'concept', 'context' and 'critique' as devices to stimulate creative ethnographic thinking that transects lines of analysis and location. It publishes work that reaches beyond academic, political and life-world divisions, and as such the series seeks to foster contributions from across socially and critically engaged fields of practice.

Contemporary Ethnographies
Moorings, Methods, and Keys for the Future
Francisco Ferrándiz

Trans Vitalities
Mapping Ethnographies of Trans Social and Political Coalitions
Elijah Adiv Edelman

Stories, Senses and the Charismatic Relation
A Reflexive Ethnography of Christian Experience
Jamie Barnes

Queer Word- and World-Making in South Africa
Dignified Sounds
Taylor Riley

Decolonial Queering in Palestine
Walaa Alqaisiya

For more information about this series, please visit: www.routledge.com/Theorizing-Ethnography/book-series/THEOETH

Decolonial Queering in Palestine

Walaa Alqaisiya

LONDON AND NEW YORK

First published 2023
by Routledge
4 Park Square, Milton Park, Abingdon, Oxon OX14 4RN

and by Routledge
605 Third Avenue, New York, NY 10158

Routledge is an imprint of the Taylor & Francis Group, an informa business

© 2023 Walaa Alqaisiya

The right of Walaa Alqaisiya to be identified as author of this work
has been asserted in accordance with sections 77 and 78 of the
Copyright, Designs and Patents Act 1988.

All rights reserved. No part of this book may be reprinted or
reproduced or utilised in any form or by any electronic, mechanical,
or other means, now known or hereafter invented, including
photocopying and recording, or in any information storage or
retrieval system, without permission in writing from the publishers.

Trademark notice: Product or corporate names may be trademarks
or registered trademarks, and are used only for identification and
explanation without intent to infringe.

British Library Cataloguing-in-Publication Data
A catalogue record for this book is available from the British Library

ISBN: 978-1-032-21085-8 (hbk)
ISBN: 978-1-032-22658-3 (pbk)
ISBN: 978-1-003-27358-5 (ebk)

DOI: 10.4324/9781003273585

Typeset in Sabon
by Apex CoVantage, LLC

To beautiful Yousef, may you rest in wonderland, till we meet and walk again.

Contents

Acknowledgements		viii
1	Introduction: Weaving Queer into Decolonisation	1
2	Mapping Hetero-Conquest	21

PART I
Unsettling — 49

3	Native Queer Refusal	51
4	Queering Aesthesis	79

PART II
Imagining Otherwise — 109

5	Towards Radical Self-Determination	111
6	Futural Imaginaries	146
7	Conclusion: Decolonial Queer Beginnings	191

Index	204

Acknowledgements

I am deeply grateful to Silvia Posocco for believing in this project and supporting it from the outset. I am equally grateful to each of the activists and artists who inspired this journey. My heartfelt thanks go to alQaws and the brilliant Haneen Maikey, whose work and analysis on queer decolonisation remain unequalled.

A special mention goes to the institutions that supported the fruition of this book: The Council for British Research in the Levant and the LSE Middle East Centre.

I also wish to thank the Durham Doctoral Studentship and the two supervisors, Chris Harker and Cheryl McEwan, who supported this work in its earlier form some years back as a dissertation.

Many thanks go to academic colleagues, journal editors and mentors who have supported the promotion and/or refining of some of the ideas presented in this book: Eric Hooglund, Mark Griffith, Mikko Joronen, Zeina Zaatary, Sandeep Bakshi, and Suhraiya Jivraj. Thanks to Routledge and to each of the editors of the Theorizing Ethnography book series and to the two anonymous reviewers who supported this project.

Last but not least, deep thanks go to Matteo, Waed, and other friends and family for their support and love.

1 Introduction
Weaving Queer into Decolonisation

اكويرين وكويريات غضبانات للتحرير . وبدنا ثورة شعبية نقضي ع الذكورية

We are angry queers chanting for liberation. We want a popular revolution to destroy patriarchy

On Wednesday the 29th of July 2020, Palestinian queers took to the streets to chant for freedom, liberation, and end of violence against communities. Such a protest, entitled 'A Rallying Cry for Queer Liberation,' was led and organised by Palestine's queer collectives: alQaws for Sexual and Gender Diversity in Palestinian Society and Aswat: Palestinian Feminist Centre for Gender and Sexual Freedoms.[2] Palestinian feminist grassroots collective Tala'at also joined in the call to 'raise our voices against the patriarchal, colonial and capitalist oppressions on our bodies and lives' (alQaws, 2020b: n.p.). Despite the challenging circumstances, including the COVID-19 pandemic restrictions on social distancing, dozens of protestors gathered at Sahit Al Asir in Haifa to raise their voices for freedom and revolution. They beat their drums as they marched while holding Palestinian keffiyeh,[3] rainbow, and Palestine flags along with signs scripted in Arabic saying, 'Our bodies are not to be used as tools for your political gains;' 'We come from all over Palestine;' 'We raise our voice against normalisation with the colonisers;' and 'Would you care to explain how I am meant to be part of a Western conspiracy to stop human reproduction?' The political messages enfolding the protest infused the mix of emotions and affective energies of love, anger, and rejoice protestors carried along with them as they marched rebelliously undeterred by the scrutinising gazes of passers-by and their cameras. The protest was not the first of its kind but was one that certainly marked a significant moment in the history of Palestinian queer organising. It came in the context of a full-on year of heated and relentless debating around the question of gender and sexual diversity in the Palestinian socio-political context, the details of which will be unpacked in the coming chapters of this book. Yet the protest reflected the growing power of the Palestinian queer movement and showed

DOI: 10.4324/9781003273585-1

2 Introduction

unprecedented capacity to mobilise widely to centre the voices and experiences of Palestinian queers.[4] Overall, the event marked a historical moment for the Palestinian queer movement, playing a role in societal transformation that can no longer be ignored or dismissed. This book takes at its core the urgency and need to centre the Palestinian queer cry for liberation, revealing its meanings and significance to the decolonisation of Palestine.

Zionist settler colonisation of Palestine holds at its premise eliminatory power structures vis-à-vis an indigenous[5] Arab Palestinian Other. These power structures are also mired in gendering and sexualising processes, which enable conquest in both its negative (genocidal) and positive (regulatory) forms to continue (Wolfe, 2006). This book engages activists' and artists' work to argue for the necessity of weaving queer into decolonisation, what I term as 'decolonial queering.' It draws on work conducted with Palestine's most prominent queer grassroots organising: alQaws for Sexual and Gender Diversity in Palestinian Society. AlQaws has worked for over two decades to disrupt this 'colonial violence [that] can help us understand how Israel divides, oppresses, and erases Palestinians on the basis of gender and sexuality' (alQaws, 2020a: n.p.). AlQaws's existence has attracted little attention from Arab scholars, including influential Palestinian feminists whose work unravels fundamental connections between gender and the settler colonial context of Palestine (see Jad, 2018; Shalhoub-Kevorkian, 2009; Abdo, 1994). Being a Palestinian woman myself and having grown up in Palestine, I see how the lack of engagement with the work of alQaws, and queer politics in general, reflects a general tide—scholarly and societal—of questioning the relevance of *sexuality* politics to our context. Queer remains a Western conceptual import, which is not only considered irrelevant but also risks recolonising us and imposing Euro-American cultural and political agendas (Massad, 2007). Moreover, suspicion towards sexuality politics, and LGBTQ organising more specifically, stems from views of the Palestinian (homo)sexual as Israelised—that is, in connection to Israelis—and thus a potential collaborator with the enemy; a view that is yet-to-be dismantled (see Alqaisiya *et al*, 2016). Identifying as an open feminist queer space, with explicit attention to LGBTQ issues, alQaws is viewed with a scepticism that dismisses them as bound to Israel, the settler colonial Zionist state, or copies of Euro-America. This book emerges in response to such attitudes that marginalise queer politics and their relevance within Palestine.

By raising the question on decolonial queering, the book engages with some wider debates regarding queer, queering, and what they signify in relation to global formations. In so doing, it argues against the constant measuring of queer in relation to Western and/or mainly American gay liberationist models (Jagose, 1997; Massad, 2007). This book's reading of queer politics in relation to decolonisation corresponds instead to Roy's and Ong's conceptualisation of the process of 'worlding' (2011). Worlding departs from 'the conventional view of the world as spatialised into binary orders,' in which everyday practices are aimed towards alternative social visions or worlds.

Worlding is 'linked to the idea of emergence, to the claim that global situations are always in formation' (Ibid.: 12). A reading of queer Palestinian work through this lens suggests that perhaps it is more constructive to understand queer politics as worlded in multiple ways, affirming 'spatializing practices that mix and match different components' rather than confined strictly to 'a single unified process' (Ibid.). This raises the possibility of 'remapping relationships of power at different scales and localities' (Ibid.). Therefore, this might lead us to understand the worlding of native decolonial queering alongside the worlding of the queer international without assuming either one solely occupies the global dimension from which to make claims.

This book focuses on the worlding of Palestinian native queerness. It invites us to comprehend its value since international scholarly research on Palestinian queer activism remains limited and with little significant empirical work generated from grounded knowledge of local contexts. By contrast, the rise of Israeli pinkwashing narratives, which promote Israel as gay friendly as opposed to homophobic and barbaric Palestine, has garnered attention from scholars who read queer as intersecting with race, sexuality, nationalism, globalisation, terrorism, and mechanisms of state-sovereignty and/or surveillance (Puar, 2011; Hochberg, 2010). Despite the usefulness of shedding light on the transgressive potentialities of Palestinian queerness, thus allowing the Palestinian queer to finally speak (Amireh, 2010), very few scholarly works offer in-depth analysis of the politics and aesthetic productions that puncture the silence on how decolonisation interacts and mutually informs the question of queerness in Palestine.

Palestine, Queer, and Decolonisation

Grounded knowledge in the interweaving of queer and decolonisation allows to complicate the utility of certain approaches to the study of queerness in Palestine. Critical investigations of the question of queerness in Palestine emerged in relation to the broader field of queer studies and its attempt to mobilise 'a broad social critique of race, gender, class, nationality, religion as well as sexuality' (Eng *et al*, 2005). These critiques explore how LGBTQ politics normalise state practices and its dominant relations of power and refer to those state-normalising LGBTQ practices as 'queer liberalism,' drawing on Lisa Duggan's notion of 'homonormativity' (2003). While Duggan charts how queer liberalism in many Western contexts promises the possibility of a 'privatised, depoliticised gay culture' (2003: 50), Jason Ritchie applies her insights to the Israeli context to trace how the rise of a visible gay culture indicates a 'privatised, depoliticised model of homosexuality' (2010: 560). Building on Duggan's concept, Jasbir Puar coins queer nationalism or 'homonationalism' and investigates the collusion of queerness with nationalist Israeli policies in the framework of self-branding as gay friendly, i.e., pinkwashing. Reviewing the literature focusing on the 'rise of the gay equality agenda in Israel [that] is concomitant with increasing repression of the

4   *Introduction*

Israeli state towards Palestinians' (2011: 133), Puar describes pinkwashing as a form of homonationalism:

> The relationship of the rise of gay and lesbian legal rights as well as popular visibility that happens in tandem with increasingly xenophobic policies in regard to minority communities within the nation-state and the Others that threaten the borders of the nation-state from outside— is exactly what I have theorised, within the context of the United States, as well as some European states, as 'homonationalism.'
>
> (Ibid.)

Puar suggests that homonationalism sheds light on queer's 'complicity and contingency with dominant formations,' thus moving away from queering as a political alternative or as that which is 'exclusively as dissenting, resistant, and alternative' (2005: 121). In the introduction to the themed issue 'Queer Politics and the Question of Palestine/Israel,' Gil Hochberg (2010) mobilises a similar approach to queerness. The introduction maps various contributions that explore how queerness complies with dominant structures of oppression and point to the violence in the constitution of the Israeli queer-self qua nation and liberalism. For example, they examine the role of the military checkpoint in shaping 'hegemonic heteronormative and masculinist modes of the nation' in Palestine/Israel (Ibid., 504). The major contribution of those analyses lies in how they scrutinise queer Israeli practices in a critical manner and identify the growing impact of international movements against Israeli pinkwashing considered a form of homonationalism. However, these analyses remain positioned in frames that do not fully account for Palestinian queer grounded knowledge; they obscure the specificity of the native Palestinian condition and the centrality of settler colonialism to understanding Zionist gendered and sexualised governing of Palestinians. One significant limitation entails the adoption of a comparative lens juxtaposing Israel to Palestine, thus Israel/Palestine or Palestine/Israel. This frame, in turn, situates queer Palestinians vis-à-vis queer Israelis in the realm of an ongoing conflict and/or homos for the nation. Hochberg's themed issue identifies queerness as premised on the promotion of a 'politics of coexistence beyond ethnonational and religious borders' (Ibid: 500). Her argument appears to stem from the idea of an ongoing conflict between Israel/Palestine, which reduces the power relations in Palestine to the presence of two equally powerful parties with conflicting 'ethno-nationalist/religious' aspirations. This framing unfortunately betrays a lack of understanding of the settler colonial history of Palestine, which manifests further in how Hochberg reflects on the use of the word Israel/Palestine in the introduction to the issue:

> The use of the slashed name might be problematic, precisely because Palestine does not mark an existing viable national entity, it is nevertheless important, for it keeps the two names, Israel, and Palestine, in

Introduction 5

motion and in relation to each other, refusing to adhere to the partitioned logic of the present political reality.

(Ibid.: 501)

To put Israel/Palestine in motion beyond the partitioned present reality conjures a sense of parity between two equal parties. It fails to consider how a settler colonial structure pursues the ongoing elimination of Palestine, thus imposing its structural unviability. Hochberg's themed issue claims to provide a neutral reading of the history of the conflict or, as she writes, surveys the national divides. I argue that this analysis, on the one hand, fails to grasp the relevance of being *Palestinian* for Palestinian queers. On the other hand, it does not capture the complex positionality of the Palestinian queer vis-à-vis the nation, meaning Palestine. These aspirations for a queer Palestinian national movement, in fact, challenge the premise of homonationalism theorising. While the latter enables a critique directed at forms of Euro-American solidarity with Palestinian queer work, it nonetheless risks situating native decolonial queer aspirations within a problematic juxtaposition of 'homos for Palestine' versus 'homos for Israel' (see Puar and Mikdashi, 2012: n.p.). Overall, analyses of queerness that heavily centres critiques of nation (Puar), as well as that which aims to trump it (Hochberg), fail to grasp the relevance of the national question that Palestinian queer positionality articulates from the very *queered* location of a colonised subject/nation.

The struggle for liberation in Palestine cannot and *should not* be understood within frames reproducing critiques of binaries of national politics. The underlying identification of Palestinian native queerness, in fact, emerges from the day-to-day experiences with a Zionist settler colonial state, which is based on the denial of an Arab Palestinian nation and their belonging to a homeland (*watan*). This denial captures the queered positionality of the native's sense of nationality by virtue of being inscribed within the conditions of forceful *ghurba* (exile). Palestine and Palestinians are caught up in perpetual exile both within the *watan*—due to systematic displacement mechanisms of the settler presence—and outside it as they desperately continue to wait for return.[6] Such a dilemma of perpetual exilic condition captures not only the irreducibility of a general national affiliative sense to the problematique of assimilationist national politics, but it also helps to approach Palestinian sense of home and national affiliation as a space for 'yearning, belonging and radical thinking and becoming' (Shalhoub-Kevorkian and Ihmoud, 2014: 377). Furthermore, critiques of Israeli queer liberalism anesthetise its connection to the history of settler colonialism. They instead lay premise in the contradictory nature of Israeli queer liberalism, highlighting how the ongoing racist and oppressive representation of Palestinians undermines Israeli liberal ideals.[7]

This book argues that to begin from decolonial queering requires having a proper contextualisation of Zionist/Jewish history of settler colonialism. In so doing, one comes to realise how racist representations of Palestinians do not contradict liberal ideals, rather they lay at the core of Israeli liberalism,

6 *Introduction*

re-instantiating its colonial premise. In other words, native grounded queering shows how Israeli liberalism and democracy are always generative of conflicting narratives around Israel/Palestine. Hochberg's issue approaches the discursive circulation of the conflict through an examination of narratives from two national sides that claim 'exclusive ownership of land,' pointing to the theological weight of the conflict and/or revealing native status of the Palestinian inhabitants (501). The same native Palestinian inhabitant would reject such a purported objective surveying of conflicting narratives because it risks allowing all these narratives to lay the same truth claims to conflict. Thus, it equates a settler colonial approach to any other discourse (i.e., the theological weight of the conflict). This approach not only reproduces the amnesia of settler colonialism for the native Palestinian but also leads to problematic framings of queerness. For example, the emancipatory power of queerness is now identified in how queer Palestinians and Israelis should come together to rise above both continued colonisation of Palestinian lands and denial of Palestinian existence and their right of return to their homelands. Consequently, such an approach discloses the temporal inadequacy in accounting for settler colonial racism that is sometimes enabled within critical frames of queer liberalism. This applies to Ritchie's conclusion on how the 'racialised Arab emerges as the most salient and dangerous other at the moment the homosexual, once the nation's sexual other, gains increasing acceptability' (2010: 556). Without grounding Israel's liberal and democratic values into its settler colonial history, critiques of queer liberalism offer a simplistic understanding of colonial racism toward Palestinians. By centring queer in the question of settler colonialism, it becomes possible to interrogate the temporal dimension of those analyses without obscuring how the creation of Israel was premised on racism toward Palestinians.

Similar problems emerge from homonormativity and homonationalism critiques and frameworks. Relying on Duggan's notion of homonormativity, Puar's homonationalism challenges queer visibility regarding oppression perpetuated against 'minority communities within the nation-state' (Puar, 2011: 135). Similarly, Hochberg's issue speaks of 'tracing the ties that inevitably links the oppression of sexual minorities to the oppression of other social minorities' (2010: 495). By framing Palestinians as a social minority, this approach risks ignoring systematic minoritisation of a native other: i.e., a structure of systematically reducing Palestinians to minorities including via ethnic cleansing, denial of return, and the demographic policies of a Jewish majority (see Salamanca *et al*, 2012; Gordon and Ram, 2016). Sidestepping the indigene's historical location, these frameworks fail short of accounting for settler colonialism, refusing to define Palestinian queerness as a social minority within the Jewish/Zionist entity. By contrast, there are studies positing settler colonialism as the basis of the formation of modern queer national subjects, what Scott Lauria Morgensen calls settler homonationalism (2010, 2013), and comparing queer Palestinians and Two-spirit (North American indigenous) people. Such analyses, however, do not capture how

Introduction 7

native queering challenges aspects of the theory of homonationalism. In fact, this approach mainly stems from the positionality of queer white settlers (Morgensen, 2014) whereby the analytical and political investment appears to be in white settler responsibility to respond to their location and proximities to settler sexualities. One must ponder whether native Palestinian queers face the same conundrums of queer modernity and/or (homo)nationalisms that white settlers in North America face today.

The main aim of this book is to offer in-depth analyses based on empirical and theoretical interventions from within the situated context, history, and internal practices of Palestinian queer work. Consequently, it reveals the inadequacy of applying theoretical frameworks that have evolved within North America's queer, albeit critical, trajectories and end up reproducing the analytical primacy of Anglo-American epistemes (Allouche, 2020). Mikdashi and Puar (2016) challenge the hegemonic formation of queer theory in relation to the global hegemony of the United States, proposing instead an engagement with Middle East area studies and/or Global South that should not collapse to US epistemic frames. In the same article, they propound a vision of queer theory in relation to homonationalism critique that should *by now* help queer theory—ala Middle East/area studies—transcend common fixation on gendered and sexual injury or subject. They ponder:

> Does queer theory (*still*) [emphasis added] require a sexual or gendered body or a sexual or gendered injury—particularly if part of the project of homonationalism is to produce and stabilise transnational, imperial, and settler colonial forms of sexual and gendered injury?
>
> (2016: 220)

In centring Palestinian queer work and injured subjects, this book shows that to seriously take Palestine as a site for queer theorising means to challenge the analytical problems that queer carries, which wind up reproducing US centrality even when it aims to undo such epistemological biases. Puar and Mikdashi's frustration with queer Middle East stuck-ness in the reproduction of identities—i.e., 'still requiring sexual or gendered body'—resonates with the very progression in Western theory from queer as identity to a deconstructive critique. In centring the plight of the indigenous queer body, this book gestures towards a theory of decolonial queering as emerging to reveal and work against the historical continuity of what I call Zionist hetero-conquest. In doing so, it challenges the very binarism of subject/subjectless that is characteristic of debates within queer Western scholarship. To identify a scope of native queering that is tantamount to decolonisation means to challenge queer critiques' investment in queer as liberal, nationalist, right-winger, and/or settler. While the scope of these frames identifies and challenges queer theorising as it emerges in relation to dominant structures (homonationalist, liberal, and/or settlers), the analytical scope of this book proposes the exact opposite. It preserves queer-ing/ed in all its

8 Introduction

forms (noun, verb, adjective) to indigenous struggle to decolonise from a gendered/sexed and racialised/classed positionality. Thus, it not only argues for the transgressive possibilities that a queering and/or the queered native subject enables but also advocates for theoretical and methodological foregrounding of decolonial queering. In other words, to start from the sexual and gendered injured indigene body entails mapping that body in relation to the web of queer*ed* bodies linked to native geo-temporal *dis*location within the structure of hetero-conquest. Therefore, as the analysis of alQaws's work and the aesthetic examples will reveal in the coming pages, the injured indigene body does not collapse to the problematics of identity that deconstructive queer critiques aim to challenge in relation to conundrums of homonationalism and/or queer liberalism. This corresponds to the fact that queer native body is located within the realm of wretchedness and nonbeing (Fanon, 1963). Hence, unlike the need to overcome the collapse to identity (queer as a noun), it is rather always already queered form the start. The book locates native's sexual and gendered injury in relation to overall colonised queered condition within the historical continuity of the settler colonial present, thus digging also for indigenous queering methodologies that initiate new possibilities. Decolonial queering, therefore, is the labour that indigenous queering activists, LGBTQ+, feminists, artists, designers, and thinkers initiate for the purpose of unsettling hetero-conquest. They do so by virtue of generating other possibilities, including the very initiation of a native emancipated self, beyond Nakba.[8] Decolonial queering departs from the sole investment in a deconstructive critique, rather it is firmly aligned with a decolonial approach in its aim to reconstruct and build possibilities for native healing and resurgence.

The mapping of queer into decolonisation that is at the heart of this book also widens and extends debates about queer vis-à-vis decolonisation theories and politics. Decolonisation in this book proceeds from an understanding of settler colonial processes (Wolfe, 2012) and the queered positionality of the indigene Other vis-à-vis processes of sexual and racial normalisation that define settler colonialism (Finley, 2011: 35). From the point of view of those undergoing decolonisation, queering is a struggle against those settler colonial power structures privileging patriarchy and heterosexuality, and thus hetero-colonialism (Driskill *et al*, 2011; Arvin *et al*, 2013). Decolonisation enfolds queering—and vice versa—as it tries to unsettle the material and symbolic paradigms enforcing continued colonisation of native bodies, lands, and desires. Queer indigenous politics encapsulate the dissent lines seeking to 'disrupt external and internalised colonialism, heteropatriarchy, gender binaries and other forms of oppression' (Driskill *et al*, 2011: 19). By understanding the role 'colonial heteropatriarchy' (Ibid.) plays in the question of colonised liberation, we can foreground the necessity of queer dissonance to decolonisation and the meaning(s) of liberation. Decolonisation means imagining beyond the naturalisation of social hierarchies, including sexual and gender binaries, that

Introduction 9

the settler colonial presence imposes (Lugones, 2010). For these reasons, it is important to identify decolonial queering in relation to the politics of refusal and remapping charted by native feminisms to identify forms of indigenous resurgence beyond the structures of the settler colonial state (Simpson, 2014; Goeman, 2013).

The search for indigenous resurgence underpinning the inquiry on decolonial queering emanates from the injured positionalities of those working to delink and heal from the settler colonial wound (Mignolo and Nanibush, 2018). In theorising delinking, Mignolo draws on the work and thinking of Frantz Fanon, identifying the geared sensibility of the colonised to undo settler encroachment on and wounding of the native's subjecthood (in Gaztambide-Fernández, 2014). In the strive to heal from the colonial violence perpetuating its injury, decolonial queering also interacts with the politics of queer disorientations put forth by Sarah Ahmed (2006). Queer disorientations, as Ahmed describes them, mark deviations from proscribed lines of orientations, thus power structures and their re-instantiation within abiding subjects. For example, she discusses how heterosexuality marks a continuation of patriarchy, while orientalism and racism generate an orientation around whiteness and histories of empire. Ahmed's theorising is useful when approaching queer in relation to coloniser/colonised dynamics (Fanon, 1967) and the reproduction of colonised orientations to the very processes allowing the continuity of their subjugation. Moreover, the Otherwise Imaginings that this book navigates in the form of politics and aesthetic productions of decolonial queering resonate with the 'future possibilities that queering enfolds beyond the here and now' (Muñoz, 2009). José Esteban Muñoz (Ibid.) charts the significance of queer investment in politics and relationality via the aesthetic work of queer of colours striving for queerness as a utopian political project. This book takes at its core the task of documenting the utopian possibilities that queer Palestinian work enables as it sits at the intersection of 'the traditional and the modern' (Grosfoguel, 2011: 17), thereby challenging nation-statist idealisation of pure and authenticated precolonial past and/or postcolonial future.

To map queering in relation to decolonisation means to investigate how Palestinian queer thinking and praxis challenge the re-inscription of colonial modalities of power in Palestinian strive for liberation. In other words, decolonial queering troubles any attempt to decolonise Palestine that re-instantiates the very paradigms of its subjugation. Decolonial queering builds on the accumulative work of indigenous feminist theorising activating reimaginings of lands and bodies, particularly in relation to projects of national liberation and/or indigenous projects of sovereignty. Mishuana Goeman contends that practices of remapping lead native nations to 'rethink spatializing and organising our communities around heteropatriarchal structure of nation-state model' (2013: 37). Similarly, Jennifer Nez Denetdale (2009) and J Kēhaulani Kauanui (2018) argue that native nationalism

10 *Introduction*

relies on traditionalist views that only reinforce homophobic and masculinist presumptions, thus replicating the exclusionary methods of the US settler colonial state model. Palestinian feminist analyses critically question national narrations of authentic Palestinian identity and set of relations that sever Palestinian emancipation (Jad, 2011, 2018; Abdulhadi, 1998), calling instead for an analytics and praxis of homing that is enabling of Palestinian becoming (Shalhoub-Kevorkian and Ihmoud, 2014).

Furthermore, in bringing activist and artistic works together, the book emphasises the role of the aesthetic, underscoring the value of sensory experiences to the enquiry into decolonial queering. My understanding of aesthetics in relation to politics draws on the work of Jacques Rancière arguing that the regime of aesthetic entails the distribution of sense, which is inherently connected to the ways in which the 'police' regime organises the hierarchical orderings of 'sense' (Rancière, 1999, 2004). Shalhoub-Kevorkian (2016) brings attention to the often-forgotten regime of 'occupying the senses' in Palestine by showing the necessity of examining the aesthetic dimensions of settler colonial domination. As such, feminist enquiries into settler colonialism should also tap into the sensory and embodied means of practicing control, which involve management of language, sight, sound, time, bodies, and spaces of its subjects (Ibid.). This exploration of the sensory dimension of settler colonial domination permits us to engage with the relevance of the aesthetic when thinking native resurgence. The aesthetic productions that this book explores, ranging from photography, video and performance art, caricatures, songs, and fashion design, engage the queering dimension to artistic productions. They go beyond traditional examination of forms of Palestinian aesthetics (e.g., Dabkeh[9] dance, kuffieh[10] wearing) to explore the relevance of the sensual, emotive, and embodied to reimagining Palestine's futurity. Therefore, they demonstrate the relevance of re-emerging as a decolonial queering *aesthesis* (Mignolo and Vazquez, 2013; Mignolo interviewed by Gaztambide-Fernández, 2014), one that shifts away from colonial modes of sensing as it gestures towards making room (Ahmed, 2010) for imagining Palestine *Otherwise*.

Decolonial queering maps those Otherwise Imaginings and the impact they have not only on an ongoing struggle for decolonisation and liberation, but also on advancing queer indigenous knowledge and theories that challenge the legacies of colonialism in research (Tuhiwai Smith, 2012). In its focus on unpacking meanings of queer as emerging from the specificity of Palestinian positionality and context, this inquiry contributes to advancing the intellectual sovereignty of indigenous knowledge. Indeed, indigenous queer critique is grounded in how 'the decision to exercise intellectual sovereignty provides a crucial moment in the process from which resistance, hope and most of all imagination issues' (Driskill *et al*, 2011: 8). Therefore, the conceptual tools articulating the weaving of queer into decolonisation that this book outlines further link to the methodological basis of a decolonial ethnography upon which it stands.

A Decolonial Ethnography

The decolonial queering stories that this book navigates emanate from ethnographic work done with the group alQaws for Sexual and Gender Diversity in Palestinian Society since 2012 up to the present.[11] In 2012, I met for the first time with alQaws's founder and now former director,[12] Haneen Maikey, and began to participate in some of its spaces and workshops in the West Bank. Being part of alQaws's spaces and activities enabled me not only to formulate connections with people whose work continues to inspire me in many ways, but it taught me first-hand why decolonial methodologies matter. AlQaws activists rightly have a suspicious and highly cautious approach to Western-based researchers. This attitude stems from how researchers often failed to seriously take Palestinian queer activism as a site for theory that does not or, rather, *should not* necessarily fit the interpretive machinery of Western—including leftist and critical—theory. During my participation at a panel with other alQaws members in 2015, Omar reflected in relation to the Massad critique saying: 'If Massad had bothered to come and talk to us, he would have seen that we agree on many things.' This book proceeds from the value of what Omar postulated; that is, having talked to the people who are at the centre of its inquiry. To do so, however, is not a simple act of performing a unilateral or a superficial conversation whereby the so-called researchers proceed from their *own* need to collate data and produce what qualifies as legitimate research. Linda Tuhiwai Smith writes profusely about the need to challenge those very legitimate frameworks often inscribed in reproducing dominant and colonising worldviews (2012). Writing from an indigenous and critical feminist perspective, Tuhiwai Smith posits how decolonising research is concerned with the need to develop 'a more critical understanding of the underlying assumptions, motivations and values that inform research practices' (50). Approaching one's 'participants,' therefore, for talking is not a simple process, rather is one that requires the capacity to actively *engage* for the purpose of attending to 'a theory from the South or below,' one whose purpose is to centre the voices and analytical reflections of local conceptions of realities (Comaroff and Comaroff, 2012). My engagement with alQaws spaces did not simply mean 'involvement' (Mctaggart, 1991) but rather paved the way for a collaborative mode of engagement 'explicitly oriented towards social change' (Kindon *et al*, 2009: 90). Such a mode entailed what is called participatory-action research, where research produces knowledge *with* rather than *on* people. In this regard, I was invited to participate alongside other activists at local (e.g., alQaws Sexuality School, Beit Jala) and international events (e.g., anti-pinkwashing event, London). The creation of knowledge about alQaws *with* alQaws also took place by writing a collaborative piece with two of its members where we identify 'as Palestinian activists and academics who are committed to engaged analyses and praxis towards decolonizing gender and sexuality in our communities' (Alqaisiya *et al*, 2016: 125).

12 Introduction

My insider positionality as a Palestinian woman not only enabled my participation to alQaws spaces but also shaped the principal location of this inquiry as a journey *about home*. To write about home means to acknowledge one's situatedness in the world, challenging the omnipresent, all-seeing, and conquering gaze of what Haraway defines 'god trick,' a way of seeing the world from the 'unmarked positions of Man and White' (1988: 581). Such an objective or impartial view of research, in fact, coheres well with an 'objectificationist' (Alonso Bejarano *et al*, 2019) or as Ndlovu-Gatsheni described: research as hyphenated to indicate undressing others to the level of nakedness (2017: n.p.). Ethnography on indigenous peoples carries this legacy of dirtiness and colonial researching through imperial eyes (Tuhiwai Smith, 2012: 91). My own field encounter with other researchers who felt a thrill about uncovering sexual taboos in Palestine and/or the hidden lesbian scene in the city of Hebron[13] showed me how much research continues to be immersed in this imperial worldview. This book echoes Simpson's call for a need to re-evaluate the urge for ethnographic detail that fails to acknowledge 'the asymmetrical power relations that inform the research and writing about native lives and politics' (2014: 105). In doing so, it centres the significance of an *ethnographic refusal*, corresponding to the need to attend to 'an ethnographic calculus of what you need to know and what I refuse to write' (Ibid.).

Both my ability to scrutinise ethically such imperial worldviews, along with this inquiry's investment in centring the decolonial dimension to the question of queerness, stems from my positionality as a Palestinian. In fact, my own field experience was marked by certain research limitations related to my West-banker 'Green ID,' which prevented me from accessing geographical spaces that a Western researcher would have the power to navigate easily. Therefore, it is important to go back to Linda Tuhiwai Smith's definition above on how decolonising methodologies are based on 'a more critical understanding of the underlying assumptions, motivations and values that inform research practices.' While a lack of accessibility to data would qualify as a limitation, a true understanding of this book in relation to its embodied native location and motivations would underscore its richness. This is further exemplified by how the unleashing of another Zionist atrocity in the summer of 2014 shaped this research. During that time, when Israel brutally aggressed and bombed Gaza for 51 consecutive days, both I and my research were simply paralysed. My identity as field-researcher was put aside, while I dealt with immense sorrow, anger, anxiety, insomnia, and endless political discussions. The scale of the violence and the unfolding tragedy not only placed practical and physical limitations on my research, due to the imposition of harsher travel restrictions by the settler colonial authority, but it also triggered grave emotional and psychological distress. The emotional burden of being home and witnessing yet another large-scale act of violence, our continuous Nakba, created a huge crisis in relation to the research and its utility: *the subaltern will not, ever, be able to speak* (Field diary, 2014).

Ironically, it was during these times of feeling utter defeat and rage, reaching a point of wanting to 'quit it all,' that forced me to understand better that the real motivation of this journey about home was/is to *arrive home, somehow*. Writing down my autobiographical reflections became a vessel for channelling not only my fears, frustrations, and anger[14] but also my/our relentless need for hope: 'I believe in change, it just takes time and needs an awful lot of persistence and patience,' as Haneen once said. Through these difficult times, I realised my proximity to the people I had met within alQaws spaces, as we would watch the news together and, at times, join in spontaneous protests down the street. The conversations that I had with activists and artists: face to face, online chats, and phone calls supplemented the active engagement with written/visual material productions of theirs as well as the willingness to continue these conversations up to this moment.

My engagement within alQaws spaces has led me to see the central role that art plays in activist spaces. AlQaws not only conducts projects that involve collaborations with artists from across Palestine, but a lot of its individuals are artists themselves or feel inspired by certain artwork that represent decolonial queering. Each individual artwork that this book engages is based on conversations conducted with the artists. Thus, the analysis is based on their own view of what their work does but also, in some instances, on how other activists see and interpret it. Overall, the book is based on both active engagement and listening to the perspectives of those involved. Active listening requires humility and capacity to learn from the real theorists in the field, thus the activists and artists that this book engages with are their own ethnographers, writers, thinkers, and creative inventors. *It is them* who, on a day-to-day level, daringly employ scientific inquiry and the will of the imagination to produce knowledge and something of value about themselves for themselves and their/our communities. This book, therefore, does not want to attempt to be the basis upon which communities were enabled for a better future. To say so is to be oblivious to the very limitations and intwined problems with which it is engraved: linguistic barrier and the writer's Western-based institutional location. The book's simple task is to share with the reader the power and will of the decolonial queer theorising and praxis enabled by the plethora of Palestinian activists and artists who are taking the lead on bettering Palestine and its decolonial queer future.

A Note on Sexual Identity

This book's decolonial ethnographic framework tallies with its approach to queering from a native-centred positionality. That is, the queer positionalities and or sexual and gendered injuries at the core of the book do not necessarily collapse to the very problematics of identity markers that Western queerness grapples with. As Omar noted in the same panel with an answer to one of the questions posed by the audience regarding the usage of labels, including queer, that correspond to Western ones: 'Yes, but queer and/or

14 *Introduction*

LGBTQ in the context of Palestine means something else. They enfold a totally different subject.' It is therefore important to remind the reader—especially those well-versed in the Anglo-American production of LGBTQ identities—that while these labels[15] are sometimes used to frame the work and self-definitions of activists, this book does not undertake the task of *revealing* to its readers the sexual identities of individual activists and artists. To do so means to fix the Palestinian queer subject(s) to the very power paradigms they are trying to battle. These power paradigms range from pinkwashing policies' production of the Palestinian homosexual that Israel ought to save to international LGBT organising fixation with questions, such as 'Who is the real Palestinian queer?' 'Are Palestinian queers oppressed like us?' 'Can we identify with Palestinian queer struggle?'[16]

This book, therefore, is not about doing the work of un-closeting, hence revealing 'the true' sexual identities of its subjects. That is not to say that the book will deny the right of individuals to share their sexual orientations in contexts where they opt to do so. As the reader will see throughout the book, there will be moments where activists' names—along with sexual identity—is shared in lieu of their own desire to assert these identifications. At the same time, the book's overall interest does not lie in revealing anthropological insights about sexual lives of Palestinians, which adheres to the approach of researching through imperial eyes. This also applies to the author's own ambivalence about declaring a sexual identity to the reader. Such an ambivalence derives from having accessed and worked within alQaws spaces without being conditioned to define my sexual identity. Yet it also bespeaks a refusal to declare that emanates from the violent projections I have faced first-hand within Western, particularly white, LGBTQ spaces. This book proceeds from the need to prioritise the value and significance of Palestinian queer collective work, which nonetheless ties with individual lives and embodied positionalities within the specific situations of decolonial queering.

Chapter Outlines

The following Chapter 2 sets to contextualise the historical continuity of what I term as hetero-conquest in Palestine. The chapter's focus and scope of analysis corresponds to the very need to anchor queering into decolonisation by foregrounding the settler colonial context that defines Palestinian Nakba. The chapter is divided into two main parts. The first part historicises Zionist project's production of a sex/gender system that correlates with the temporal and spatial constituents of conquest. The second part of the analysis is concerned with exploring how Palestinian struggle for liberation—from the First Intifada to the present reality of the Oslo peace accord era—re-instantiate hetero-conquest. Overall, the chapter's novelty lies in centring the lens of gender and sexuality to historicising Palestine's settler colonial present. Its unpacking of the political/aesthetic frameworks infusing hetero-conquest enables the reader to follow on the significance of decolonial

Introduction 15

queering works as shown in the rest of the chapters, which are divided across two themes: Unsettling (Part I) and Imagining Otherwise (Part II).

Part I: Unsettling

Chapter 3 analyses alQaws's activism, the story of its emergence and ongoing work in order to show the relevance of decolonial queering politics in challenging and unsettling paradigms of hetero-conquest. It starts by focusing on the emergence and evolution of alQaws's positionality as a queer and Palestinian grassroots movement, which rejects both Israeli LGBT spaces and Western frames of gay organising. It outlines how its anti-pinkwashing work not only questions Israeli narratives of gay progressiveness versus Palestinian homophobia but also reveals the complicit role of international actors in reproducing such colonising hierarchies. Queer Palestinian calls for boycott and anti-normalisation work challenge essentialising critiques around the Gay International as well as some strands of homonationalism-centred critiques. Overall, the chapter reveals how Palestinian queer activism offers strategies and analyses of value to the politics of native queer refusal.

Chapter 4 examines the work of several artists: Nadia Awad's cinematic lens, Alaa Abu Asad's photography and video art, Tariq Knorn's performance art, alQaws's activist/artist musical tracks, and the story of the late dancer Ayman Safiah. Through an engagement with these artists and their work, I unpack the value of a queering aesthesis, which seeks to enunciate a politics of native sense that queers and interrupts the aesthetic-political field of settler colonial encroachment on the native's being. Such politics, I argue, function on multiple levels: first, it challenges the Zionist configuration of sex and sense, where the projections of sexual pluralism and moral superiority of Israeli humanist values coalesce. Second, it articulates the native's bodily ways of doing, being and enunciating epistemologies for revival and life. In doing so, it grounds the willingness to challenge the native's own political imaginary as it succumbs to the imperatives of a settler sensual regime bent on instilling the native's *ghurba* (exile) from her land, (hi)stories, and desires.

Part II: Imagining Otherwise

Chapter 5 analyses alQaws's role in decolonising *from within* and demonstrates how its local practices aim to offer an alternative vision of free Palestine, thus imagining otherwise. The chapter unpacks the underexplored dimension of internalised pinkwashing, showing how activists' critical engagement with this concept reflects the work of decolonisation that Palestinian queers lead in the local context of Palestine. Internalised pinkwashing is symptomatic of colonised re-instantiation—on subjective and objective scales—of the very hierarchies of hetero-conquest. The chapter examines the significance of alQaws's decolonial queering work in relation to healing from the colonial wound. It traces everyday decolonial queering practices aimed

16 *Introduction*

at decolonising desire, building communities, and rebuilding the homeland. The exploration of activist modus operandi reveals the significance of alQaws's work as it offers a channel for queering Palestine's futurity.

Chapter 6 provides an analysis of the role of Palestinian queer artistic productions play in distributing futural imaginaries of decolonial queering. It starts by examining alQaws's *tarwiha* narratives, which activate the value of the emotive and affective to crafting alternate conceptions of Palestinian selfhood, going beyond the strictures of hetero-conquest. The chapter then draws on Tarik Knorn's artistic productions and their role in provoking a political message, which is grounded in decolonising sexuality and carving anti-capitalist consciousness against 'La La Land' hyper-consumption reality. It finally engages Omar Ibin Dina's *zey al tashrifat* to reveal the role of fashion design in queering processes of male- and state-making, thus opening up room for other fabrications to predominant gendered and sexual scripts of Palestine's futural imaginaries. The main contribution of these artistic practices lies in how they channel imaginaries that enfold conceptions of subjectivities and the space and time of sociality that remain obscured within prevalent understandings of what Palestinian freedom entails.

Chapter 7 evaluates the significance of decolonial queering politics in Palestine. It presents three theses with a twofold aim: first, to capture the value of the analysis on the activism/art presented in previous chapters; and second, to examine theoretical and empirical implications of decolonial queering across the fields of Palestine and Middle East studies, queer and feminist theories, and the politics of decolonisation. The overall goal of this chapter is not simply to conclude but also to pave the way for beginnings *to come*. The examination of the politics and aesthetics of decolonial queering is a small contribution within the wider community of activists, artists, and scholars who are committed to imagining decolonial queer possibilities and the meanings they bear for the future of the world.

Notes

1 Chants in Arabic from the protest 'A Rallying Cry for Queer liberation' which was held on 29 July 29 2020. See Facebook Link: www.facebook.com/ 550374051685982/videos/751220839054738 (Accessed 29 May 2020).
2 See Facebook call to protest: www.facebook.com/events/2587890398126558/ (Accessed 29 May 2020).
3 Palestinian traditional scarf chequered in white and black and is a symbol for Palestinian national struggle for liberation.
4 Link to video campaign: www.facebook.com/550374051685982/videos/ 210493773677942 (Accessed 29 May 2020).
5 I use indigenous, indigene and native interchangeably throughout the book.
6 This is seen in the abundance of Palestinian cultural productions on *ghurba*, capturing the ephemeral exilic condition of Palestine and Palestinians.
7 In this regard, Jason Ritchie (2010: 559) indicates how 'Israel is perpetually caught between an assemblage of racist discourses and practices, which limits

Introduction 17

membership in the nation and its rights and benefits to Jews, and liberalism, which in turn posits the equality of all the state's citizens, including its Palestinian minority.' See Ritchie, 'How do you say come out of the closet in Arabic.' Similarly, Rebecca Stein (2010: 521) identifies Israel's gay decade in the 1990s as contradictory because recognition for gays came with further oppression toward the Palestinians. See Stein (2010) 'Explosive Scenes from Israel's Gay Occupation.'
8 Arabic word for catastrophe. It marks the creation of the Zionist state.
9 Palestinian traditional folk dance.
10 Palestinian national scarf.
11 Due to Covid-19 pandemic, engagement with alQaws's activism has taken the form of online ethnography.
12 A new director named Haneen Sader has taken over since December 2020.
13 During conversations I had with a French and an American researcher in 2013.
14 As Audra Simpson reminds, 'ethnography in anger can have a historically and politically productive effect' (2014: 119).
15 Including the Arabic words such as *mithli* and *mithliyah* (for homosexuality) took place against the presence of other derogatory terms such as *shadh* (pervert).
16 The implications behind the question to Omar, but also this dynamic revealed itself in solidarity activist visits to Palestine.

Bibliography

Abdo, N., 1994. 'Nationalism and Feminism: Palestinian Women and the Intifada—No Going Back?,' in *Gender and National Identity: Women and Politics in Muslim Societies*, edited by V. M. Moghadam. London: Zed Books and Oxford University Press.

Abdulhadi, R., 1998. 'The Palestinian Women's Autonomous Movement: Emergence, Dynamics, and Challenges.' *Gender & Society* 12(6): 649–673.

Ahmed, S., 2006. *Queer Phenomenology: Orientations, Objects, Others*. Durham, NC: Duke University Press.

Ahmed, S., 2010. *The Promise of Happiness*. Durham, NC: Duke University Press.

Allouche, S., 2020. 'Seven Analytical Recommendations for the (Un)Queer-(y)ing of the Middle East.' *Kohl: A Journal for Body and Gender Research* 6(1): 31–37.

Alonso Bejarano, C., Lopez Juarez, L., Mijangos Garzia, M., and Goldstein, D., 2019. *Decolonizing Ethnography: Undocumented Immigrants and New Directions in Social Science*. Durham, NC: Duke University Press.

Alqaisiya, W., Hilal, G., and Maikey, M., 2016. 'Dismantling the Homosexual Image in Palestine,' in *Decolonizing Sexualities: Transnational Perspectives, Critical Interventions*, edited by S. Bakshi, S. Jivraj, and S. Posocco. London: Counterpress.

alQaws, 2020a. 'Analysis Paper.' *alQaws for Sexual and Gender Diversity in Palestinian Society*. Available at: www.alqaws.org/articles/Beyond-Propaganda-Pinkwashing-as-Colonial-Violence?category_id=0&fbclid=IwAR0ba1z3ydkTUxJnGy97gBzcA qIKP6O7NbcA29F0_qKh2Kar8eend74Bx_s (Accessed 29 April 2020).

alQaws, 2020b, 29th July. 'Press Release: Queer Palestinians Gather in Haifa Calling for Safety and Liberation.' *alQaws for Sexual and Gender Diversity in Palestinian Society*. Available at: www.alqaws.org/news/Queer-Palestinians-gather-in-Haifa-calling-for-safety-and-liberation?category_id=0 (Accessed 29 April 2020).

Amireh, A., 2010. 'Afterword.' *Journal of Lesbian and Gay Studies* 16(4): 635–647.

Arvin, M., Tuck, E., and Morrill, A., 2013. 'Decolonizing Feminism: Challenging Connections between Settler Colonialism and Heteropatriarchy.' *Feminist Formations* 25(1): 8–34.

18 Introduction

Comaroff, J., and Comaroff, J., 2012. *Theory from the South: How Euro-America is Evolving Toward Africa*. London: Routledge.

Denetdale, J. N., 2009. 'Securing Navajo National Boundaries: War, Patriotism, Tradition, and the Diné Marriage Act of 2005.' *Wicazo Sa Review* 24(2): 131–148.

Driskill, Q. L., Finely, C., Gilley, B., and Morgensen, S. (eds.), 2011. *Queer Indigenous Studies: Critical Interventions in Theory, Politics and Literature*. Arizona: The University of Arizona Press.

Duggan, L., 2003. *The Twilight of Equality: Neoliberalism, Cultural Politics and the Attack on Democracy*. Boston: Beacon Press.

Eng, D., Halberstam, J., and Muñoz, J. (eds.), 2005. 'What's Queer about Queer Studies Now?' *Social Text* 23(3–4): 84–85.

Fanon, F., 1963. *The Wretched of the Earth*. New York: Grove Press.

Fanon, F., 1967. *Black Skin, White Masks*. London: Pluto Press.

Finley, C., 2011. 'Decolonizing the Queer Native Body (and Recovering the Native Bull-Dyke) Bringing Sexy Back and Out of Native Studies Closet,' in *Queer Indigenous Studies: Critical Interventions in Theory, Politics and Literature*, edited by Q. L. Driskill, C. Finely, B. Gilley, and S. Morgenson. Arizona: The University of Arizona Press.

Gaztambide-Fernández, R., 2014. 'Decolonial Options and Artistic/Aesthetic Entanglements: An Interview with Walter Mignolo.' *Decolonization: Indigeneity, Education & Society* 3(1): 120–140.

Goeman, M., 2013. *Mark My words: Native Women Mapping Our Nation*. Minneapolis: University of Minnesota Press.

Gordon, N., and Ram, M., 2016. 'Ethnic Cleansing and the Formation of Settler Colonial Geographies,' *Political Geography* 35: 20–25.

Grosfoguel, R., 2011. 'Decolonizing Post-Colonial Studies and Paradigms of Political-Economy: Transmodernity, Decolonial Thinking, and Global Coloniality.' *Journal of Peripheral Cultural Production* 1(1): 1–39.

Haraway, D., 1988. 'Situated Knowledges: The Science Question in Feminism and the Privilege of Partial Perspective.' *Feminist Studies* 14(3): 575–599.

Hochberg, G., 2010. 'Introduction: Israelis Palestinians, Queers: Points of Departure.' *Journal of Gay and Lesbian Studies* 16(4): 493–516.

Jad, I., 2011. 'The Post-Oslo Palestine and Gendering Palestinian Citizenship.' *Ethnicities* 11(3): 360–372.

Jad, I., 2018. *Palestinian Women Activism: Nationalism, Secularism Islamism*. New York: Syracuse University Press.

Jagose, A., 1997. *Queer Theory: An Introduction*. New York: New York University Press.

Kauanui, Kēhaulani, 2018. *Paradoxes of Hawaiian Sovereignty: Land, Sex, and the Colonial Politics of State Nationalism*. Durham, NC: Duke University Press.

Kindon, S., Pain, R., and Kesby, M., 2009. 'Participatory Action Research.' *International Encyclopedia of Human Geography* 90–95.

Lugones, M., 2010. 'Toward a Decolonial Feminism.' *Hypatia* 25(4): 742–759.

Massad, J., 2007. *Desiring Arabs*. Chicago: University of Chicago Press.

Mctaggart, R., 1991. 'Principles for Participatory Action Research.' *Adult Education Quarterly* 41(3): 168–187.

Mignolo, W., and Nanibush, W., 2018. 'Thinking and Engaging with the Decolonial: A Conversation Between Walter D. Mignolo and Wanda Nanibush.' *Afterall: A Journal of Art, Context and Enquiry*. Available at: www.afterall.org/article/

thinking-and-engaging-with-the-decolonial-a-conversation-between-walterd-mignolo-and-wanda-nanibush (Accessed 19 April 2021).

Mignolo, W., and Vazquez, R., 2013, 15 July. 'Decolonial AestheSis: Colonial Wounds/Decolonial Healings.' *Social Text-Periscope*. Available at: http://socialtextjournal.org/periscope_article/decolonial-aesthesis-colonial-woundsdecolonial-healings/ (Accessed 29 April 2021).

Mikdashi, M., and Puar, J. K., 2016. 'Queer Theory and Permanent War.' *GLQ: A Journal of Lesbian and Gay Studies* 22(2): 215–222.

Morgensen, S., 2010. 'Settler Homonationalism: Theorizing Settler Colonialism within Queer Modernities.' *A Journal for Lesbian and Gay Studies* 16(1–2): 105–131.

Morgensen, S., 2013. 'Settler Colonialism and Alliance: Comparative Challenges to Pinkwashing and Homonationalism.' *Jadaliyya* [Online]. Available at: www.jadaliyya.com/pages/index/11016/settler colonialism-and-alliance_comparative-chall (Accessed 24 June 2021).

Morgensen, S., 2014. 'White Settlers and Indigenous Solidarity: Confronting White Supremacy, Answering Decolonial Alliances, Decolonisation, Indigeneity Education and Society.' Available at: https://decolonization.wordpress.com/2014/05/26/white-settlers-and-indigenoussolidarity-confronting-white-supremacy-answering-decolonial-alliances/ (Accessed 29 April 2021).

Muñoz, J., 1999. *Disidentifications: Queer of Color and the Performance of Identity*. Minneapolis: University of Minnesota Press.

Muñoz, J., 2009. *Cruising Utopia: The Then and There of Queer Futurity*. New York: New York University Press.

Ndlovu-Gatsheni, S., 2017. 'Decolonising Research Methodology Must Include Undoing Its Dirty History.' *The Conversation*. Available at: https://theconversation.com/decolonising-research-methodology-must-include-undoing-its-dirty-history-83912 (Accessed 29 April 2020).

Puar, J., 2005. 'Queer Times, Queer Assemblages.' *Social Text* 23(3–4): 121–139.

Puar, J., 2007. *Terrorist Assemblages*. Durham: Duke University Press.

Puar, J., 2011. 'Citation and Censorship: The Politics of Talking about the Sexual Politics of Israel.' *Feminist Legal Studies* 21(1): 133–142.

Puar, J., 2013. 'Rethinking Homonationalism.' *International Journal of Middle East Studies* 45(2): 336–339.

Puar, J., and Mikdashi, M., 2012. 'Pinkwatching and Pinkwashing: Interpretation and Its Discontents.' *Jadaliyya* [Online]. Available at: www.jadaliyya.com/pages/index/6774/pinkwatching-and-pinkwashing_interpenetration-and- (Accessed 24 June 2016).

Rancière, J., 1999. *Disagreement: Politics and Philosophy*. Translated from French by J. Rose. Minneapolis: University of Minnesota Press.

Rancière, J., 2004. *The Politics of Aesthetics*. London: Bloomsbury.

Ritchie, J., 2010. 'How Do You Say Come Out of the Closet in Arabic.' *A Journal of Lesbian and Gay Studies* 16(4): 557–575.

Roy, A., and Ong, A., 2011. *Worlding Cities: Asian Experiments and the Art of Being Global*. Chichester, West Sussex: Wiley-Blackwell.

Salamanca, O., Qato, M., Rabie, K., and Samour, S. (eds.), 2012. 'Past Is Present: Settler Colonialism in Palestine.' *Settler Colonial Studies* 2(1): 1–8.

Shalhoub-Kevorkian, N., 2009. *Militarization and Violence Against Women in Conflict Zones in the Middle East: A Palestinian Case Study*. Cambridge: Cambridge University Press.

20 Introduction

Shalhoub-Kevorkian, N., 2016. 'The Occupation of the Senses: The Prosthetic and Aesthetic of State Terror.' *The British Journal of Criminology* 57(6): 1279–1300.

Shalhoub-Kevorkian, N., and Ihmoud, S., 2014. 'Exiled at Home: Writing Return and the Palestinian Home.' *Biography* 37(2): 377–397.

Simpson, A., 2014. *Mohawk Interruptus: Political Life Across the Borders of Settler States*. Durham, NC: Duke University Press.

Stein, R., 2010. 'Explosive: Scenes from Israel's Gay Occupation.' *Journal of Gay and Lesbian Studies* 16(4): 517–536.

Tuhiwai Smith, L., 2012. *Decolonizing Methodologies: Research and Indigenous People*. London: Zed Books.

Wolfe, P., 2006. 'Settler Colonialism and the Elimination of the Native.' *Journal of Genocide* 8(4): 387–409.

Wolfe, P., 2012. 'Purchase by Other Means: The Palestine Nakba and Zionism's Conquest of Economics.' *Journal of Settler Colonial Studies* 2(1): 133–171.

2 Mapping Hetero-Conquest

This chapter provides the necessary contextual analysis of the Palestinian Nakba through the framework of what I identify as 'hetero-conquest.' The chapter is divided into two main parts drawing on various historical events and contextual examples that demonstrate the centrality of gender and sexuality to understanding Palestine's settler colonial reality. The first part addresses the Zionist project in Palestine since its inception up to now and how it produces a sex/gender system that tallies with the temporal and spatial constituents of the structure of native elimination in both negative (genocidal) and positive (regulatory) forms (Wolfe, 2006). I have a twofold aim in this part: to provide a queer reading of the Zionist desiring project, demonstrating the entwining of space, time, and sex to the epistemological and ontological foundation of conquest; and to situate analyses of contemporary discourses on LGBT liberty in the settler colony within the historical continuity of Zionist hetero-conquest. The second section examines the reproduction of hetero-conquest in the struggle for Palestinian liberation, which relies on sexed/gendered hierarchies and thus consolidates a heteropatriarchal vision of Palestinian national identity. Through analysis of political events spanning from the First Intifada to the Oslo peace accords, I show how Palestinian liberation succumbs to reproducing the politics of sex, space, and time that maintain, rather than challenge, the structural continuity of Nakba. The conclusion reflects on how unpacking hetero-conquest and its re-instantiation corresponds to the very need to anchor queering into decolonisation, as analyses of activism and aesthetics in the forthcoming chapters will further demonstrate.

Time, Space, and Desire in the Zionist Project

The word *Nakba*—Arabic for catastrophe—is a specific moment in history (1948) of Palestinian indigenous dispossession and their making into refugees, dispersed all over the world and denied their basic right of return, which allowed the establishment of 'Eretz Israel' (Greater Israel). Palestinian Nakba is also the structure that defines the fabric of the 'new colonial society on the expropriated land base' (Wolfe, 2006: 388). The structural reality of Nakba can be traced in the Zionist carving of space in which to

DOI: 10.4324/9781003273585-2

22 Mapping Hetero-Conquest

pursue the embodiment of a settler colonial politics of time. The creation of a Jewish state in Palestine was, from the standpoint of its founding father Theodore Herzl, a means to overcome inherent Jewish failure—following movements like Haskalah[1]—to assimilate into the ideals of modern Western society. Studies of Herzl's life reveal his strong aspiration to establish himself as the new man of the Enlightenment, sharing Christian European disdain for those stereotypical Jewish characteristics that were presumed to obstruct assimilation into gentiles' society (see Kornberg, 1993; Bowman, 2011).

Like other Western Jews aspiring to assimilation, Herzl categorised Jewishness into two types: Western, with which he identified, and Eastern, known as the *Ostjude*. The latter type of Jewishness bore an 'unspeakably low and repulsive' character (Herzl in Pawel, 1993: 345), one whose reform was necessary even by means of mass baptism into the Catholic Church. Once all efforts to change the ghettoised nature of Jews failed and, instead, Herzl witnessed the rise of anti-Semitic movements in Europe, he conceived a programme called Zionism, which developed further his existing ideas for Jewish transformation outside Europe. Herzl advocated for Jews to leave Europe in order to establish a state 'where they can finally reveal themselves as Europeans' (Bowman, 2011: 69). Herzlian Zionism is not only anti-Semitic at its core—assuming that anti-Semitism could be extinguished by eradicating those Jewish traits said to incite it, but it is also revealed as an agent of Western Time, enshrined in and reproductive of the colonial and racial dynamics of 19th-century Europe.

In Herzl's words, a Jewish state in Palestine would stand as a 'defence of Europe in Asia, an outpost of civilisation against barbarism' (Mendes-Flohr and Reinharz, 2011: 601). Herzl relies on the evolutionary schema of nineteenth-century temporalising rhetoric (see Fabian, 1983; Nanni, 2012) and reproduces the hierarchical classifications of Modern versus Backward, West versus East that helped legitimise colonial projects. Thus, to break the Jewish destiny that relegates them outside the contours of the 'here and now' of European Western Time, constantly collapsing into their 'there and then' pre-modern stereotypically Eastern character (Fabian, 1983: ix), Zionism becomes a force of mapping salvation for a 'chosen people' through a settler colonial project. The Jew travels and settles in Palestine to meet the requisites of European temporal intelligibility. In doing so, the Jew embodies a movement across sacred time and its secularised variants. In other words, the establishment of a state in the East, in the very geography of the Orient, permits the European Jew to occupy the position of 'tabulating space.' That is, according to an evolutionary scheme, measuring others through 'a temporal slope, a stream of Time—some upstream, some downstream' (Ibid.: 17). Hence, to observe and contain the barbarism of the Orient enables the Jew to unlock a temporal position in which they—European Jewry—were trapped within Europe and finally reveal themselves as agents of Western Time.

The politics of Time that underpins the Zionist project provides a window for examining the settler colonial presence over Palestine, meaning forcible *absentation*[2] of Palestinians and the physical/geographical transformation

Mapping Hetero-Conquest 23

of Palestine into Israel. In fact, Zionism carves up the very geography of historic Palestine as per the hierarchical taxonomies embedding its politics of Time. By adopting spatial mechanisms of Wall(ing) as fortification and separation and Tower(ing) as gazing down, devouring, and containing, the newly revealed Jewish European self sits on higher chrono-geographical grounds than those it *literally* deemed beneath it (Rotbard, 2003), that is, those at the lower end of the temporal slope. Wall and Tower are fundamental elements to understand Zionist chrono-geographical conquest. The architectural characteristic of walling sits at the core of the Zionist obsession with erecting enclosed spaces, such as 1948 military rule; environmental planning of Tel Aviv; and walls, checkpoints, and permit systems in the OPT[3] (Ibid.) without mentioning the infamous blockade of Gaza. At the same time, towering is the epitome of Israeli colonies functioning as 'panoptic fortresses' (Weizman, 2002: 5). Being on top of mountains and hilltops, towering functions as a gaze over surrounding landscapes and Arab towns to maintain and exercise power. The materiality of Israeli-configured space fuses the temporal modalities that generated it in the first place. The Israeli regime of gazing over Palestine/Palestinian enclaves manifests the structural reality of Palestinian Nakba within the regiments of Zionist settler colonial presence and denoting Palestinian coercive removal from history. This act of gazing used to tame, observe, and contain the barbarism of the Orient, as Herzl declared, also imbues gendered and sexualised performances that reveal the crucial role of desire within the Zionist project.

In *Land and Desire in Early Zionism*, Boaz Neumann brings into focus what he calls an existential aspect of the Zionist project in Palestine: the 'pioneer's desire for the land' (2011: 3). According to Neumann, conquest does not entail violence and native erasure, rather it is presented as an act of 'creation, construction and redemption' of 'land without organs through creating its organs' (Ibid.: 80). His study focuses on what Hebrew defines as *halutzim*—pioneers, those who were 'the first' to engage in activity in 'the land of Israel' (Ibid.: 3). To study the *halutzim*'s relationship with the land means to explore the essential constituents of the way Zionism and Israel are experienced in space and the human body (Ibid.: 7). For this reason, he writes, 'When we Israeli Jews of today gaze at the Land of Israel, we see it largely through the eyes of *halutzim*. When we feel it with our bodies and souls, we sense it largely through their sensibilities' (Ibid.). For *halutzim* pioneers, the Zionist narrative is a romantic endeavour; it is a 'story of falling in love romantically and even sexually, with the land of Israel' (Ibid.: 52–53). By imagining and desiring an 'always female, virgin beloved mother earth,' the *halutz* seeks to 'pierce that virginity and cause their beloved to fall in love with, and even wed them' (Ibid.). Those imaginings capture how the pioneers related to the land through love, sexual fantasies, and desires. Neumann draws upon the cases of Zionist leaders, such as David Ben Gurion and Berl Katznelson, and describes their relationship with land as the 'groom' who will deliver into the 'mother-belly of the betrothed soil'

24   *Mapping Hetero-Conquest*

(Ibid.: 53). *Halutzim*'s passion for the land is also described in relation to its wondrous beauty, which freed the pioneers being hypnotised by 'the mysterious force inherent in the Orient as a whole' (Ibid.: 63).

Drawing on Neumann's account, I aim to map out those performances of gender and sexuality that constitute Zionist conquest as a desiring project. His thesis shows how an 'oppositional, binary gender system' (Butler, 1999: 30) activates *halutzim*'s conquest. Far from being natural and free-floating, *halutzim* desire cannot be separated 'from the political and cultural assumption in which it is invariably maintained' (Ibid.: 6). Configurations of the *halutz* as the penetrator of the virgin motherland create and maintain a power dynamic based on exclusion and hierarchy, achieving the goals of settler colonial conquest. In other words, performances of femininity and masculinity that instruct pioneer desire for the land also underwrite the production of the settler colonial power regime. Desiring is a marker for 'rebirth' of the new Jew whose newly built nation should stand as 'a defence of Europe in Asia, an outpost of civilisation against barbarism' (Mendes-Flohr and Reinharz, 2011: 601). It is a fundamental element of the reproduction of those European geo-temporalities of conquest, whence desiring the oriental land permits the Jew to demonstrate its European-ness. Pioneer unification with, and desiring of, the land is said to regenerate the New Jewish body, figured without organs, signifying a living corpse and disunity, the result of exile and degeneracy. It also simultaneously redeems the 'sick,' 'desolate' state of the 'land without organs' (Neuman, 2011: 93). The land, therefore, stands bare and naked awaiting and yearning for the pioneer-redeemer, who will enable the organs to appear again (Ibid.: 97). It is 'a land without a people' that awaited, yearned for, and desired the 'people without a land' (Ibid.). Pioneer conquest as creation emerges within a discursive and fantastical imagining of desiring and being desired by the bare land in order to fulfil 'a moral conquest as a result of which human beings lived and created cultural values' (Ibid.: 80). More importantly, as Neumann explains, the Arab incapacity to desire and conquer the land, in the same way the *halutz* could, informs such a moral conquest:

> The emptiness of the land, its status as a land without organs, was magnified by the Arab presence within it. In the *halutzim* eyes, the local Arabs had not only failed to build, create, and redeem the land but were incapable of doing so—because they lacked desire. Thus, the Arabs had not conquered the land and could not conquer it . . . largely owing to character traits such as laziness and primitiveness, expressed in a lack of technological capability.
>
> (Ibid.: 84)

This passage captures desire as the origin story of Zionism, representing both the new Jew, who desires the land, and the land that yearns to be desired by its Jewish conqueror. To trouble and queer Neumann's account

Mapping Hetero-Conquest 25

means grasping how desire is the effect of conquest in its violent form and comprehending how violent assumptions constitute the Zionist 'story of origin' (Butler, 1999: 46).[4] Violent eliminatory logic underpins Neumann's untroubled account of Jewish-Israeli desire constituting its intelligibility. His framing of conquest as moral and non-violent naturalises violence and native dispossession and enables conquest as settler colonialism to operate. Thus, conquest as moral renders legitimate Zionist presence in Palestine, permitting the structural continuity of Nakba. The Zionist desiring project gains its legitimacy through a naturalised account of gendered relations, presenting figures of the penetrator (masculinised) pioneer and the penetrated (feminised) native land, which also enables the marking of other bodies and desires as illegitimate. Pioneer penetration of the woman-land signifies both Arab impotence and lack of desire; or, as Neumann claims:

> As a virgin, the land expected to be penetrated; the Arabs were impotent. As a bride the land demanded love; the Arabs did not love it they even neglected it.
>
> (2011: 85)

This gendering and sexualising discourse reify the temporal and spatial constituents of Zionist settler colonialism. Such an impotence vis-à-vis the land informs how Zionism ontologises Arab presence qua absence: 'their very presence on the land served only to make their "absence" more palpable and actually intensified pioneer desire' (Ibid.). Pioneer desire, constructing legitimacy of a moral conquest (creation), derives from the Arabs' superfluous presence on the land, which renders them absent and/or containable within the gaze of the Israeli-Zionist conqueror. The potency of the Jewish-Zionist presence can only be articulated in relation to its antithesis: the impotence of the present-absent Arab.

The temporal paradigm of West versus Orient defines the potency of the Zionist presence, constituting its reality in relation to conquest. Desiring the so-called virgin land creates a boundary between the Israeli-Zionist (settler) presence as potent and the Palestinian (indigenous) absence as impotence. Moreover, this settler potency produces a Zionist geography (state of Israel) as Zionist pioneers boast of their ability to fertilise and birth the land of Israel by using expensive European ploughing techniques, which the 'primitive Arab' lacked (Ibid.: 84). The latter's ploughing techniques merely give a 'pretence of penetrating the soil,' rendering pioneer conquest of land 'a human cultural enterprise of great value, a civilising enterprise' (Ibid.). The very phrase 'conquest of land' resonates with the Hebrew phrase of *Avodah Ivrit*[5] (Hebrew Labour), capturing early Zionist politics of Jewish exclusive labour dating back to the 1930s (Brym, 1988). Sustained by the figure of the New Jew who is strong and works the land, this early conquest of labour played a fundamental role in clearing natives from the land and instituting

26 *Mapping Hetero-Conquest*

zones of insulated Jewish-only lands—Kibbutzim—that then became the base on which to 'fashion their ethnocratic state—in waiting—in Mandate Palestine' (Wolfe, 2012: 133). This inevitable link between desire—as hetero-normalising and productive of gendering processes—and the birthing of an exclusively Jewish state[6] is important to keep in mind when analysing settler colonial conquest in its violent and exclusionary form. If we understand first the desire for the woman-land, we grasp not only the epistemological and ontological foundation of settler colonial conquest in Palestine, but it also unveils what can be termed the hetero-conquest foundations of the Zionist project in Palestine. In such a frame, it is possible to recognise how contemporary Israeli discourses of modern sexuality and branding Israel with gay haven narratives—known as pinkwashing—are necessarily located within the politics of time, space, and desiring charted thus far. Therefore, pinkwashing narratives should not be approached solely via those frames (homonationalism and queer liberalism) that examine how queer emerges to normalise the nation-state. Their essential definition as Israeli/Jewish/Zionist encapsulates a continuum of structural reality of Nakba and its modalities of time, space, and desire rather than an identifiable moment in Israeli queer liberal time. The following discussion demonstrates the continuity of Zionist hetero-conquest via an exploration of contemporary mobilisation around LGBT liberty.

The Ga(y)ze of a Liberal Democracy

> Go to Tel Aviv and have sex with hunky Israeli guys, they are so masculine they are soldiers.
> (Michael Lucas, director of *Men in Israel*, in Schulman, 2012: 117)

Michael Lucas is the director of the 2009 pornographic film *Men of Israel*. An American Jew, known for his loyalty to Israel and keenness to obtain Israeli citizenship through its law of return,[7] Lucas often spoke of the significant role his films play in relation to promoting Israel's 'humanist values' (Portwood, 2013: n.p.). He claims, 'when it comes to gay rights, Israel is one of the most progressive countries' (Ibid.). Lucas offers his films, including *Men of Israel*, as examples to confront some of the misconstrued assumptions about Israel. He states:

> Tel Aviv is maybe the gayest city in the world, but some people lump Israel in with other Middle Eastern countries where gay life is vastly more secretive and dangerous and where gay people are subject to harassment, assault and imprisonment.
>
> (Ibid.)

Lucas's *Men of Israel* celebrates an 'all-Israeli gay porn,' with an 'all-Israeli cast' and across 'all-Israeli geographies' (Hoffman, 2009: n.p.). It helps

Mapping Hetero-Conquest 27

'viewers see Israel, its geographic features and history, a place not much different from Prague or Palm Springs: an invitation as an LGBT vacation destination where handsome men have sex' (Ibid.). Furthermore, Lucas does not shy away from speaking out against those whom he describes as 'romanticizing the same Palestinians that hang gay people on cranes, but demoniz[e] Israel which is a safe haven for gay people' (Glazov, 2011). Instead, he claims, 'Israel is a beacon of LGBT emancipation in an area that's a very dark corner for our gay and lesbian brothers and sisters' (Jerusalem Post, 2011: n.p.).

These narratives demonstrate how representations of Israel as a gay haven correspond to a Zionist settler colonial teleology, generating—once again—the spatio-temporal paradigms central to Zionist conquest, as discussed earlier. Lucas's porn movie features images filmed in 'telegenic scenes of Tel Aviv and Haifa' (Kaminer and *The Forward*, 2009: n.p.) for promoting Israeli tourism, and it refers to an 'abandoned village' on the outskirts of Jerusalem, which can also be seen in the background of some of the promotional poster of the film.[8] He describes this 'abandoned village' in an online blogpost:

It was a beautiful ancient township that had been deserted centuries ago. . . . However, that did not stop our guys from mounting each other and trying to repopulate it. Biology may not be the lesson of the day but these guys shot their seeds all over the village.

(2009: n.p.)

Although Lucas describes this village as abandoned for centuries, it is in fact a former Palestinian village, Suba, whose population was ethnically cleansed in 1948 (see Blumenthal, 2013: 215). Lucas's statement constitutes an act of erasure that simultaneously establishes Israel as a particular kind of (liberal, gay friendly) presence. His film and statements resonate with an array of narratives framing Israel as a liberal democracy via its record on gender and sexuality rights. For instance, in his 2011 speech to the Joint Session of US Congress, after emphasising the strong alliance that connects his country to America, Israel's Prime Minister Benjamin Netanyahu stated that Israel does not need democracy or nation building; 'we've got it.' (Congressman Joe Walsh, 2011). Israel's assumed ability to build democracy like its Western allies in North America and Europe is positioned in relation to a 'lack' in the rest of the region. In fact, Netanyahu declares, 'in a region where women are stoned, gays are hanged, and Christians persecuted, Israel stands out, it is different . . . free press, open courts, rambunctious parliamentary debates' (Ibid.). The statements of both Lucas and Netanyahu present Israel as an LGBT destination that mirrors places like Prague and Palm Springs. At the same time, such discourses also entail the creation of distance from a surrounding region, which they observe as 'a dark corner' for sexual minorities.

Lucas's film and related narratives promote the gayness of Israel as a modern liberal democracy and represent a manifestation of Zionist ongoing

28 *Mapping Hetero-Conquest*

conquest of Palestine as explored above through Neumann's account. This is where the Jewish-Israeli exclusive and 'rightful' presence over Palestine, by virtue of carving an all-Israeli topography, fuses a temporalising rhetoric (civilised versus primitive), which underpins the sense of desiring as the creation and continuing repopulation of the woman/land with *halutz* seeds. People like Lucas automatically qualify for Israeli citizenship, a process that Israel grants through the implementation and maintenance of its settler colonial laws. Yet citizenship comes with the settler state and its subjects' investment in the promotion of conquest through humanist and progressive values Neumann described. It is hardly surprising, therefore, to see Lucas's dedication to the production of cinematic work promoting the beauty of Israeli geography. It is the demarcation of a barbaric Other, a supposed primitive Middle East region, that allows Lucas, and so the Zionist state, to articulate Israeli progressiveness towards gay rights. As Lucas warns, Palestine should not be romanticised for the way it 'hangs its gays.'

It is against the backdrop of such an analysis that it is possible to trace the continuity of Zionist hetero-conquest of, and/or the ongoing Nakba for, Palestine. The Israeli liberal ga(y)ze is part of a structural demonisation and absentation of Palestine and Palestinians, turning them into savages 'hanging gays on cranes' and therefore, unlike 'Israel,' not eligible to build a nation and achieve the goals of liberal democracy. Through such a logic, Palestine and Palestinians, unlike Lucas, have no right to exist and/or be granted a right to return to those spaces that are now proclaimed part of Israel. The emptiness of the deserted village, therefore, continues to instigate the desire for conquest, meaning Jews spreading Jewish seeds for repopulation (Neumann, 2011). Irrespective of gender and/or sexual identification of Israeli-Jewish subjectivity, settlers' inherent desire to spread their seeds and repopulate the land, construed as vacant, manifests the masculinist and heteronormative positionality of settler colonial violence in Palestine.[9] The need to spread Jewish-Israeli seeds marks legitimated settler conquest versus native dispossession. It tallies with the biopolitical regulation of the native other through their remaking into settler state (non)citizens and their continuous erasure and management within dictated boundaries of the sovereign settler state.[10]

While my aim thus far has been to situate the Zionist settler colonial project—from the nineteenth-century *halutz* desiring schema to Lucas's movie—within the structural continuity hetero-conquest, the following pays particular attention to its re-instantiation within the Palestinian liberation struggle.

Imagining Liberation: Re-Instantiating Hetero-Conquest

The Intifada—Arabic for uprising or sudden shaking—represents one of the most significant events in Palestinian political history and the struggle for self-determination. It also enables an understanding of the consolidation of a masculinist and hetero-paternalist image of the Palestinian liberation struggle. Analysis of the Unified National Leadership of the Uprising

Mapping Hetero-Conquest 29

(UNLU) communiqués reveals how the Palestinian masculine agent produces the nation and its symbols, which are cast as female-guardian (e.g., 'mother-land'). Liberation is imagined as a woman who needs protection from colonial penetration. UNLU communiqués describe the motherland, who gives birth to the national hero, *Fida'iyeen*, as she 'rejoices twice: first on the day of her son's death and again on the day of the declaration of the state' (Malhi-Sherwell, 2001: 162). They further 'congratulate' Palestinian women on their role in mothering and birthing the nation, while urging nationalist 'sons' to launch the revolution, marking through their deaths the nation's glory and dignity (Lockman and Beinin, 1989; Massad, 1995). If the death of the 'son' marks dignity, 'pregnancy' describes the Intifada, and the coloniser's attempt to suppress it is an 'abortion' (Lockman and Beinin, 1989: 360). Palestine's colonisation is the 'rape' of the land (Rubenberg, 2001: 219). The Intifada was also likened to a wedding whose anniversary continues to be celebrated in relation to a Palestinian wedding '*ors al Intifada*.' In doing so, liberation becomes a celebration of heterosexual consummation, giving birth to the 'children of the revolution' (Palestine National Council, political communiqués, 1988, in Lukacs, 1992: 415). This language indicates how Palestinian national identity stems 'from masculinised memory, masculinised hope and masculinised humiliation' (Enloe, 1993: 44). The bodies of women intertwine with the symbolic body of the nation because 'it is women who reproduce nations biologically, culturally and symbolically' (Yuval-Davis, 1997: 2). Yet the agency to enact such (re)production of the nation is always and already a masculine privilege.

Exploring the central role family and women's reproductive abilities play in defining the Palestinian visions of national liberation also requires an examination of the National Charter of the Palestine Liberation Organisation (PLO). The document defines Palestinian identity as a 'genuine, essential and inherent characteristic; [it is] transmitted from parents to children' (in Lillian Goldman Law library: n.p.). Article 5 of the charter also indicates that, 'The Palestinians are Arab nationals who until 1947 normally resided in Palestine regardless of whether they were evicted or have stayed there. Anyone born after that date of a Palestinian *father*—whether inside or outside Palestine—is also Palestinian' (my emphasis: Ibid.). These definitions prove how the 'cyclical life of the family' stands at the centre of identifying the true, authentic qualities of the Palestinian (Lindholm Schulz, 1999: 34). The continuity of 'genuine' Palestinian identity hinges on the biological process of procreation 'from parents [father, mother] to children.' However, as 1947 signals a historic rupture, configured as a biological violation of the nation-as-woman or the Zionist 'rape of the mother-land,' the charter assigns the role of passing Palestinian identity only to the 'father.'

The exclusion of the mother not only demonstrates the privileges assigned to masculine agents in the process of nation building (Massad, 1995), but also reveals the activation of hetero-paternal relations, where the father plays the central role in producing and maintaining the socio-political order (Arvin *et al*, 2013). Through this lens of '*al-ard al-mughtasaba*' (the raped

30 Mapping Hetero-Conquest

land), Intifada nationalist narratives construct national heroes who are retrieving 'honour, dignity and respect' for Palestine. For example, one narrative of the Intifada valorised the Palestinian *Fida'iyeen* (freedom-fighters) who represent the restoration of Palestinian dignity. It is the same masculinised memory and humiliation that, while it seems to elevate the body of the woman to that of the nation, does so to maintain a position of superiority and sole control over the nation-building process. Women assume a secondary, supportive role in the narrative of nationalism. It is important to note, however, that my aim in showing this masculinist discourse does not by any means underplay the key role Palestinian women played during the Intifada (see Kuttab, 1993; Jean-Klein, 2001).

The nationalist narrative that privileges the role of masculine agents to liberate the raped motherland interacts with the Zionist discourse of conquest explored earlier. The mobilisation of Palestinian society using a nationalist discourse reliant on values of pride and honour resonates with the ways the very colonising power has come to foster these values. For instance, Arafat's insistent use of rape as a metaphor to describe the colonisation of the land builds on those blunt sexual representations upon which Zionism relied to envision its conquest. As Zionism envisioned the land as a woman in need of pioneer insemination, so Palestinians constructed a vision of liberation as recuperating the honour of the raped motherland. To assess further how the concept of honour (re)produces itself, we also need to consider how Israel exploits this Palestinian discourse in order to recruit collaborators and defeat the Palestinian Intifada. The Arabic term *Isqat*, which translates literally as downfall, is widely known amongst Palestinians to describe those coerced into collaboration by the Israeli secret services. Israel blackmails people and brings about their downfall through collaboration, using knowledge of those who violate certain societal codes, such as drug use, alcohol use, premarital sex, and homosexuality amongst others. This fear of *Isqat* triggers social and moral panic, rendering topics concerning sexual abuse— and, more generally, sexuality—difficult to handle or even to talk about in Palestinian socio-political spheres (Shalhoub-Kevorkian, 2009: 15). Fear of *Isqat* also functions against those groups, including unmanly men and unwomanly women, meaning those who failed to repeat the gendered performances deemed necessary for the nation's self-definition through ideals of honour and purity. During the period from the first to the Second Intifada (1990–2000), various Palestinian factions started adopting cleansing strategies against stigmatised groups that were seen as an easy target for coerced collaboration with the enemy. Similar to Israeli methods, these factions blackmailed and threatened those engaged in non-conforming behaviours, including sex workers and those with expressions of gender or sexuality that were suspected to be homosexuals. The usage of such tactics further enforced patriarchal perceptions of sexuality whereby 'these immoral behaviours are defined as a threat that needs to be uprooted from political activism' (Alqaisiya *et al*, 2016: 127). Palestinian appropriation of the values of

Mapping Hetero-Conquest 31

honour and dignity triggered a vicious cycle as it further legitimised Israeli intelligence to continue blackmailing into collaboration those Palestinians who were afraid of being publicly exposed.

The famous Palestinian proverb *al-ard heya al-ard*, meaning 'land is honour,' is a good example of how codes of sexual purity instruct national self-imagining within the existing frame of Zionist conquest. The discursive intensification of *manly* men, whose refusal to be emasculated by the Israeli colonial machine manifests in their ability to protect their *ard* (land/honour) from violation, comes through heightened confrontation with the coloniser. *Manly* men are juxtaposed with roles ascribed to *womanly* women, who are saluted and recognised in their capacity to procreate and guard the nation's martyrs and prisoners. The production of art, including political posters and artistic productions that represent the struggle in gendered terms, enforce the discursive dramatisation of gendered bodies vis-à-vis the nation's liberation. For instance, they juxtapose (Figure 2.1) the hero, who is willing to sacrifice his blood for the sake of redeeming the nation, with the woman in her traditional Palestinian dress *thawb*, depicting the woman/land (see Figure 2.2, Figure 2.3, Figure 2.4, and Figure 2.5). The recurrent use of such imagery in Palestinian art, particularly from the mid-1970s to mid-1980s, becomes a key signifier for an authentic Palestinian national identity by marking the retrievability of a Palestinian pre-conquest past (Malhi-Sherwell, 2001: 165).

The consolidation of an origin story, or a past 'before the rape,' in Palestinian nationalism takes place in hetero-paternal terms. That is, in referencing an 'imaginary past' presumed to be pure and free of settler colonial contamination, Palestinian nationalist rhetoric reinforces its constitution within the frames of hetero-patriarchy and hetero-paternalism that rely on a narrow definition of the male/female binary (Arvin *et al*, 2013: 13). By imagining 'a state of origin' where the land is figured as a woman in her peasant dress, they justify the continuous (re)production of the gendered and sexed narratives that buttress hetero-conquest (i.e., the strong masculinist agent of the revolution versus the woman-land who reproduces children of the revolutions). Figures 2.2–Figure 2.5 illustrate how those posters reiterate a message that relegates women to the role of mothering and guarding the nation (in Figure 2.2 depicted through the symbol of the ancient olive tree rooted in the soil of Palestine), as well as being guardians and producers of future-generations of the to-be-liberated land (Figure 2.3 and Figure 2.4). Figure 2.5, a popular image of 'the mother with a baby in her arms,' combines two fundamental elements: the role of the woman in giving birth and the infant national hero who will grow to retake the feminine nation (Yuval-Davis, 1997). Nationalist agendas also frame the repudiation of non-conforming gendered identities when launching *ors al Intifada*, as political factions seek to purify and cleanse the constituents of genuine Palestinian identity. They produce gendered performances vis-à-vis the nation along with the exclusionary praxis upon which gender solidification takes place

32 *Mapping Hetero-Conquest*

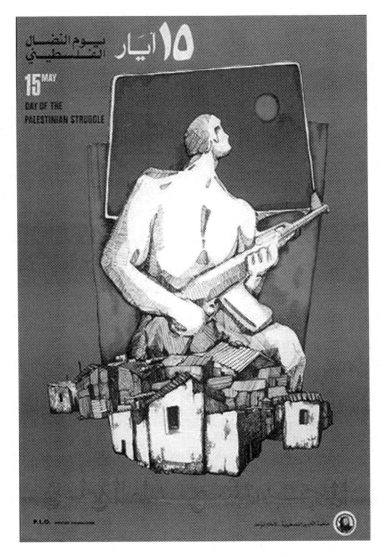

Figure 2.1 Arabic Caption Reads: 'Glory to the Martyrs of the Homeland'
Source: Menhem (1976)

'as the truth effects of a discourse of primary and stable identity' (Butler, 1999: 174). The reification of a discourse of nation-statism generates the hetero-paternalism of an intelligible Palestinian identity together with its exclusionary and hierarchal elements.

While the Palestinian Intifada served as a reminder to Israel of the threat that awaits it from a people who will never cease to fight to liberate their

Mapping Hetero-Conquest 33

Figure 2.2 Woman/Land
Source: Haboub, 2013

land,[11] this vision for liberation, however, matured into a new formula when its same masculinist agents signed the Oslo Accords in the early 1990s. PLO recognition of Israel within the parameters of the Oslo Accords brought Fatah leaders to transition from founding fathers of Intifada into occupying the role of Palestinian National Authority (PNA)[12] figures holding semi-autonomy over stipulated enclaves. It also witnessed the creation of a new era: Palestinian liberation succumbed to blatant recognition and normalisation[13] with the settler colonial regime.

34 Mapping Hetero-Conquest

Figure 2.3 Woman as Guardian of Nation
Source: Al Muzin (1979)

Mapping Hetero-Conquest 35

Figure 2.4 Mother Intifada
Source: Mansour (1988)

Modernising and Securitising a Recognisable State

Oslo marks the rise of an elitist urban strata seeking to build a structure that contains and renders Others, those through whom the struggle and revolution gained its meaning in the first place. The signing of the agreements, triggering recognition of Israel and a turn to an agenda of peaceful dialogue, went hand in hand with pushing crucial issues off the negotiating

36 *Mapping Hetero-Conquest*

Figure 2.5 Return-Mother With Baby
Source: Ibid.

table, particularly the status of East Jerusalem and the right of return of refugees. The embrace of the Oslo peace and security discourses by Arafat and the Fatah elite marked the unofficial abandonment of refugees and peasants upon whom the resistance leadership relied for its 'symbols and signs of authenticity' (Sayigh, 1997: 102). The PNA's aspiration to institutionalise their authority over enclaves of territory (Areas A and B) left refugees, particularly those in Lebanon, to 'feel that their suffering in the camps was cynically used by this leadership to bolster its credentials in the OPT' (Khalili, 2007: 54). Thus, peasants and refugees started sharing a similar fate to women as authenticating symbols and origin stories, consolidating

Mapping Hetero-Conquest 37

their symbolic importance rather than their political agency. Their role as symbols of misery and exile became more crucial as long as it provided legitimacy to the masculinist, elitist, and urban strata of state-makers working de facto under the coloniser's control. It thus is not surprising to see current, de facto, PNA leader Mahmoud Abbas explicitly announcing from his Ramallah-base his authority's confident recognition of the Israeli state and the legitimacy of its future. This recognition, he declares, is opposed to any 'ridiculous' claims that the PNA seeks to bring Palestinian refugees back or to act as a threat to the security of the Israeli state (BBC News, 2014). In fact, the rise of the PNA to power on the back of a peace treaty with Israel signalled a remarkable transition from masculinist agents of the revolution to occupying the position of statesmen/capitalist elites who uphold and promote a politics of liberation that embeds aspirations for state recognition (Khalidi and Samour, 2011). This new route of envisioning liberation via the parameters of state-making relies on the need for a recognition of legitimacy by the very power, and its international political allies, that subjugated Palestine in the first place.

This politics of blatant normalisation and recognition of Israel's legitimacy on behalf of the Palestinian leadership permits us to map out the re-instantiation of hetero-conquest in Palestinian politics of emancipation through the statist aspirations of its leaders. Oslo is the catalyst for the establishment of a PNA regime that relies on, and maintains, the colonial politics of time and space, which, as discussed above, are central to hetero-conquest. This maintenance and reproduction of a system that maintains the logic of colonial governance can be captured in the agenda of securitisation that the new PNA regime represents through its official endorsement of the 'deterring terrorism agenda'[14] whose simultaneous support by both the United States and Israel indicates the institutionalisation of a protection regime for the settler state. At the same time, this securitising agenda comes together with a modernising outlook, which a segment of PNA affiliated capitalist elites adopted in order to showcase Palestine's readiness for recognition as a state.

One major example of the PNA's modernisation is the figure of Salam Fayyad, former International Monetary Fund economist. Under US pressure, Abbas appointed Fayyad to the Ministry of Finance and subsequently made him prime minister by presidential decree after Hamas took control of the Palestine Legislative Council in the 2006 elections. Fayyad's policies and plans became known as Fayyadism, a term coined by *The New York Times* columnist Thomas Friedman (2010: n.p.). Fayyadism involved a series of projects that resonated within a developmental state-building programme. They echoed the notion of 'economic peace' (Lunat, 2010: n.p.) that Israeli Prime Minister Benjamin Netanyahu advocated, according to which economic development should lead to statehood recognition for Palestinians. Fayyadism re-enforced the 'inequitable and elite-based structures of power' (Tartir, 2014: 38), which further consolidated the power of the PNA. It reveals the underlying client-state nature of the PNA to Israel, as the latter

38 *Mapping Hetero-Conquest*

subcontracts its colonial occupation to the former through modernising and/ or securitising projects. These produce a vision of the 'eventual Palestinian state' as 'a free and open market economy,' thus emphasising 'the Palestinian private sector as the engine for economic growth' (Ibid.: 16).

The development project for the new Palestinian city, also identified as the 'promised city' of Rawabi (meaning 'hills' in Arabic), is an example of these politics of modernising Palestine for future statehood recognition. The Qatari Diar Real Estate Investment Company and the Palestinian American billionaire and entrepreneur, Bashar Al-Masri, developed the city in 2010 to capture a vision of futural Palestine within the agendas of modernity and progress. Under the slogan 'live, work and grow,' Rawabi is designed to meet the dreams of 'Palestinian families,' providing 'opportunities for "affordable" home ownership, employment, education and leisure and an attractive environment' (Rawabi News, 2022). Projects such as Rawabi encapsulate new conceptions of Palestinian socialites within the Oslo structure. Figure 2.6 illustrates those billboards in Ramallah promoting visions of a happy Palestinian family that has received bank loans to purchase a house. Rawabi crafts 'an orientation' towards the modern nuclear family as 'a happy object' and maintains the structure of state-making political elites (Ahmed, 2010: 45). The billboards show photographs of the modern nuclear (maximum three or four children) Palestinian family against the backdrop of the 'most luxurious residential apartments' (Figure 2.6). The photographs put on display,

Figure 2.6 Happy Family Real Estate Poster in Ramallah
Source: Palestinian photographer Lama Abu Odeh

Mapping Hetero-Conquest   39

or make visible for their viewers, the ideal of happy family as an object to aspire to or as 'a fantasy of the good life' (Ahmed, 2010: 51). They outline the directionality of the idea of happy family as something that bears affective value. What is significant to explore, however, is how such directionality is laid out via the objects that allow its circulation. In this case, not only do the billboards themselves bespeak family as a happy object, but they also enforce increased investment in neoliberal capitalist projects (such as Rawabi). They encapsulate a modern and elitist version of Palestinian subjectivity, one that qualifies for 'international recognition.' Masrai states, 'Rawabi also sends a message to the international community. We are not what they are led to believe, a bunch of terrorists. We are ready to build our state. Here is the proof' (in Sherwood, 2016: n.p.). 'Rising' to represent 'Palestine's potential' (Ibid.), Rawabi captures an imagined idea of Palestinian futurity as a universal notion of progress, which supposedly legitimises the rightfulness of the Palestinian state to be. This demonstrates how the Palestinian politics of modernisation and development, for the sake of a future state, reproduce the temporal paradigms and notions of progress of Zionist hetero-conquest. One of the comments about Rawabi captures its rise to overlook the Israeli city of Tel Aviv (Savir, 2015: n.p.). Remarking on Rawabi's proximity to Tel Aviv is a way of describing not only a spatial proximity but also a temporal one. In other words, Rawabi depicts the Palestinian ability to build a progressive modern city like the one embodied by Tel Aviv.

The construction of the 'promised Palestinian city' relies on enforcing cooperation and peaceful economic relations with the settler entity. Masri bluntly announces 'every construction project in Palestine must have components from Israel' (In Kozaczuk, 2015: 32). The construction of the Palestinian 'promised city' not only bears components from Israel, as Masri declares, but also generates, as Palestinian architect Yazid Anani and Al Khateeb[15] argue (see Figure 2.7 and Figure 2.8), the very spatialities of settler colonialism:

> There are striking similarities between new housing projects and already existing settlement patterns. When comparing Pasgot, a Jewish settlement, with Rawabi, a new Palestinian city, we notice how they engage the landscape in similar ways. There is a strong similarity with the colonial mechanism of gazing at space, fragmenting space, controlling the mountain tops, creating gated communities, and fostering elitism in the planning of these housing projects.
>
> (Anani, 2011: n.p.)

Anani further clarifies, drawing on other examples of Palestinian architecture, how Palestinian political structures have come to rely on the same spatial mechanism of the colonisers. Rawabi's over the hill location resonates with settlement locations over the peaks of mountains and hilltops, which are able to rise above and observe an Other. Moreover, Anani examines

40   Mapping Hetero-Conquest

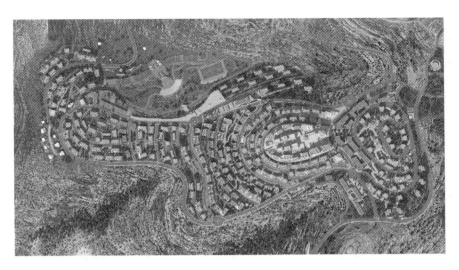

Figure 2.7 Rawabi
Source: Palestinian architect Yousef Al Khateeb (2012)

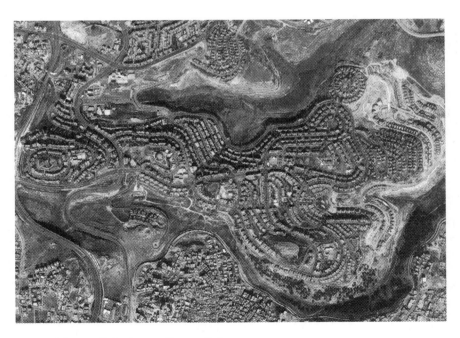

Figure 2.8 Israeli Settlement Pasgot Ze'ev
Source: Palestinian architect Yousef Al Khateeb (2012)

Mapping Hetero-Conquest   41

how the *Mukat'a*, headquarters of the PNA in Ramallah, reifies Zionist wall and watchtower system explored earlier. Such architecture depicts the way the 'political entity fears its own people,' hence comes the use of a defence system against passers-by or citizens (Ibid.). However, I must stress the interplay of temporal and spatial constituents to/of hetero-conquest. The continuity of hetero-conquest can be traced in this new Palestinian regime whose imagining of a future (state of Palestine) relies on the very structures that allow negation of Palestine to continue. The distribution of the happy family notion not only fulfils a linear continuation of Palestinian identity in the cyclical life of the family, but more crucially, it reflects the modern aspect of this happy family, which can afford and own the luxury home of its dreams.

This modern aspect is caught within the larger web of power, which uses capitalist modernisation to enforce its own hegemony. Controlling female and queer bodies and utilising the notion of honour against political activists has been instrumental to the Palestinian Authority's increasing suppression of social and political dissent from the Oslo structure and its corrupt political elites. The PNA's rallying of women's rights through presidential decrees affirming the Palestinian National Authority's support of international treaties, such as the 1325 resolution and CEDAW,[16] was simply a means to legitimise the PNA's modern and international outlook to the world. Indeed, as Chapter 5 will further reveal, the PNA's signing of such treaties did not impede its security regime from targeting women and queer political organising, which reached its zenith in 2019. The suppression of women and queer protestors must be situated within the growing strife between young Palestinian activists and the Authority's peace agenda, which dates back to 2012 protests against the visit of Israel's vice prime minister, Shaul Mofaz,[17] to Ramallah. The visit, the purpose of which was to resume stalled negotiations between the PNA and Israel, was met by hundreds of young protestors marching against it and carrying the slogan, resonating with that of the Egyptian revolution, 'down with police rule' (Abu Samra, 2012: n.p.). The protests, which resumed the following year with youth marching around the *Mukat'a* in Ramallah, were marked by the PNA police and *Mukhabarat*— the secret services and the regime—using targeted beating and sexual assault of female protestors who were in the front line of these protests. Slandering of women protestors by the PNA security apparatus took the form of calling them 'prostitutes' because some of them, as the police forces claimed, used derogatory language against the police and 'cursed the divine' (Abu Ghosh, 2013: n.p.). The defiling of protestors' honour becomes a tool used by the PNA to reaffirm its hegemonic domination of the public sphere by virtue of controlling those social outcasts and Western-funded agents[18] who are supposedly threatening the values of traditional Palestinian society. Hence, the mobilisation of sex panics against those seen as immoral and sexually promiscuous, in the wake of the Oslo securitising and modernising regime, becomes instrumental in PNA violence and socio-political control within the structure that maintains Nakba for Palestine.

42 *Mapping Hetero-Conquest*

Conclusion: Hetero-Conquest Anchors Decolonial Queering

In this chapter I have given a contextual understanding of settler colonialism in Palestine within the scope of what I call hetero-conquest. In doing so, I argue for the need to ground the politics and aesthetics of decolonial queering, where—as the forthcoming chapters reveal—queering is woven into decolonisation from within the forces maintaining Nakba over Palestine. Theories of queer critiques emerging from Global North contexts of racism and homonormativity fall short of accounting for settler colonialism as an amalgam of politics of space, time, and desire—i.e., hetero-conquest—against which stands the value of decolonial queering, initiating a radical liberatory critique. Historicising the spatio-temporal constituents of the nineteenth-century Zionist desiring project not only reveals the gendering and racialising mechanisms of early *halutz* conquest but also situates contemporary narratives of sexual modernity in the settler colony within the historical continuity of its temporal, spatial, and sensual regime. As the forthcoming chapters reveal, Palestinian queer activism and artistic productions emerge to frame native positionality and the will to refuse and unsettle the forces maintaining this regime, including through the reproduction of the coloniser's frames of emancipation and recognition in both intimate and geopolitical spheres. Decolonial queering, therefore, posits critical questions to native subjects regarding the freedom they envision and to which they relate, permitting them to see the restrictive strictures of freedom endowed via the misrecognition of one's own history and true struggle.

Strands of Latin American and Native American studies have undertaken to examine decolonial epistemologies offered via queer indigeneity and/or Chicana borderlands (Anzaldua, 1987; Perez, 2003). However, it is essential to recentre Palestine and its geopolitical/geocolonial specificity within this debate, allowing the hetero-conquest framework to anchor the agenda of queering Palestine. This book's overall aim is to excavate the politics and aesthetics whose capacity to unsettle the settler colonial ga(y)ze entwines with the will to see beyond the failure of converting the openings created by mass mobilisations into moments of real change. Thus, rather than collapsing the Intifada into the national rhetoric that reified hetero-conquest by carving a directionality toward Oslo, destroying any possibility of genuine liberation, decolonial queering calls for an imagination of Palestine to emerge within new radical semantics, geopolitics, and intimate desiring. Decolonial queering, as such, seeks praxis for liberation by inviting both Palestine and Palestinians to recognise and re-evaluate the value of her/their own (hi)stories, geographies, and bodies.

Notes

1 Jewish Enlightenment is an example of an influential tide of Jewish intellectualism, spanning from the 1770s to the 1880s, which sought to 'assimilate into European society in dress, language, manners and loyalty to the ruling power.'

See Shira Schoenberg (2016) *Modern Jewish History: The Haskala*, Jewish virtual library. Available online at: www.jewishvirtuallibrary.org/jsource/Judaism/Haskalah.html (Accessed 1 December 2021).

2 That is, to render native population in Palestine absent by force in order to supplant them with Zionist settlers. This is perfectly captured by the infamous Zionist slogan: 'a land without a people for a people without a land.' Furthermore, Zionist categorisation of internally displaced Palestinians (IDPs) as present-absentee captures settler colonial policies of preventing those IDPs, although granted Israeli citizenship, from returning to their previously owned homes and properties. They were recognised as present within the borders of the state, however, their 'absence' from property previously owned, which was the inevitable result of a process of systematic expulsion and being prevented from returning throughout the military period, deemed them 'absent' and so unable to recover their property. Therefore, native presence, perpetually caught in absence, instructs legitimised displacement and denial of return while Jews—from anywhere in the world—qualify for citizenship. (For more on IDPs and military period see Khoury, 2012; Pappe, 2006.)

3 Occupied Palestinian Territories

4 In the same context, Butler clarifies that the story of origin is 'a strategic tactic within a narrative that by telling a single, authoritative account about an irrevocable past [before the legal state of origin] makes the constitution of the law appear as a historical inevitability.'

5 See definition in *The Encyclopaedia and Dictionary of Zionism and Israel* (2005) Avoda ivrit Definition. Available at: www.zionism-israel.com/dic/Kibbush_Haavoda.htm (Accessed 1 December 2021).

6 The passing of Jewish national law, adopted officially in July 2018, known as the Nation-State Bill, which declares Israel is a nation state of Jewish people, is nothing new, as its roots are in the very foundation of the settler colonial state being exclusively Jewish (i.e., Israel's basic law: https://main.knesset.gov.il/en/activity/pages/basiclaws.aspx).

7 Israel's Law of Return stipulates that any Jew, from anywhere in the world, has the right to proclaim 'Aliyah' and become a legal Israeli citizen. See: www.knesset.gov.il/laws/special/eng/return.htm (Accessed 14 June 2021).

8 See here: www.amazon.ca/Israel-2011-Calendar-Lucas-Entertainment/dp/1935478249 (Accessed 14 June 2021).

9 Discussion on Netta Brazilai, winner of Eurovision 2018, in Chapter 3 further illuminates this point.

10 Laws such as the Citizenship and Entry into Israel, which bans the issuance of 'family unification' documents for Palestinians (see: www.knesset.gov.il/laws/special/eng/citizenship_law.htm) and absentee property laws disallowing Palestinian reclamation of properties they owned prior to their displacement by the Jewish state (see: https://unispal.un.org/UNISPAL.NSF/0/E0B719E95E3B-494885256F9A005AB90A) all cohere with the settler-state's larger war on Arab demography.

11 For the Israelis, the Intifada appeared as a reminder of what their first prime minister David Ben Gurion once said: 'A people which (sic) fights against the usurpation of its land will not tire so easily.' See BBC News (2008) 1987: The Intifada. Available online at: http://news.bbc.co.uk/1/hi/world/middle_east/7381369. stm (Accessed 1 December 2021).

12 I refer to PNA and Authority interchangeably throughout.

13 In reference to security coordination that PNA de facto leader Mahmoud Abbas described as 'sacred' in one of his speeches (see Miller, 2014). In the sphere of economic cooperation between Palestinian capitalists, with nascent ties to the PNA, and Israel despite the global call for BDS (See Dana, 2014a).

44 Mapping Hetero-Conquest

14 This is captured in more recent reforms of the PNA security apparatus, which took place after the Second Intifada to enable what US and Israel perceived as the need to dismantle any prospect for terror. Former prime minster Sharon advocated this at the 2003 conference: '1. Dismantling all existing security bodies loyal to Arafat,' which he described as terrorists following their engagement in armed struggle against Israel during the Second Intifada; '2. Appointing a New Minister of Interior to oversee the dissolution and outlawing of Palestinian military wings;' and '3. Immediate renewal of Palestinian Israeli security cooperation.' He stressed that 'the security reform must accompany a sincere and real effort to stop terrorism, while applying the "chain of preventive measures" outlined by the Americans: intelligence gathering, arrest, interrogation, prosecution and punishment.' (Dana, 2014a: n.p.).
15 In his essay on Rawabi, the Palestinian architect and artist Youself Al-Khateeb, makes a similar argument to Anani. Al-Khateeb uses two aerial photos, one of an Israeli settlement—Pasgot Ze'ev—and one of Rawabi in order to show striking similarities between the two (see Figure 2.7 and Figure 2.8).
16 UN Convention on the Elimination of All Forms of Discrimination against Women
17 Infamous for his targeted killing strategy against Palestinians
18 In the follow up to these protests, activists including the late Basil Al Araj were interview on the local Palestinian TV along with spokesperson of PNA security forces who accuses Basil and other activists of being Western agents (Al Falastiniat Tv, 2013).

Bibliography

Abu Ghosh, R., 2013. 'On the Pavement of Al-Mukata'a.' *Quds News* [Online]. Available at: https://qudsn.net/post/26948/%D8%B9%D9%84%D9%89-%D8%B1%D8%B5%D9%8A%D9%81-%D8%A7%D9%84%D9%85%D9%82%D8%A7%D8%B7%D8%B9%D8%A9 (Accessed 1 December 2021). Source in Arabic.
Abu Samra, Q., 2012. 'In Ramallah Too. "Down with Police Rule".' *Anadolu Agency* [Online]. Available at: www.aa.com.tr/ar/archive/%D9%81%D9%8A-%D8%B1%D8%A7%D9%85-%D8%A7%D9%84%D9%84%D9%87-%D8%A3%D9%8A%D8%B6%D9%8B%D8%A7-%D9%8A%D8%B3%D9%82%D8%B7-%D8%AD%D9%83%D9%85-%D8%A7%D9%84%D8%B9%D8%B3%D9%83%D8%B1/358169 (Accessed 1 December 2021). Source in Arabic.
Ahmed, S., 2010. *The Promise of Happiness*. Durham, NC: Duke University Press.
Al falastiniat Tv, 2013. 'Haki Al Makshuf.' *Al falastiniat Tv*. Available at: www.youtube.com/watch?v=1IY1HTuE4Mw&t=1180s (Accessed 22 December 2012).
Al Muzin, A., 1979. 'The Workers.' *The Palestine Poster Project Archive*. Available at: www.palestineposterproject.org/poster/the-workers (Accessed 1 December 2021).
Alqaisiya, W., Hilal, G., and Maikey, M., 2016. 'Dismantling the Homosexual Image in Palestine,' in *Decolonizing Sexualities: Transnational Perspectives, Critical Interventions*, edited by S. Bakshi, S. Jivraj, and S. Posocco. London: Counterpress.
Anani, Y., 2011. 'Designing Civic Encounter.' *Academia the Mirror* [Online]. Available at: www.artterritories.net/designingcivicencounter/?page_id=13 (Accessed 1 December 2021).
Anzaldua, G., 1987. *Borderlands/La Frontera: The New Mestiza*. San Francisco: Aunt Lute Books.

Mapping Hetero-Conquest 45

Arvin, M., Tuck, E., and Morrill, A., 2013. 'Decolonizing Feminism: Challenging Connections Between Settler Colonialism and Heteropatriarchy.' *Feminist Formations* 25 (1): 8–34.

BBC News Arabic, 2014. 'Abu Mazeen: We Do Not Want to Drown Israel with Refugees.' Available at: www.bbc.com/arabic/middleeast/2014/02/140216_abbas_refugees_flood (Accessed 1 December 2021).

Blumenthal, M., 2013. *Goliath: Life and Loathing in Greater Israel*. New York: Nation Books.

Bowman, G. W., 2011. 'A Place for the Palestinians in the Altneuland: Herzl, Anti-Semitism, and the Jewish State,' in *Surveillance and Control in Israel/Palestine: Population, Territory and Power*, edited by E. Zureik, D. Lyon, and Y. Abu-Laban, 65–79. New York: Routledge.

Brym, R. J., 1988. 'The Transformation of Menial Labour in Israel.' *Newsletter – Association for Israel Studies* 3(2): 12–15.

Butler, J., 1999. *Gender Trouble: Feminism and the Subversion of Identity*. New York: Routledge.

Congressman Joe Walsh, 2011. *Prime Minister of Israel Benjamin Netanyahu Speech at the Joint Session of Congress*. Available at: www.youtube.com/watch?v=0BaMLlnb_KI (Accessed 1 December 2021).

Dana, T., 2014a. 'The Beginning of the End of Palestinian Security Coordination with Israel?' *Jadaliyya*. Available at: www.jadaliyya.com/pages/index/18379/the-beginning-of-the-end-of-palestiniansecurity-c?fb_comment_id=57197082624523 9_575963662512622 (Accessed 1 December 2021).

Dana, T., 2014b. 'The Palestinian Capitalists That Have Gone Too Far.' *AlShabaka—The Palestinian Policy Network*. Available at: https://al-shabaka.org/briefs/palestinian-capitalists-have-gone-too-far/ (Accessed 1 December 2021).

Enloe, C., 1993. *The Morning After: Sexual Politics at the End of the Cold War*. California: University of California Press.

Fabian, J., 1983. *Time and Other: How Anthropology Makes Its Objects*. New York: Columbia University Press.

Friedman, T., 2010. 'The Real Palestinian Revolution.' *The New York Times* [Online]. Available at: www.nytimes.com/2010/06/30/opinion/30friedman.html (Accessed 1 December 2021).

Glazov, J., 2011. 'Michael Lucas: A Gay Man for Israel.' *FRONTPAGE Magazine* [Online]. Available at: www.frontpagemag.com/fpm/93081/michael-lucas-gay-man-israel-jamie-glazov (Accessed 1 December 2021).

Haboub, A., 2013. 'BADIL Poster Contest.' *The Palestine Poster Project Archive*. Available at: www.palestineposterproject.org/poster/badil-poster-contest-2013-haboub (Accessed 1 December 2021).

Hoffman, W., 2009. 'GREAT EXXXPECTATIONS: Israeli Stud Make a New Kind of Porno.' *Tablet Magazine* [Online]. Available at: www.tabletmag.com/jewish-life-and-religion/10955/great-exxxpectations (Accessed 1 December 2021).

Isseroff, A., 2005. 'Zionism and Israel—Encyclopaedic Dictionary: Avoda Ivrit Definition.' Available at: https://zionism-israel.com/dic/Kibbush_Haavoda.htm (Accessed 1 December 2021).

Jean-Klein, I., 2001. 'Nationalism and Resistance: The Two Faces of Everyday Activism in Palestine During the Intifada.' *Cultural Anthropology* 16(1): 83–126.

Jerusalem Post, 2011. 'Michael Lucas: Israel Is a Beacon of LGBT Emancipation.' *The Jerusalem Post* [Online]. Available at: www.jpost.com/International/

46 Mapping Hetero-Conquest

Michael-Lucas-Israel-is-a-beacon-of-LGBT-emancipation (Accessed 1 December 2021).

Kaminer, M., and The Forward, 2009. 'Can Gay Porn Save Israel's Image?' *HAARETZ* [Online]. Available at: www.haaretz.com/news/can-gay-porn-save-israel-s-image-1.7471 (Accessed 1 December 2021).

Khalidi, R., and Samour, S., 2011. 'Neoliberalism as Liberation: The Statehood Programme and the Remaking of the Palestinian National Movement.' *Journal of Palestine Studies* 40(2): 6–25.

Khalili, L., 2007. *Heroes and Martyrs of Palestine*. Cambridge: Cambridge University Press.

Khoury, A., 2012. 'The Internally Displaced Palestinians in Israel.' *BADIL Resource Centre* [Online]. Available at: www.badil.org/en/component/k2/item/1873-art6.html (Accessed 24 June 2017).

Kornberg, J., 1993. *Theodor Herzl: From Assimilation to Zionism*. Bloomington: Indiana University Press.

Kozaczuk, D., 2015. 'The Hegemonic Ideal of Neoliberal Space of Peace. Rawabi, Palestine, a Case Study.' MSc thesis, The School of Oriental Studies [Online]. Available at: www.academia.edu/19535210/The_Hegemonic_Ideal_of_Neoliberal_Space_of_Peace._Rawabi_Palestine_a_Case_Study (Accessed 1 December 2021).

Kuttab, E. S., 1993. 'Palestinian Women in the "Intifada": Fighting on Two Fronts.' *Arab Studies Quarterly* 15(2): 69–85.

Lillian Goldman Law library, 2008. 'The Palestinian National Charter: Resolutions of the Palestine National Council July 1–17, 1968.' *Yale Law School*. Available at: https://avalon.law.yale.edu/20th_century/plocov.asp (Accessed 1 December 2021).

Lindholm Schulz, H., 1999. *The Reconstitution of Palestinian Nationalism*. Manchester: Manchester University Press.

Lockman, Z., and Beinin, J., 1989. *Intifada: The Palestinian Uprising Against Israeli Occupation*. Boston: South End Press.

Lukacs, Y., 1992. *The Israeli-Palestinian Conflict: A Documentary Record, 1967–1990*. Cambridge: Cambridge University Press.

Lunat, Z., 2010. 'The Netanyahu-Fayyad "Economic Peace" One Year On.' *Electronic Intifada* [Online]. Available at: https://electronicintifada.net/content/netanyahu-fayyad-economic-peace-one-year/8673 (Accessed 1 December 2021).

Malhi-Sherwell, T., 2001. 'Imagining Palestine as the Motherland,' in *Self Portrait: Palestinian Women's Art* (Exhibition Catalogue), edited by Tali Ben Zvi and Y Lerer, 160–166. Tel Aviv: Andalus Publishing.

Mansour, S., 1988. 'Mother Intifada.' *The Palestine Poster Project Archive*. Available at: www.palestineposterproject.org/poster/mother-Intifada (Accessed 1 December 2021).

Massad, J., 1995. 'Conceiving the Masculine: Gender and Palestinian Nationalism.' *Middle East Journal* 49(3): 467–483.

Mendes-Flohr, P., and Reinharz, J., 2011. *The Jew in the Modern World: A Documentary History*. Oxford: Oxford University Press.

Menhem, E., 1976. 'Day of The Palestinian Struggle.' *The Palestine Poster Project Archive*. Available at: www.palestineposterproject.org/poster/day-of-the-palestinian-struggle (Accessed 1 December 2021).

Miller, E., 2014. 'Abbas Avows to Uphold 'Sacred' Security Coordination with Israel.' *The Times of Israel*. Available at: https://www.timesofisrael.com/abbas-vows-to-uphold-sacred-security-coordination-with-israel/ (Accessed 1 December 2021).

Nanni, G., 2012. *The Colonisation of Time: Rituals, Routine and Resistance in the British Empire*. Manchester: Manchester University Press.

Neumann, B., 2011. *Land and Desire in Early Zionism*. Translated from Hebrew by H. Watzman. New England, US: Brandeis University Press.

Palestine Student League, 2012. 'We Will Return.' *The Palestine Poster Project Archive*. Available at: www.palestineposterproject.org/poster/we-will-return-even-if-it-takes-us-a-while (Accessed 1 December 2021).

Pappe, I., 2006. *The Ethnic Cleansing of Palestine*. London: Oneworld.

Pawel, E., 1993. *Labyrinth of Exile: A Life of Theodor Herzl*. New York: Farrar, Straus and Giroux.

Perez, E., 2003. 'Queering the Borderlands: The Challenges of Excavating the Invisible and Unheard.' *Frontiers: A Journal of Women Studies* 24(2/3): 122–131.

Portwood, J., 2013. 'Michael Lucas on Gay Men in the Promised Land.' *Out Magazine* [Online]. Available at: www.out.com/entertainment/movies/2013/04/03/michael-lucas-gay-men-undressing-israel (Accessed 1 December 2021).

Rawabi News, 2022. Available at: www.Rawabi.ps (Accessed 1 December 2021).

Rotbard, S., 2003. 'Wall and Tower,' in *A Civilian Occupation: The Politics of Israeli Architecture*, edited by R. Segal and E. Weizman. New York: Verso.

Rubenberg, C., 2001. *Palestinian Women: Patriarchy and Resistance in the West Bank*. London: Lynne Rienner.

Savir, M., 2015. 'The Golden Palestinian City Overlooking Tel Aviv.' *i 24 Middle East News* [Online]. Available at: www.i24news.tv/en/news/international/middle-east/84497-150904-the-golden-palestinian-city-overlooking-tel-aviv (Accessed 1 December 2021).

Sayigh, Z., 1997. *Armed Struggle and the Search for State: The Palestinian National Movement 1949–1993*. Oxford: Oxford University Press.

Schoenberg, S., 2016. *Modern Jewish History: The Haskala, Jewish Virtual Library*. Available at: www.jewishvirtuallibrary.org/jsource/Judaism/ Haskalah.html (Accessed 1 December 2021).

Schulman, S., 2012. *Israel/Palestine and the Queer International*. Durham, NC: Duke University Press.

Shalhoub-Kevorkian, N., 2009. *Militarization and Violence Against Women in Conflict Zones in the Middle East: A Palestinian Case Study*. Cambridge: Cambridge University Press.

Sherwood, H., 2016. 'Story of Cities #49: The Long Road to Rawabi, Palestine's First Planned City.' *The Guardian* [Online] Available at: https://www.theguardian.com/cities/2016/may/24/story-cities-rawabi-planned-city-palestine (Accessed 13 July 2017).

Tartir, A., 2014, 'Criminalising Resistance, Entrenching Neoliberalism: The Fayyadist Paradigm in the Occupied Palestinian West Bank.' PhD thesis, The London School of Economics and Political Science [Online]. Available at: http://etheses.lse.ac.uk/3179/ (Accessed 1 December 2021).

Weizman, E., 2002. *Optical Urbanism, Open Democracy*. Available at: www. opendemocracy.net/ecology-politicsverticality/article_804.jsp (Accessed 19 December 2021).

Wolfe, P., 2006. 'Settler Colonialism and the Elimination of the Native.' *Journal of Genocide Research* 8(4): 387–409.

Wolfe, P., 2012. 'Purchase by Other Means: The Palestine Nakba and Zionism's Conquest of Economics.' *Journal of Settler Colonial Studies* 2(1): 133–171.

Yuval-Davis, N., 1997. *Gender and Nation*. London: Sage Publications.

Part I
Unsettling

3   Native Queer Refusal

Introduction

This chapter engages the work and analysis of the most prominent queer organising group, alQaws for Sexual and Gender Diversity in Palestinian Society, to reveal their meaning in relation to what I call native queer politics of refusal. I begin by charting the story of alQaws's emergence as recounted by the activists and the founder of the group, Haneen Maikey. The group's journey of emerging as an independent collective that is firmly grounded in the native positionality of its Palestinian subject is situated within the context of local socio-political dynamics in the follow up of Oslo's failure. Yet alQaws's journey for self-recognition in relation to Palestine marks a rejection of working within apolitical frames of organising that maintained the structure of Palestinian Nakba. Analysis of alQaws's politics and their meanings in relation to queer, Palestine, and decolonisation is further consolidated in relation to the advancement of anti-pinkwashing/pinkwatching activism and boycott, divestment, sanctions (BDS) anti-normalisation work. AlQaws-led activism and analyses to expose pinkwashing is fundamental to the decolonial queering praxis rooted in unveiling the violence upon which the Zionist sexuality regime is founded. Emblematic of such violence is the propagation of Israel as a saviour myth, whose hijacking of native queer pain not only serves to sustain and naturalise settler colonial conquest of native bodies and lands but also explains the global expansion of the same regime. Palestinian queer work and boycott campaigning addresses the complicity of international normalising of Israel's sexuality regime. It does so by challenging the very modern/homophobic notion that is also symptomatic of the hegemony of the international colonial ga(yz)e intersecting forms of racism, patriarchy, and capitalism. AlQaws's politics of queer refusal encompasses native resistance to mainstream approaches of Western LGBT rights anchored in peacebuilding and developmental agendas informing Global North countries' investment in Palestine. In so doing, it makes audible a native queer voice that is mobilising queerness as grounded in decolonisation politics from Palestine to the rest of the world.

DOI: 10.4324/9781003273585-4

52 *Native Queer Refusal*

To Be Queers in Palestine

> In 2001 alQaws was part of an Israeli Zionist organisation in Jerusalem [Jerusalem Open House (JOH)]. The funny story is that they advertised a job looking for a Palestinian—the job description referred to an Arabic speaker or something along those lines—a community organiser who could reach out to Palestinians LGBT. Since I was exploring my sexuality, it was the right timing and perfect 'professional hat' to hide under in order to explore my sexuality . . . so, in 2001 we started as a tiny, local, service-oriented, apolitical project. We were exploring our sexual orientation in a Zionist Israeli apolitical organisation [audience bursts laughing]. It is a joke but it's true, [and this was] in one of the most hectic political periods, during the Second Intifada. We were a bunch of queers sitting in a community centre discussing sexual orientation. I think what happened at the end of those various meetings, as we went to downtown Jerusalem, was crucial for us. Soldiers were stopping us and our friends who came from the West Bank—back then the apartheid wall was not yet officially in place—they were not even able to come. So, this entire political situation was coming in, imposing itself into these discussions and it was hard to ignore it. What we did then was to contain it, work with it, and see how we could be queers in Palestine and what it meant to be queer in Palestine and Palestinian queer.
>
> (alQaws, 2014a: n.p.)

Haneen Maikey, founder, and director of alQaws since 2008, provides a detailed explanation of the gradual development of the groups' current political trajectory. This process, she jokes, did not come about because of 'us feeling happy and drunk and wanting suddenly to be radical;' it was the outcome of '10 years of real field-work experience that—most of the time—was far from radical, if not very politically problematic' (Ibid.). As Haneen's words above reveal, this intense political period brought the group to interrogate its confinement within Israeli LGBT spaces, which was primarily based on sexual orientation, triggering instead a need to work with what it means to 'be queers in Palestine.' During the period of the Second Intifada (2000–2005), Zionist forces targeted and killed Palestinians everywhere,[1] intensifying further the reality of Palestinian Nakba through wider imposition of checkpoints, settlement expansion, and further encroachment on Palestinian land. This period also represented—for many Palestinians—the official demise of the Oslo Accord-inflicted peace era. The launch of the Oslo peace process in the early 1990s raised hopes for a resolution to the Israeli/Palestinian conflict founded on what was claimed as mutual respect, economic peace, and coexistence. The ensuing wave of optimism led many Palestinian and Israeli human rights and feminist civil society groups to team up and launch collaborative projects. AlQaws was one such project. However, as the Second Intifada unfolded concurrently with the joint alQaws-JOH initiative, this collaboration eroded.

Oslo had become a marker of the surrender of Palestinian leadership to the reproduction of a system that sustains the power of colonial governance,

Native Queer Refusal 53

which are central to the re-instantiation of hetero-conquest, as discussed in Chapter 2. Under Oslo, Palestinian Nakba continued through the intensification of Palestinian dispossession as settlement construction grew exponentially, as did barriers, walls, and checkpoints (Roy, 1999). Palestinians' launching of their uprising in September 2000 came in this context of peace as a marker of Nakba. That is, far from bringing a just solution, Oslo epitomised the colonised condition of being robbed of one's life, resources, and most basic right to return to and/or simply *be* in one's homeland. During this 'crackdown,' Israel targeted, wounded, and killed Palestinians both within the 1949 armistice lines (so-called Israel proper) and in the occupied Palestinian territories (oPt) (see Jamjoum, 2002; Allen, 2008; Adalah, 2015). Against this backdrop, members of alQaws faced growing emotional and logistical constraints, such as travel difficulties and repeated harassment by Israeli soldiers. Most importantly, their discussions of sexuality became increasingly inextricable from the political reality in which they are implicated as *Palestinians*.

The Second Intifada was a historical juncture that forced alQaws members to confront and recognise who they truly are in the face of the settler colonial machine. Having to confront what it meant 'to be queer in Palestine' and/or to be a 'Palestinian queer' was at the core of the group's re-evaluation process of its affiliation with Israeli LGBT initiatives, working within the ambit of an ostensibly apolitical organisation. To recognise who they are as Palestinians, which emanated from their embodied/political location as such, meant to undergo a process of delinking as detaching from the overall structure of violence that defined their being (Mignolo and Escobar, 2010). In other words, alQaws members began to see 'the joke' of working within a 'Zionist apolitical organisation.' Such a reality of apolitical conjoining of Israelis and Palestinians for projects of coexistence and mutual collaboration was reflective of the very façade/joke of peace that Oslo propagated. Thus, Oslo became the vessel for propagating colonised misrecognition (Fanon, 1967), locking them within the fantasy of being able to collaborate and co-exist beyond politics. However, the need for queer Palestinians to engage with their own—native—embodied reality, which is being violently dispossessed and killed, fuelled the turn away from the very structure enabling native disappearance to continue. Haneen explains that within JOH spaces alQaws members started to see how the 'coloniser/colonised dynamic reproduced itself in terms of what language we could and could not use' (alQaws, 2014a: n.p.). 'We could not use the word "occupation" because this "apolitical" Zionist organisation would not allow it' (Ibid.). The discursive refusal of the colonised reality of Palestine relied on the very structures that reproduced, in material and symbolic terms, the reality of native disavowal. Palestinian queers' need to recognise and engage with who *they truly are*, i.e., in relation to such disavowal, enable them to see 'the joke' encapsulating their (non)being in the realm of apolitical Zionism. In doing so, they undergo a process of revealing the reality of peaceful

54 *Native Queer Refusal*

violence (Fanon, 1963), whereby the fantasy of 'peace' and 'apolitical coexistence' serve only to maintain Zionism and so a violent encroachment on the native's being.

Recognising one's native and so queered position in the world meant querying the very terms of organising in the ambit of 'apolitical' sexuality organising, which served to maintain the structure of Nakba. Experiences with Israeli LGBT groups had exposed alQaws to unitary gay politics, that is, an espousal of a progressive stance on LGBT questions while maintaining the settler colonial violence underpinning Zionist discourse and practice. Ghaith Hilal recounts how the aftermath of a 2009 homophobic incident, in which a Jewish-Israeli gunman killed two people at a gay bar in Tel Aviv, exemplifies that dynamic,

> A commemorative event followed this incident and some Palestinian LGBT individuals, who wanted to express their solidarity, were banned from participating in fear of them talking politics. At the same time, the event was full of those same Israeli politicians who praised the killings of Gazans[2] a few months earlier. Now, they had come to proclaim a 'Do Not Kill' message to the rhythm of the Israeli national anthem at the vigil.
>
> (Conversation with Ghaith, 2015)

It is important to note that the Israeli anthem, 'Hatikvah,' is a Zionist song that celebrates exclusive Jewish entitlement to Palestine identified as the 'land of Zion.' Naftali Herz Imber, a Ukrainian Jew, wrote 'Hatikvah' (meaning hope in Hebrew) in 1880 to represent 'the undying hope of the Jewish people, through the long years of exile that they would someday return to independence in their homeland' (Jewish Virtual Library: n.p.).[3] This song represents yet another example of a Zionist hope for a return to History, which reflects salvation qua Time, marking, as discussed in the previous chapter, the initiation of hetero-conquest. 'Hatikvah' stands for the Zionist reinvention of Jewish collective identity within a biblical frame (Masalha, 2007); it legitimises a Jewish sovereign state on the back of a hetero-conquest regime. AlQaws's gradual split from JOH spaces, which officially took place in 2007, signalled not only a moment of recognising the need to detach and delink from the coloniser's structures of violence but also signified an urge to 'engage in an epistemic reconstitution' (E-IR, 2017: 2). For alQaws, then, grounding Palestine in queerness and queerness in Palestine grew ever more urgent as it became increasingly clear that the apolitical single-issue approach was oblivious if not reproductive of the settler colonial reality of Palestine and Palestinians. Hence, decolonial queering required transcending exclusivist gay identifications and constructing possibilities for gay resignification, captured in the organisation's full name when it established itself as a separate entity in 2007: alQaws for Sexual and Gender Diversity in Palestinian Society (*al-qaws lil-ta'addudiyya al-jinsiyya wal-jindiriyya fil mujtama'a al-filastini*). While *qaws quzah* is the Arabic word for rainbow, a now universally recognised symbol associated with LGBT politics, alQaws's rainbow embraces sexual and gender diversity (*alt'adudiyya al-jinsiyya wal jindariyya*) and, in addition, positions itself clearly within Palestinian society (*fil mujtama' al-filastini*). Thus, it grounds sexuality in a socio-political context that does not elide the settler colonial reality of Palestine. In this process of naming, alQaws re-signified the exclusionary politics of gayness and the standard LGBT framework to 'question the structures of knowledge and subject formation (desires, beliefs, expectations)' (E-IR, 2017: 2) that maintained Nakba. By expanding the rainbow to include native positionality and subject position, alQaws redeployed dominant norms to render the work of decolonial queering more politically effective (Butler, 1992).

Countering Pinkwashing

alQaws's emergence as an independent collective coincides with the Zionist practice of branding itself as a modern, progressive society and gay haven while simultaneously depicting Palestinian society as reactionary and homophobic. The tactic, which Palestinian queer activists identify as pinkwashing, seems to have begun in 2002 when Israel recruited its Jewish LGBT community to help promote itself using so-called pink-progressive and LGBT-friendly tropes. In 2005, the effort culminated in an official multimillion-dollar campaign rebranding Israel as a modern democracy and gay destination (see pinkwatching.com). Presenting itself as 'the only democratic and LGBT-friendly country in the Middle East' (Ibid.) while simultaneously continuing to expand the colonisation of Palestinian land, Israel legitimises its illegal and oppressive practices against Palestinians whom it depicts as homophobic. An emblematic example of alQaws's efforts to expose pinkwashing, widely known as pinkwatching campaigning, took place at an activist led event during Israel's apartheid week in 2015. Both myself and alQaws member, Omar Khoury, were invited as panellists for the event, which was organised by students at the London School of Economics and Political Science. Following the presentations that questioned the myth of Israeli innocence and normalcy, a member of the audience, who self-identified as Israeli, stated, 'Israel has the right to promote its image and be proud of being open, just like any other country would promote itself. . . . Why should there be anything wrong with that?!' Omar responded by pointing out that Israel was 'not like any other normal country . . . because its branding campaign always relies on proliferating certain images and narratives of Palestine and Palestinians.' In our collaborative piece, Haneen, Ghaith, and I frame pinkwashing as:

> An ontologically racist and colonial project . . . a familiar Zionist tactic that reframes the relationship between Israel and Palestine from 'coloniser-colonised' to one that distinguishes between those who are

56 *Native Queer Refusal*

'modern and open,' and those who are presented as 'backward and homophobic.' Thus, it simplifies and anesthetises the fundamental violence based on which colonialism thrives.

(Alqaisiya *et al*, 2016: 131)

alQaws-led activism to expose pinkwashing is fundamental to decolonial queering praxis as engraved in unveiling the violence upon which the Zionist sexuality regime is founded. Ghiath Hilal unpacks fully the functionality of this violence through the deployment of modern/democratic tropes to propagate the notion of the colonial saviour. It depicts Israel as the gay refuge that will save LGBT Palestinians from their own homophobic/backward society. As Ghaith says, 'Israel uses narratives of progress and its self-image as a gay haven and a democracy to persuade queer Palestinians that they will always be victims of their homophobic societies and that neither alQaws nor our communities can accommodate their needs' (Conversation with Ghaith, 2015). The saviour fantasy enforces a victimhood positionality for queer Palestinians, who, deprived of agency, must look to Israel since their needs cannot be accommodated in their own society. AlQaws's activism produces significant analysis that shatters the myth of Israel as a gay refuge for Palestinians (Maikey, 2019: n.p.). The group challenges the production of films and documentaries that disseminate this reality of Palestinian suppressed LGBT, whose only way to find shelter from their homophobic families is by seeking refuge in the gay haven city of Tel Aviv. One such example is the activists' collective statement with regards to a 2015 movie named *Oriented*,[4] which traces the lives of three gay Palestinians who live in Tel Aviv.

We are concerned that this film positions Tel Aviv as the 'gay haven' for queer Palestinians, falsely implying a 'tolerant' and 'open' city that graciously allows self-identified Palestinian queers—both victims and strong activists—to live and thrive. This directly contributes to the pinkwashing propaganda campaign (perhaps even serving as its newest face) and is an unfortunate erasure of Palestinian queer narratives. Unlike this film's narrow picture, our work, our priorities, and our successes refer to the many Palestinian queers—who live, thrive, create, struggle, and fight on a daily basis for their freedom—without relation to Tel Aviv. Change cannot happen in a pinkwashed city, nor can it fit into a cliché discourse about 'change' in documentary films. The change we strive for is not narrow and superficial; it is rooted in our slow, deep and cumulative work on sexual and gender diversity within our own communities and context.

(alQaws Opinion Piece, 2015: n.p.)

AlQaws's statement captures the reality of a native queer politics for emancipation that is anchored in the conscious disavowal of there being any relationality to the coloniser's space, 'fight on a daily basis for their freedom—*without* relation to Tel Aviv.' At the same time, the analysis reveals how settler subjects are at pains to demonstrate solidarity with native queer suffering. For instance, in the follow up to recent incidents of violence towards Palestinian LGBT groups and individuals, Israeli institutionalised support was noticeably heightened, and several solidarity marches began to take place. Haneen writes how the discourses reproduced in such acts of solidarity, where Jewish-Israeli analyses and institutional support dominate, cement the colonial self-generated fantasy of the Zionist state as a refuge space for Palestinian queers constituted as inherently denied the freedom that their coloniser can offer (Maikey, 2019: n.p.). Spaces of multicultural Israeli-ness coming in solidarity with Palestinian suffering exemplify a facile settler sense of empathy with the pain of the native Other. What I call, following Razack's (2007) 'Stealing the Pain of Others,' the settlers' theft of natives' pain.

Razack draws on Hartman to contemplate the appropriation of the slaves' suffering by their own owner/master. The latter's ability to stand as witness and approximate the former's suffering emanate from the very power position they occupy in relation to the fungible body of the slave. What underlines this facile intimacy with their slaves is a process of affirming the master's humanitarian and morally superior character at the expense of an objectified and objectifiable—conquerable—Other. This, in turn, obscures the former's inherent complacency in the slave's suffering, thus such an act of empathy and identification 'dehumanise them [the slaves] even further' (2007: 376). In other words, an element of pleasure instructs the master's sense of embracing the pain of their slave. This relates to the former's position of observer and consumer, which has historically cemented the master's role in relation to a voyeuristic enjoyment of the slave's suffering. Zionist narratives of saving and protection LGBT Palestinians indicate this same relational dynamic. It reifies a Jewish-Zionist all-embracing sense—à la its Jewish and democratic constitutional definition—that remains morally superior and thus more worthy of legitimacy than a native sovereign constituency. The settler colonial hijacking of native pain reaffirms legitimacy and naturalises settler conquest. The following example serves as an illustration. During the summer of 2014, I received a phone call from Haneen who shared with me a story that was circulating in relation to the death of the Jerusalemite child, Muhammad Abu Khdeir. In the follow up to the death of the child, who was kidnapped and burnt to death at the hands of Israeli orthodox settlers, a story began to circulate in some Israeli circles that Muhammad had been killed by his family because he was gay. As Haneen suggests, 'this episode confirms the violence perpetuated by the pinkwashing narrative from an ostensibly progressive stance, whereby Israel and Israeli, who are killing, displacing and dispossessing Palestinians, are saving them from a society that otherwise kills them' (Conversation with Haneen, 2014).

The circulation of an image of Abu Khdeir on social media, with the tag in Hebrew 'Arabs killed him because he was gay,' demonstrates the affective parameters of a settler rescue-empathy that is not to be separated from the

58 Native Queer Refusal

very genocidal structure it serves and perpetuates. This rescue-empathy logic also interlinks with the production of a native sense of guilt, which intermeshes with a settler sense of innocence. The latter abrogates settlers from their responsibility in native dispossession by virtue of endowing conquest with a HuManist value, encapsulating the Human/Man notion of the settler colonial trap (Mignolo, 2006). In other words, settlers' rescue-empathy locks the native within the socio-political imperatives that 'toys with colonised psyche' (Shalhoub-Kevorkian, 2016: 1296) and destroys their sense of being a people (Smith, 2005: 3). The native's sense of guilt inscribes the compulsion to re-enact, on subjective (Palestinian queer need for refuge in Tel Aviv)[5] and objective (PLO signing of Oslo) scales, the inevitability of the native's failure to govern and/or imagine a sovereign sensual self. AlQaws activists reveal the insidious impact that drives pinkwashing policies; 'Pinkwashing tells queer Palestinians that personal (and never collective) liberation can only be found by escaping from their communities and running into their coloniser's arms.' They further add in the same statement that

> The pervasive myth of Palestinians finding 'queer refuge' in Israeli cities flies in the face of the actual policies of the colonial state, which are premised on the exclusion and destruction of Palestinians—queer, trans, or otherwise. The fantasy of Israeli humanitarianism falls apart as soon as the colonial situation is taken into account. There is no 'pink door' in the apartheid wall.
>
> (alQaws, 2020a: n.p.)

alQaws's anti-pinkwashing analysis not only shatters the myth upon which Israel's violence continues but also encapsulates the ensuing native queer revolutionary agency that the colonial saviour fantasy denies it. Pinkwashing as discussed thus far dictates that queerness vis-à-vis Palestine is either non-existent or only conceived via colonisers' HuManist rescue-empathy frame, thereby locking the native within the psycho-political imperatives of hetero-conquest. Decolonial queering encapsulates native politics of unsettling the colonial ga(y)ze, which fixes onto the Other their reality in relation to homophobia and death. In returning that gaze, alQaws counters

> This chiding discourse [that] re-colonises our bodies by implicitly suggesting that queer Palestinians look to Israel as our saviour . . . a familiar and toxic colonial fantasy—that the coloniser can provide something important and necessary that the colonised cannot possibly provide for themselves.
>
> (alQaws, 2014c: n.p.)

Anti-pinkwashing work embodies the queer ontological condition of the present-absent[6] native Palestinian because it troubles more than represents the logic of identifications through which a saviour-self construes its victim

Native Queer Refusal 59

(gay) Other. This is relayed in the ways in which alQaws counters pinkwashing from a position that challenges the singling out of sexuality as the main site of Palestinian oppression.

> Singling out sexuality ignores the stranglehold that Israel's militarised colonial regime has on the lives and privacy of Palestinians more generally throughout Palestine. Blackmailing and extorting an individual based on their sexuality is, of course, a naked act of oppression. But it is no more or less oppressive than blackmailing and extorting an individual based on their lack of access to healthcare, disrupted freedom of movement, exposure of marital infidelities, finances, drug use, or anything else . . . singling out sexuality suggests that 'sexuality' should be the most important priority for Palestinian organisations—including ours—in our struggle against Israeli apartheid, colonisation, and dispossession. It also suggests that sexuality can be singled out from Israeli apartheid, colonisation, and dispossession.
>
> (Ibid.)

This outright refusal to fall into the trap of single-issue politics is seen in alQaws's assertion that 'representing Palestinian gays is not our mission' (Field notes, 2015). The group invites all Palestinians, whether gay identifying or not, to take part in its events and analysis around sexuality, colonialism, and pinkwashing. Thus, another fundamental aim of the politics of decolonial queering is to dismantle normative discourses and colonial regimes of power that set the parameters for imagining Palestinian gay subjectivity in the first place.

The present-absent positionality that Palestinian anti-pinkwashing, also known as pinkwatcher, occupies challenges the arguments that reduce anti-pinkwashing to an identitarian—meaning homonationalist—dynamic. In their important Jadaliyya article in 2012, Jasbir Puar and Maya Mikdashi stated that 'pinkwashing and pinkwatching speak the language of homonationalism. One does so in the name of Israel, the other does so in the name of Palestine' (2012: n.p.). Drawing on Puar's theory of homonationalism, they argued that pinkwatching becomes a venue that consolidates Palestinian gay identities and thus reproduces the logic of the pinkwashing narrative in reverse. While the latter promotes gay identities affiliated with the Israeli state, the former operates from the opposite side of the spectrum, promoting gay identities for Palestine. However, even though homonationalism investigates how queer participates in dominant power structures—nationalism and imperialism—it fails to consider what meanings queer assumes from the standpoint of native, queered positionality, and grassroots work. Consequently, it fails to capture the relevance of decolonial queering politics and locks pinkwatching work within the very same terrain of power that homonationalism critiques. It 'obscures specific, politically relevant features of pinkwatching activism that are particular to Palestine and Palestine

60 *Native Queer Refusal*

solidarity work' (Schotten and Maikey, 2012: n.p.). A homonationalism-centred critique ignores alQaws's own self-definition as an initiative that encompasses the entirety of historic Palestine or, as Maikey describes it, a national queer movement that extends to every corner of Palestinian territory (alQaws, 2014b: n.p.). Such an identification allows alQaws to project a unified nation/notion of Palestine against the Israeli settler colonial order and its geography of dispossession and fragmentation. Reducing pinkwatching to a kind of obverse image of pinkwashing negates alQaws's very deliberate strategy. More specifically, an anti-national conceptual approach overlooks the centrality of nationalist struggles—albeit beyond a re-instantiation of the colonial nation-static model—to decolonial resistance from the standpoint of native people (Driskill, 2010). Thus, decolonial queering complicates queer deconstructionist critique as defined and evaluated solely through the lens of an anti-national stance. Such a stance, as argued in Chapter 1 and as this chapter later shows via a critique of Atshan's anti-puritan stance, succumbs to reifying an understanding of queerness beyond national divides, which in the case of Palestine/Israel proves to be hugely problematic; it reproduces the very settler colonial tropes that Palestinian queers are battling against.

Furthermore, alQaws's anti-pinkwashing activism leads the struggle for anti-normalisation politics that lay bare the power of queer counter-identifications. The annual call to boycott Tel Aviv Pride and Israeli gay tourism, together with the rejection of the discourses connecting Palestinian queers to the pinkwashed city of Tel Aviv, are strategies that alQaws deploys to unsettle the very paradigms—of LGBT pride and acceptance—that reproduce Nakba for Palestine and Palestinians. They are forms of activism whose queerness, as Muñoz (2009: 94) also writes, desires 'another way of being in the world and time' and strives for a different way of being. As part of their Boycott Tel Aviv Pride 2016 campaign, for example, alQaws activists and international allies released a video in which the statement 'Sunbathe at the gay beach and spend the night in luxurious boutique hotels built on the ruins of ethnically cleansed Palestinian villages' is followed by the question 'Why are you proud of Tel Aviv?' (alQaws, 2016). Anti-pinkwashing activism highlights the problematic discourses on gay rights as celebrated in pinkwashed spaces such as Tel Aviv while simultaneously laying bare the historical violence that has been anaesthetised from the consciousness of those espousing progressive gay rights. Pinkwatching discloses what has been obfuscated in the promotion of Tel Aviv as a top gay destination, whose pride brochures and tourist guides fail to mention that the city

> . . . is also an hour away from the world's largest open prison, Gaza, and it is built on stolen land. They forget to mention that the gay soldiers you dance with in the pride parade check, arrest, and kill Palestinians on a daily basis.
>
> (ibid)

Native Queer Refusal 61

Decolonial queering counters the Zionist sexuality regime by centring a Palestinian queer voice that is enacting a politics of refusal (Simpson, 2014). Such politics of refusal lay the ground for the ushering of native resurgence beyond the violence—of Tel Avivian pride and LGBT freedom—fixing the native out of place. Maikey put it succinctly in a Facebook post in 2013, 'The definition of "Pride": never went to, and never will attend the TLV [Tel Aviv] Pride' (Facebook post, 2013). They further reveal how numerous institutions and LGBT bodies (such as the Ministry of Foreign Affairs, Ministry of Tourism, Tel Aviv Municipality, as well as the Aguda, Israel's LGBT task force) participate in the branding campaigning and warn against working with them. Such political (op)positionality grounds queerness in an understanding of decolonisation that signals the refusal to settle for a narrow framework of disidentification. While the logic of queer disidentification aims to avoid the 'trap of assimilation or adhering to different separatist or nationalist ideologies' (Muñoz, 1999: 18), alQaws's anti-normalisation politics highlight the necessity of counter-identification (Smith, 2010: 56). It is through the latter lens that alQaws's work troubles normalised public perceptions of the Israeli state and its gay-friendly image: in other words, alQaws positions itself in relation to Palestine in order not to turn Palestinians into an accepted small minority. Instead, it strives to unsettle the very nature of the settler colonial power structures underlying Israel's branding campaigns. The collective's aim is not to carve out a minority position within the settler state but to continually question the givenness of that state as Omar said, interrupting its presumed rightfulness to continue to exist on the structural basis of Palestinian Nakba. In espousing a counter-identification lens, alQaws's politics encapsulate the power of decolonial queering as it emanates from the recognition of one's native positionality, which simultaneously drives the need to 'refuse to allow a wedge to be driven between the self and society' (alQaws, 2020a). Part and parcel of this work of refusing colonial fragmentation is the work that decolonial queering leads in relation to the international role in enacting willfull ignorance (Vimalassery *et al*, 2016) of their complacency within the constitutive structures of native dispossession.

The Hegemonic International Ga(y)ze

alQaws's efforts also address what can be called the hegemonic role of the international in cementing the pinkwashing practices referenced above. Such hegemony encompasses the entwining of international politics of aid in Palestine with systematic international support and normalisation with the state of Israel. The signing of the Oslo Accords between Israel and the PLO not only held out the promise of peace as Nakba, as discussed thus far, but also ushered in a deluge of international assistance premised on a linear view that peace would lead to security and reward Palestinians with development. Focused on post-conflict scenarios and the Palestinian state-building enterprise, international aid providers disregarded the facts on the grounds that

62 *Native Queer Refusal*

Oslo only exacerbated problems: the continued expansion of settlements and dispossession of Palestinians as a result of occupation, annexation, and criminalisation (see Le More, 2008). Ignoring Israel's expansionist policies, as well as the structural flaws inherent to Oslo, served to further entrench the settler colonial project (see Tartir, 2014). The Oslo agenda structured the foreign aid directed to Palestinian civil society in such a way as to require recipients, both NGOs and grassroots groups, to undertake what Tariq Dana has described as 'predefined tasks in service of the "peace process,"' generating almost-total dependency (2015: 195). Dana goes on to say, 'major political assignments previously associated with the dynamics of anti-colonial struggle' were replaced 'with ostensibly apolitical approaches based on the politics of peacebuilding' (Ibid.). As international donors sought to fund activities deemed crucial to state building in post-conflict societies (see Roy, 1999; Taghdisi-Rad, 2011), they widened the scope of their interest to human rights and, particularly, to sexuality rights, further shaping the course of development in the Palestinian context. Based on recent interactions with international donors, human rights organisations, and international media outlets, alQaws started reflecting critically on this growing interest in what is labelled the 'gay scenery' in Palestine.

> The coloniser's standards and achievements became the yardstick by which the colonised were measured and had to conform, ignoring the fact that the same 'anti sodomy' laws were removed from the Jordanian Penal code—which the PA inherited—in in 1957.
>
> (Maikey, 2012: 122)

The logic of 'development and peace' thus demanded of the Palestinians that they look to their colonisers as role models rather than engage in decolonisation. In one of our Skype conversations, Ghaith sent me a link to read and commented,

> This article[7] [in an online magazine] by this American writer, who wants to explore Gay Palestine, is now providing readers on Palestine, which he considers to be only the West Bank, with a description of fun places as opposed to what we get in the news. He refers to these gay scenes and cafes of Ramallah, which are supposed to challenge what his American audience usually expect to see happening in Palestine. That is, homophobia, xenophobia and terror . . . It is funny that the writer even suggests contacting alQaws as one of the Palestinian gay rights groups. I think they never googled us! [laughing]
>
> (Conversation with Ghaith, 2015)

This article that Ghaith draws on explains the underlying—pinkwashing—assumptions associated with the emerging gay Palestinian scenery, homophobia, xenophobia and terror. During another discussion, Ghaith and Haneen also indicated how international donors are accomplices to the very pink-washing policies that the Palestinian queer movement is trying to combat,

(H): There is a growing donor obsession with the Ramallah gay scenes, and some of them think that it can become like Tel Aviv! . . . This is a dangerous rhetoric on two levels: first, it repeats the old mantra of us needing to somehow catch up with Tel Aviv, re-affirming the colonising notion of civilised/uncivilised; second, this also feeds the logic of fragmenting further Palestine, creating a hierarchy within Palestine that is reproduced by measuring closeness to the so-called Tel Avivian progress.

(G): It is true and I think the emphasis on Ramallah is another way of echoing the Ramallah/Gaza binary, where Palestinian fragmentation is augmented by their capacity to develop.

(H): It reminds me of how some Israeli officials commented in response to Palestinian demands to stop the aggression and lift the siege on Gaza. One of them declared, 'Let's wait for when you have gay parades in Gaza first!'

(Conversation with Haneen and Ghaith, 2015).

Erasing the violence that facilitated the creation and existence of that city, the donor narrative held up Tel Aviv as an example of the threshold of development to which Palestinians should aspire. In brief, the development discourse whitewashed the reality of settler colonialism that is central to Tel Aviv's being. Moreover, such comparisons signalled the fragmentation of Palestinian spaces, reinforcing a growing binary between Ramallah (more liberal) and Gaza (conservative and Islamist). Such a binary underpins inter-Palestinian fragmentation, which Oslo and US donor money facilitated. AlQaws members also draw attention to the kinds of sentiments that international LGBT organising echo in the aftermath of violence against Palestinian queers, implying that 'now it is time to speak about Palestinian homophobia and persecution of gays and abandon this rhetoric on anti-normalisation with Israel' (Maikey in Queer Arabs podcast, 2020). AlQaws challenges the authority with which international LGBT organising aims to dictate the agenda on Palestinian queer politics, restricting it to the realm of Western LGBT approaches that are founded on notions of pride, visibility, and homophobia. Activists' analyses unpack the duality of the West and the Rest upon which a notion of progress for those riding the wave of fighting homophobia is based.

The duality of the US, the West, and the civilised friends of gay people is being used against the Iraqi people and government, who are instead homophobic. This gives the Americans the right not to respect the will of the Iraqi people or of the Iraqi gay community to determine their own paths of struggle. Instead, they imposed the love of gayness and democracy on them, in a ready-made package, sent from America with

64 *Native Queer Refusal*

love. Similarly, Israel uses this discourse in its attempt to whitewash its crimes in front of the whole world.

(Maikey and Shamali, 2011: n.p.)

Such a developmental discourse coheres with the larger support and normalisation that international—mainly the US and European—countries provide for the settler state, including silencing and sanctioning the call led by Palestinian civil society for the global BDS of the Israeli state (https://bdsmovement.net/). AlQaws is part and parcel of that call for an anti-normalisation stance, which also spills over into the international aid sphere.[8] Accordingly, alQaws refuses to 'work [either] directly with Israeli organisations or those international bodies who do not uphold an anti-normalisation stance' (Conversation with Muhammad, 2015). In their 2019 campaigning for a boycott of Eurovision in Israel and Tel Aviv Pride, alQaws and other anti-pinkwashing allies issued a statement to call on international visitors and spectators not to 'become accomplices to Israel's spectacle of cultural propaganda' (alQaws, 2020a: n.p.). In their urgent call to boycott these events, to stop 'complicity and business as usual' with the Zionist settler colonial regime (Ibid.), alQaws issued a series of analyses around the 2018 Eurovision event where Israel's Netta Brazilai won the contest. In a piece entitled, 'Eurovision: When Pluralistic Genders and Sexualities Sing for Settler Colonialism,' Omar Al-Khatib argues that Eurovision's celebration of queerness and camp aesthetics that is representative of Israel's pluralism shows how such events maintain and reproduce sexual and gendered politics serving white supremacist and settler colonial projects (2019: n.p.).

Al-Khatib's piece and other alQaws-produced analysis on this event help to shed light on how international hailing of Israel as the utmost representative of gender and sexual pluralism serves the blatant normalisation of the settler colonial state. At the same time, their analysis reveals the colonial role that international spaces, such as Eurovision, occupy in relation to native queer Others, read as failing to catch up with the freedom that the West and Israel grants LGBT folks. The recognition given to Israel and 'proud' Israelis, such as Barzilai, as a place/subjects of sexual pluralism and modernity stand as another marker of settler sovereignty, reproducing Nakba for Palestine. Barzilai's speech upon winning, 'Thank you for accepting diversity. Next year in Jerusalem!' (Kershner, 2018), corresponds to the de facto conquest of the city and the legitimacy conferred upon it by the Euro-American powers, whose economic and cultural support have enabled settler conquest in Palestine for more than 100 years. Barzilai's victory under the premise of pride in gender and sexual plurality functions as an affective form of geopolitical mapping where Israel's place in the model of Euro-Western queer citizenship is affirmed. Eurovision is a space that 'allow[s] performers and fans alike to be part of an international order that is said to simultaneously claim and disavow regional, national, and continental identities,' enabling them 'to maintain a sense of cultural identity while critiquing essentialism' (Tobin, 2007: 28). The claim to non-essentialism and internationalism that this space maintains, however, obscures the very exclusivist either/or logic upon which non-essentialising scripts of queer geopolitical relations stand (Weber, 2015). The non-essentialism of a global queer citizenship is mediated through the sovereign parameters of a Euro-Western consensus, whose constituent grids on development, immigration, and nation-state formations underpin hierarchising processes of racial and sexual imbrications. In the case of the settler colonial project, one can go further to situate the establishment of a settler-sovereign nation-state within the structures of elimination (Wolfe, 2006)—entrenching, as argued in the previous chapter, the continuity of settler presence as hetero-conquest on native land.

Palestinian queer analysis shows how this structure of settler colonialism in Palestine is maintained through the white streaming of LGBT pluralism that the international hegemonic powers lead. Their anti-normalisation queer activism brings attention to what Magid Shihade calls 'Global Israel.' The creation of the Israeli settler state activates a structure of domineering global settler-mobility, exemplified by 'violence and repression, arms trade, and technologies of surveillance, and militarisation that shape Israeli [settler] mobility locally, regionally, and globally' (Shihade, 2015: 15). This is part and parcel of what the global BDS call against Israel strives for, that is, to bring attention to the very mobility, expansion, and intersection of Israel's power militarily, economically, and culturally. Palestinian queer work, in particular, and boycott campaigning highlights the sexual aspect of this mobility and normalising of Israel's violence. While expanding globally, this sexual regime is constructed in relation to gender and sexual modernity to reify its structure of native elimination. It makes visible, sayable, and audible (Rancière, 2004) a modern and pluralistic (gendered and sexed) self by rendering invisible and inaudible a Palestinian native Other that is being marked for erasure, disappearance, and theft of their pain.

By highlighting the limitations of mainstream Western LGBT approaches in the context of Palestine, alQaws's decolonial queering brings forward the power of the native queer voice that is bent on unmasking the epistemic violence implicit in the depiction of homophobia as 'the specific property of Arab/Muslim society' (alQaws, 2014c: n.p.). In addition, it reveals how the logic of development legitimates the ontological violence of the settler colonial and imperial order, which promotes itself as a civilising enterprise spreading democracy where it is otherwise deemed lacking (see Netanyahu Speech to US Congress, 2011). This logic informs a large majority of international assistance/aid directed toward development and peacebuilding, which enforces and whitewashes colonising hierarchies using the lexicon of progress and democracy. Pondering its response to hegemonic international investments to combat homophobia and spread LGBT rights, alQaws draws on the specificity of what it calls 'our local context.'

66 *Native Queer Refusal*

How can we frame our struggle as against homophobia when we live in a society that does not publicly discuss sexuality? Are pride parades the ultimate celebration of freedom and visibility in a context where millions of Palestinians have no access to water, health care, mobility, work, etc.? How can we understand individual visibility in a family-based society? Is coming out, as understood and practised in the West, a crucial step for a healthy and open life? What are the means to achieve an open and healthy life for LGBT people whose bodies, minds, and reality [are] colonised?

(Alqaisiya *et al*, 2016: 137)

Fundamental to alQaws's mission of unsettling the hegemony of the international is its dedication to working throughout what it identifies as historic Palestine, that is, in both the oPt and inside Israel proper. As a result, the organisation has a presence in Haifa and Jaffa, but it also functions in East Jerusalem, Ramallah, and Bayt Jala (in the oPt). Bringing together communities from both sides of the Green Line[9] demonstrates alQaws's commitment to transcending Zionist colonial fragmentation and rejecting the politics of international assistance that reifies that fragmentation.[10] That notwithstanding, alQaws also takes seriously these varied classifications of Palestinian identity and the consequent division and ghettoisation of Palestinians. As one of their members, Muhammad Halim, explains,

This does not mean that alQaws fails to acknowledge the material impact of these divisions, including the legal statuses under which different communities live, as well as the degree of deterrence these barriers impose on a lot of the work, especially the inability to reach out to Gaza, for instance.

(Conversation with Muhammad, 2014)

The organisation's spaces allow and enable a conjoining of Palestinian identities, be they 48ers (that is, those Palestinians who remained inside Israel's still-undeclared borders after 1948), East Jerusalemites, or West Bankers. Furthermore, alQaws's activism also extends to Palestinians in the diaspora, thereby bridging the gap between insiders, i.e., Palestinians within the boundaries of historic Palestine, and outsiders, i.e., Palestinians in exile. This capacity to recognise and overcome divisions and separations further demonstrates the potential of rising above the colonising frame of humanitarian assistance. AlQaws's US-based trans activist Izzat Mustafa identifies how Palestinian NGOs have been confined to the need to convince the world of 'our suffering,' thus in that process prioritising obtaining donor money; 'we forgot to speak to one another . . . we got burnt out' (Eyewitness Palestine, 2020: n.p.). Mustafa explains how alQaws sees it role in relation to this problematic dynamic that the donor agenda and the framework

Native Queer Refusal 67

of humanitarianism has created. In bringing activists from across historic Palestine and beyond together, decolonial queering, as Mustafa explains it, captures the need to reject the reality of colonial fragmentation by virtue of mobilising queerness, 'not simply an identity, but a radical approach to political mobilisation and decolonisation' (alQaws, 2020a: n.p.).

Rising in Solidarity

Emblematic of its effort to mobilise queerness as grounded in the politics of decolonisation is the solidarity networks that alQaws creates with Queer, Trans People of Color (QTPOC) collectives and groups. Through these networks, alQaws and allies contemplate the urgency for querying epistemic violence, which is bent on reproducing categories of identity classifications—gendered, racialised, and sexualised among others—to maintain the settler and neo-colonial presence (Bakshi *et al*, 2016). One such collective alQaws partners with, to disseminate the value of its decolonial queering politics, is the US-based Audre Lorde Project (ALP). Named after Audre Lorde, the Black feminist, poet, and long known warrior activist for the emancipation of oppressed people, ALP is a community Organising Centre for Lesbian, Gay, Bisexual, Two-spirit, Trans and Gender Non-conforming (LGBTST-GNC) people of colour based in the New York area. AlQaws and members of the ALP come together to carve a space for a different internationalism to the one dictated by the hegemonic colonial ga(y)ze charted earlier. Within such spaces alQaws members articulate further their politics of decolonial queering, as they capture, in Haneen's words, an active *refusal* to engage any single-issue politics, to discuss our bodies' desires outside of our local politics context, or to copy Western hegemonic concepts of LGBT organising (alQaws, 2014b: n.p.). During the same event, Haneen also refuted the common belief that alQaws's politics do not qualify it for donor money from big international actors, that is, the US Department of State. She instead emphasises with pride, 'it is *we* who actually refuse to take money from the US Department of State.' Such events for collaborative thinking and building of solidaristic networks become the vessel for channelling queerness that is firmly situated at the heart of decolonisation work and the combatting of intersecting systems of racism/colonialism, patriarchy, and capitalism. In other words, fundamental to such spaces is the creation of an *Other* queer international. One which emanates from the need to build communities whose aim is to resist *and re-exit* which encapsulates a process of delinking from the rules imposed (Mignolo, 2016)—Zionist pinkwashing—by virtue of affirming an *Other* self to that of the colonial order of Human/Man—hetero-conquest regime.

One example of such delinking praxis is the collaboration that alQaws has established with the duo of trans South Asian activists called Dark-Matter. The duo, Alok and Janani, who are also part of the ALP collective, visited Palestine in the summer of 2013. During that visit, they conducted

68 Native Queer Refusal

various writing and educational workshops which were aimed at creating a dialogue with alQaws and the Palestine-based queer movement. Fundamental to the discussions that alQaws and DarkMatter led in various spaces was the need to think about how colonialism, racism, and capitalism should be the heart of our understanding of gender and sexuality related questions (Field notes, 2013). Alok and Janani, who identified themselves as second-generation immigrants living in the US, shared with the group their own experiences with racism in US contexts and rainbows—in reference to white-stream LGBT politics—which are 'just refracted white lights' (Field notes, 2013). In the workshop, they both provided the space for participants to reflect on how Israel uses 'our bodies, stories, and desires to whitewash its settler colonial and white supremacist regime' (Field notes, 2013). AlQaws activists and members reflected on pinkwashing and how a politics of refusal to normalise with the coloniser captures the interweaving of queerness in our decolonial context. During the workshop, the Dark-Matter duo performed various spoken poetry pieces. These pieces not only spoke to their own experiences with white supremacy and coloniality as second-generation immigrants but also intersected with a lot of the analysis that alQaws's spaces channel in relation to pinkwashing as internalised, which I unpack at length in Chapter 5. Alok and Janani shared insights about how the circulation of LGBT rights as single-issue politics tallies with the reproduction of whiteness, which impacts their being as brown trans bodies. Their performances created an energy for rage and rebellion that was simultaneously mixed with laughter and enjoyment of the sarcastic, provocative, and powerful style in which they performed each piece. One piece, entitled 'White Fetish,' was particularly striking. The piece, which starts by both performers announcing 'I have a confession,' goes on to reveal the insatiable desire that one particularly racialised body has or is *meant to have* for whiteness.[11]

(J): I have this insatiable addiction to coffee.

(A): Fairtrade coffee.

(J): I want to wake up to that smell next to me. That and freshly pressed New Yorkers and Moleskine covers and sweaty yoga mats.

(A): See the truth is . . .

(A) and (J): I am a Snow Queen.

(A): I just have this, this thing . . .

(A) and (J): for white people.

(J): Can't help it, it is the way they eat steak for dinner. I know I am a vegetarian, but I'd make exceptions.

(A): I have heard that white men have huge . . .

(J): empires.

(A): I have heard that they are really good at . . .

(J): gentrification. Once a white woman asked me where I was from. No! where I was really from . . . Then she told me that she was going to

Native Queer Refusal 69

India with her no-profit that year, and I said 'Oh tell me more, Oh take me with you!'

(A): The first white boy I slept with was so excited when I told him he was sexy. Like I was the first person to say that, like ever in the entire world. You have to understand, I like it that way, like your veins are showing, like your skin could bleach out your clothes . . .

(J): like your SPF level is 9000 . . .

(A): like WHITE.

(A) and (J): It just turns me on.

(A): I like to cuddle in the ugliest sweaters with you and listen to David Sedaris. And plan our future lives together. We can rent one apartment in Brooklyn and another in the Mission and stare at the same C-shaped constellation together at night-time I want you to pick me up on the way back from your unpaid internship. I want to jam to your hip hop. I want you to tell me more about your gap year.

(J): I want to map the lines on your palms to the lines you drew in Africa. I want to get my name tattooed on your arms in Sanskrit, and then in Chinese. I want us to make Black friends together. I want us to have brunch with them.

(A): I want us to get gay-married in San Francisco. I want to pick up our tribal print tuxedos together at American Apparel. I want to vote for Obama with you! And name our ethnically adopted children Hope and Post-Race.

(J): On our wedding night, you will tell me about all the women of colour artists that make you feel like a diva, such as Beyonce. And you will awkwardly gyrate me with your hips.

(A): Later that night you will pull me aside and take nude photos of me, like that time you randomly selected me from the airport's security checkline.

(A) and (J): I LOVED THAT . . .

(A): and when we are couch surfing together on our first honeymoon night . . .

(J): I will call you master because colonialism never had a safe word . . .

(A): and you will whisper tenderly in my ear . . .

(J): Don't worry I am not racist like them.

(A) and (J): Then fuck me like you are.

The white fetishism that the poem unveils corresponds to the (settler) colonial condition under which Black and native Othered bodies are seen and constructed via the colonial ga(y)ze. Alok's and Jannani's performance captures in aesthetic terms the layers of analysis that alQaws and the ALP collective bring together when anchoring an understanding of sexuality to the very settler coloniality condition that entails erasure of native people, Black, and other racialised communities (alQaws, 2014b: n.p.). The trans South Asian immigrant duo's performance embodies the very processes of positing the

70 Native Queer Refusal

queer racialised body in relation to white-stream neoliberal LGBT subject/ politics that is maintaining the continuity of the 'race and colonialism amnesia' (Bacchetta, 2016: 265). The poem unveils the very fantasy of the coloniser's saviour trope whose very postcolonial, post-racial, and/or multicultural premise only masks the very colonialism it is based on in the first place. The flamboyant and overly sexualised tone that the performers transmit, as they dramatically play the role assigned to them in that white fetishist world, confronts the listener with the politics of race and sex inherent to colonised and racialised Other's being. Alok's and Janani's spoken poetry articulates in affective terms the abject position of the queer native, racialised Other who needs to look up to their white coloniser as saviour. In doing so, they echo activists' refusal of the HuManist rescue trope, which as the poem so eloquently reveals, is also firmly anchored in liberalism and the business of non-profit that US and Western countries champion in relation to the rest of the world that awaits saviour. In the very act of performing that position of the abjected Other, Alok and Janani confront the colonial ga(y)ze, whose desire to unveil and consume the racialised and sexualised other stems from the very entwined regimes of empire, gentrification, and border security that instructs a master/slave relationship. Such performances, for all of us in that room, encapsulated the power of native queer politics refusing to succumb to a world built around settler colonial whiteness. A refusal that ushers in the decolonial queer voice of a killjoy, 'we will not let your occupation, colonialism and apartheid be!'(pinkwatching Israel, 2017: n.p.). Furthermore, the spaces that such dialogues, conversations, and performances are built around capture refusal in an embodied affective lens. I wrote in my diary that day,

> It was in that small room on a full-on Palestinian hot summer's day where bodies were melting with sweat and craving a bit of fresh air outside on the balcony that a sense of togetherness was building up. The space was charged with curiosity to learn about oneself and the others who came from faraway places (from Palestine and beyond) and whose stories conjured something familiar, something erotic.
>
> (Diary note, 2013).

Audrie Lorde explains how the erotic functions in the space of 'sharing deeply any pursuit with one another' (1984: 89). The workshop created a space for all of us to share in the form of writing, performance, and sometimes just ranting and chatting that was charged with communal emotions of joy, rage, and frustration. It is in in that space of sharing where bridges started to build between the sharers (Lorde, Ibid.) that the value of decolonial queering politics reveal themselves in relation to the openings they aspire to 'beyond the here and now' (Muñoz, 1999). These openings further materialise in the very alternate possibilities they create. In the aftermath of their visit, DarkMatter launched an Indiegogo campaign along with a special art and activism event in New York city, whose outcome was the raising

Native Queer Refusal 71

of $6400 in support of alQaws's work. AlQaws issued a statement thanking DarkMatter and asserting that

> The success of this campaign demonstrates the relevance of our joint anti-colonial and queer organizing, and offers strong evidence of the transformative potential of establishing new and meaningful alliances throughout the globe.
>
> (alQaws, 2015: n.p.).

The openings and transformations that alQaws's decolonial queering enables challenges Arab scholarly criticism of the group, which emanates from an essentialised understanding of decolonisation and/or queering, and thus fails to see the power of native refusal.

Beyond Essentialising Critiques

Joseph Massad (2007, in Éwanjé-Épée and Magliani-Belkacem, 2013) and Sa'ed Atshan (2020) are two vocal critics of alQaws; Massad accuses alQaws of being agents of the West and Israel, while Atshan views the group's local role as far from the reality of Palestinian homosexual/homophobia. I argue that while Massad and Atshan approach their criticism of alQaws from seemingly opposing positions, their critiques emanate from a similar failure stemming from a conception of decoloniality and/or queerness that fails to balance the interactions between these two concepts. Their frames, in fact, collapse respectively into essentialist frames for envisioning liberation and/ or queering—a decoloniality devoid of queering—or a reproduction of colonised (gay) identifications—a queer devoid of decoloniality. Joseph Massad argues that Palestinian queer work, including that by alQaws, reproduces Western colonising identities in a naïve manner, defining them as 'copies of the Euro-Americas' (Massad, in Éwanjé-Épée and Magliani-Belkacem, 2013). His critique explores and denounces the complicity of gay Arab internationalists who aim at 'transforming practitioners of same sex contact into subjects who identify themselves as "homosexual" and "gay"' (2007: 162). In particular, Massad refers those movements based in Lebanon and Israel that are staffed with Palestinian citizens who

> . . . participate in the heterosexualisation of most Arabs and the homo-normativisation of a minority of them. What these organisations want to impose as part of the gay international is a regime of sexuality predicated on a recent Western ontology wherein one's sexual desires become the TRUTH of one, of one's identity and of who one is.
>
> (Massad, in Éwanjé-Épée and Magliani-Belkacem, 2013: n.p.)

Massad's analysis insists that these groups fail to counter LGBT liberationist (2007: 189) discourse, and their work merely reproduces an image of the

72   *Native Queer Refusal*

colonial order and its modes of sexual imperialism. In his more recent work, Massad refers directly to alQaws and accuses its members of being far from radical but instead Israel-based and Western-funded liberals who are nothing but an extension of gay internationalists (2015: 271). Massad's branding of alQaws as yet another gay internationalist group that merely promotes Western sexualities corresponds to a denouncement of intersectionality in the process of crafting anti-colonial identity/positionality. More importantly, such reductive reading of alQaws's work emerges from a lack of ethnographic and productive engagement with the group, which, as I charted in Chapter 1, locks the native within the very epistemic violence of empire. Sa'ed Atshan writes from a position that seemingly claims to situate itself against what his book title captures as 'the empire of critique.' In other words, Atshan rallies an anti-puritan stance that accounts first and foremost for a Palestinian subaltern queer voice. In doing so, he argues that the Palestinian queer movement, including alQaws, has problematically succumbed to the narrow prism of moral puritanism captured in what Atshan views as an excessive focus on fighting Zionism and countering pinkwashing. This, in Atshan's view, renders the work of alQaws irrelevant to the plight of the Palestinian homosexual, i.e., countering homophobia in their society rather than challenging colonialism.

While Massad's critique reduces alQaws to a group that has adopted Westernised positionalities, Atshan accuses the group of spending too much time fighting the West and the occupation and thus failing to address the needs of the barely surviving Palestinian homosexual. These two critiques may initially seem to convey opposite assessments of alQaws. I argue, however, that both Massad's and Atshan's critiques fall into the same trap. That is, they essentially fail to capture the significance of decolonial queering and the politics of native refusal it enfolds. Massad's argument relies on essentialising alQaws's work as one that entrenches queerness as a Western/coloniser imported concept with no relevance to the local context. Atshan, instead, adheres to a single-issue frame that absolves the relevance of a decolonial political frame he deems as puritan. In such a scenario, Atshan not only fails to ground a queer Palestinian critique of homophobia in activists' situated understanding of socio-political dynamics of their own context but also advocates for a 'co-resistance' frame wherein queer Palestinians should partner with Jewish-Israeli bodies as well as being more open to accepting international donor money. In doing so, Atshan as much as Massad posits alQaws's work solely in relation to the hegemonic settler colonial ga(y)ze that the group's work, from the moment of its emergence, has sought to challenge. Atshan and Massad fail to see liberation—for Palestine and/or queer Palestinians—beyond the logics reproducing hetero-conquest. That is, both their critiques construct alQaws and its role solely in relation to the coloniser (Israeli LGBT spaces) and international's donor money, which the work of decolonial queering is bent on unsettling.

The Palestinian queer movement, which can and does exist without the patronage of queer settlers. Independence from colonial civil society is necessary to meaningfully address gender and sexuality issues within Palestinian society. Proposing 'co-resistance' between queers on opposing sides of the colonial divide relies on a shallow identitarian framework that ignores the formative and innate differences that prohibit such resistance. It also upholds pre-existing structures of power and privilege that hinder queer Palestinian life.

(alQaws, 2020b: n.p.)

Conclusion

In her engagement with the native community of Kahnawà:ke Mohawk refusals of Canadian and US settler sovereignty, Audra Simpson conceptualises the productive force of refusal. 'There was something that seemed to reveal itself at the point of refusal—a stance, a principle, a historical narrative, and an enjoyment in the reveal' (2014: 107). The story of alQaws's decolonial queer emergence demonstrates how refusal of a Zionist settler regime is the labour of disavowing and *unsettling* settler modalities of sexuality that are bent on the theft of natives' land and pain. Such unsettling does not simply articulate the value of countering settler colonial violence that governs native life but also enables conceptual, politico-historical, and subjective *unseen* forces (Simpson, 2014). Native queer refusal, therefore, captures a dialectic of resistance as re-existence (Mignolo, 2016). When activists turned away from the Zionist apolitical frame, their choice was rooted in the socio-historical context of re-constituting the self and recognising who one truly is. Such a process of native self-recognition as always already *political* not only serves to unsettle the reality of peaceful violence that the hetero-conquest regime is bent on propagating, but also instructs native queer willingness to rise in power. AlQaws's anti-pinkwashing work encapsulates activists' conscious disavowal of any relation to the coloniser's space as they collectively assert the need to fight for freedom without relation to Tel Aviv. Such a disavowal enacts refusal as a counter-identification praxis whereby normalisation with the settler state/subjects ought to be refuted. It also enables centring a queer Palestinian voice from a position that troubles more than represents the logic of identifications through which a saviour-self construes its victim (gay) Other. Decolonial queering gazes back at LGBT white-streaming policies where the hegemonic power of the international ga(y)ze collides with the global legitimisation of settler coloniality regimes. Native queer voicing of their active refusal—i.e., 'we actively refuse to engage any single-issue politics; to discuss our bodies' desires outside of our local politics context; Western hegemonic concepts of LGBT organising (alQaws, 2014b: n.p.)—is situated in the context of building communal work and rising in solidarity with the multiples of communities around the globe. Such solidaristic communities are expanding the work of decolonial queering by bringing the different worlds of being/knowing that their specific situatedness at the intersection of racism and

74 *Native Queer Refusal*

hetero-coloniality captures. AlQaws's collaboration with QTPOC collectives that are refusing settler coloniality to re-emerge decolonially (Baskhi *et al*, 2016) is a manifestation of the transformative potentials that such conjoined efforts enable. Art plays a crucial role in such a process. It functions as a vital channel for enunciating a will for life beyond the strictures—including those of scholarly critiques—on indigenes' ability for decolonial (re)existence.

Notes

1 The events in October 2000 witnessed the killings of Palestinian protestors in Israel, classified as Arab Israelis, at the hands of Israeli police. see: www.adalah. org/en/content/view/8639 (Accessed 29 April 2020).
2 Israel launched a military aggression on the Gaza strip in 2008 known as Operation Cast Lead. See: https://imeu.org/article/operation-cast-lead (Accessed 29 April 2020).
3 See: www.jewishvirtuallibrary.org/israeli-national-anthem-hatikvah (Accessed 29 April 2020).
4 See: www.orientedfilm.com/ (Accessed 19 April 2020).
5 This aspect is unpacked at length in Chapter 6.
6 See Endnote 2 in Chapter 2.
7 Ghaith also sent me the following article as an example of the growing narratives on Palestine's gay scenery in general and Ramallah in particular: *Passport Magazine*, 'Exploring Gay Palestine,' https://passportmagazine.com/exploring-gay-palestine/ (Accessed 29 April 2020).
8 The Palestinian Campaign for the Academic and Cultural Boycott of Israel defines normalisation as 'the participation in any project, initiative or activity, in Palestine or internationally, that aims (implicitly or explicitly) to bring together Palestinians (and/or Arabs) and Israelis (people or institutions) without placing as its goal resistance to and exposure of the Israeli occupation and all forms of discrimination and oppression against the Palestinian people,' as translated and quoted by PACBI (2011: n.p.).
9 The Green Line demarcates Israel proper from the OPT.
10 See Chapter 5 for more detailed discussion.
11 The piece can also be accessed here: www.youtube.com/watch?v=oEjLegrOqqY (Accessed 29 April 2020).

Bibliography

Adalah, 2015. 'The October 200 Killings.' *Adalah*. Available at www.adalah.org/en/content/view/8639 (Accessed 29 April 2021).
Al-Khatib, O., 2019. 'Eurovision: When Pluralistic Genders and Sexualities Sing for Settler Colonialism.' *Mitras* [Online]. Available at: https://metras.co/%D9%8A%D9%88%D8%B1%D9%88%D9%81%D9%8A%D8%AC%D9%86-%D8%AD%D9%8A%D9%86-%D9%8A%D9%8F%D8%BA%D9%86%D9%8A-%D8%A7%D9%84%D8%A7%D8%B3%D8%AA%D8%B9%D9%85%D8%A7%D8%B1-%D8%B9%D9%84%D9%89-%D9%84%D8%AD%D9%86-%D8%A7/?fbclid=IwAR2gHTICtmUny-ZZa910POw-zuh1SOo8JLFe-PiFcfON6QJqxYjw-6yfGTlA (Accessed 29 April 2020). Source in Arabic.

Native Queer Refusal 75

Allen, L., 2008. 'Getting by the Occupation: How Violence Became Normal During the Second Palestinian Intifada.' *Cultural Anthropology* 23(3): 453–487.

Alqaisiya, W., Hilal, G., and Maikey, M., 2016. 'Dismantling the Homosexual Image in Palestine,' in *Decolonizing Sexualities: Transnational Perspectives, Critical Interventions*, edited by S. Bakshi, S. Jivraj, and S. Posocco. London: Counterpress.

alQaws, 2014a. 'Liberation in Palestine, A Queer Issue – Haneen Maikey.' *alQaws* [Online]. Available at: http://alqaws.org/videos/Liberation-in-Palestine-A-Queer-Issue-Haneen-Maikey?category_id=0 (Accessed 29 April 2020).

alQaws, 2014b. 'Queer/Anti-Colonial Struggle from the US to Palestine.' *alQaws* [Online]. Available at: www.alqaws.org/videos/QueerAnti-Colonial-Struggle-from-the-US-to-Palestine?category_id=0 (Accessed 29 April 2020).

alQaws, 2014c. 'alQaws Statement Re: Media Response to Israel's Blackmailing of Gay Palestinians.' *alQaws* [Online]. Available at: www.alqaws.org/articles/alQaws-Statement-re-media-response-to-Israels-blackmailing-of-gay-Palestinians?category_id=0 (Accessed 29 April 2020).

alQaws, 2015. 'alQaws' Opinion Piece About the Documentary "Oriented".' *alQaws* [Online]. Available at: www.alqaws.org/news/alQaws-Opinion-Piece-about-the-Documentary-Oriented-?category_id=19 (Accessed 29 April 2020).

alQaws, 2016. 'Boycott Tel Aviv Pride.' *alQaws* [Online]. Available at: www.alqaws.org/news/BOYCOTT-TEL-AVIV-PRIDE-2016?category%3C?show%20[CSF%20char= (Accessed 29 April 2020).

alQaws, 2020a. 'Alqaws Analysis Paper: Beyond Propaganda Pinkwashing as Colonial Violence.' *alQaws* [Online]. Available at: www.alqaws.org/articles/Beyond-Propaganda-Pinkwashing-as-Colonial-Violence?category_id=0 (Accessed 29 April 2020).

alQaws, 2020b. 'No Queer "Co-Resistance" with Colonizers: Confronting Normalization and Pinkwashing.' *alQaws* [Online]. Available at: www.alqaws.org/articles/No-Queer-Co-Resistance-with-Colonizers-Confronting-Normalization-and-Pinkwashing?category_id=0 (Accessed 29 April 2020).

Atshan, S., 2020. *Queer Palestine and the Empire of Critique*. California: Stanford University Press.

Bacchetta, P., 2016. 'QTOPOC Critiques of "Post Raciality", Segregation Coloniality and Capitalism in France,' in *Decolonizing Sexualities: Transnational Perspectives, Critical Interventions*, edited by S. Bakshi, S. Jivraj, and S. Posocco. London: Counterpress.

Bakshi, S., Jivraj, S., and Posocco, S. (eds.), 2016. *Decolonizing Sexualities: Transnational Perspectives Critical Interventions*. London: Counterpress.

Butler, J., 1992. 'Contingent Foundations: Feminismand the Question of "Postmodernism",' in *Feminists Theorize the Political*, edited by J. Butler and W. Scott. London: Routledge.

Congressman, Joe Walsh, 2011. *Prime Minister of Israel Benjamin Netanyahu Speech at the Joint Session of Congress* [Online]. Available at: www.youtube.com/watch?v=0BaMLlnb_KI (Accessed 29 April 2020).

Dana, T., 2014. 'The Beginning of the End of Palestinian Security Coordination with Israel?' *Jadaliyya* [Online]. Available at: www.jadaliyya.com/pages/index/18379/the-beginning-of-the-end-of-palestinian-security-c?fb_comment_id=5719708262 45239_575963662512622 (Accessed 29 April 2020).

Dana, T., 2015. 'The Structural Transformation of Palestinian Civil Society: Key Paradigm Shifts.' *Middle East Critique* 24 (2): 191–210.

76   Native Queer Refusal

Driskill, Q. L., 2010. Doubleweaving Two-Spirit Critiques: Building Alliances Between Native and Queer Studies. *GLQ: A Journal of Lesbian and Gay Studies* 16(1): 69–92.

E-International Relations, 2017. 'Interview—Walter Mignolo/Part 2: Key Concepts.' *E-IR*. Available at: www.e-ir.info/2017/01/21/interview-walter-mignolopart-2-key-concepts/ (Accessed 20 July 2021).

Éwanjé-Épée, Felix, and Magliani-Belkacem, Stella, 2013. "The Empire of Sexuality: An Interview with Joseph Massad." *Jadaliyya* [Online]. Available at: www.jadaliyya.com/pages/index/10461/the-empire-of-sexuality_an-interview-with-joseph-m (Accessed 14 July 2018).

Eyewitness Palestine, 2020. 'What Does Comprehensive Liberation Mean?' *alQaws Facebook Page* [Online]. Available at: www.facebook.com/AlQawsorg/photos/a.580950708628316/3574064132650277/ (Accessed 29 April 2020).

Fanon, F., 1963. *The Wretched of the Earth*. New York: Grove Press.

Fanon, F., 1967. *Black Skin, White Masks*. London: Pluto Press.

Jamjoum, L., 2002. 'The Effects of Israeli Violations During the Second Uprising "Intifada" on Palestinian Health Conditions.' *Social Justice* 29(3): 53–72.

Kershner, I., 2018, May 13. '"Next Year in Jerusalem!" In Israel, Eurovision Win Is Seen as a Diplomatic Victory, Too.' *New York Times*. Available at: https://www.nytimes.com/2018/05/13/world/middleeast/israel-eurovision-jerusalem.html (Accessed 29 April 2020).

Le More, A., 2008. *International Assistance to the Palestinians After Oslo: Political Guilt Wasted Money*. New York: Routledge.

Lorde, A., 1984. 'Uses of the Erotic: The Erotic as Power,' in Lorde, A., *Sister Outsider: Essays and Speeches*. Trumansburg, NY: Crossing Press:

Maikey, H., 2012. 'The History and Contemporary State of Palestinian Sexual Liberation Struggle,' in *The Case for Sanctions Against Israel*, edited by A. Lim. London: Verso Books.

Maikey, H., 2019, November 9. 'Tel Aviv Protecting Queers?' *MITRAS*. Available at: https://metras.co/%D8%AA%D9%84-%D8%A3%D8%A8%D9%8A%D8%A8-%D8%AA%D8%AD%D9%85%D9%8A-%D8%A7%D9%84%D9%85%D8%AB%D9%84%D9%8A%D9%8A%D9%86%D8%9F-%D8%A3%D8%B3%D8%B7%D9%88%D8%B1%D8%A9-%D8%A5%D8%B3%D8%B1%D8%A7%D8%A6%D9%8A%D9%84/ (Accessed 29 April 2020). Source in Arabic.

Maikey, H., and Shamali, S., 2011. 'International Day Against Homophobia: Between the Western Experience and the Reality of Gay Communities.' *alQaws Articles* [Online]. Available at: www.alqaws.org/siteEn/print?id=26&type=1 (Accessed 12 June 2017).

Maikey, H., and Taj Al'rees, 2011. 'Sexuality Movement in Palestine: From Identity Politics to Queer.' *Qadita* [Online]. Available at: www.qadita.net/featured/queers-2/ (Accessed 29 April 2020). Source in Arabic.

Masalha, N., 2007. *The Bible and Zionism: Invented Traditions, Archaeology and Post-Colonialism in Palestine-Israel*. London: Zed Books.

Massad, J., 2007. *Desiring Arabs*. Chicago: University of Chicago Press.

Mignolo, W., 2006. 'Citizenship, Knowledge, and the Limits of Humanity.' *American Literary History* 18(2): 312–331.

Mignolo, W., 2016. 'Foreword: Decolonial Body-Geo-Politics At Large,' in *Decolonizing Sexualities: Transnational Perspectives, Critical Interventions*, edited by S. Bakshi, S. Jivraj, and S. Posocco. London: Counterpress.

Mignolo, W., and Escobar, A., 2010. *Globalization and the Decolonial Option.* New York: Routledge.

Muñoz, J., 1999. *Disidentifications: Queer of Color and the Performance of Identity.* Minneapolis: University of Minnesota Press.

Muñoz, J., 2009. *Cruising Utopia: The Then and There of Queer Futurity.* New York: New York University Press.

PACBI, 2011. 'Israel's Exceptionalism: Normalizing the Abnormal.' *Palestinian Campaign for Academic and Cultural Boycott of Israel* [Online]. Available at: www.pacbi.org/etemplate.php?id=1749 (Accessed 24 June 2017).

Pinkwatching Israel. [Online]. Available at: www.pinkwatchingisrael.com (Accessed 24 June 2017).

Puar, J., and Mikadashi, M., 2012. 'Pinkwatching and Pinkwashing: Interpretation and its Discontents.' *Jadaliyya* [Online]. Available at: www.jadaliyya.com/pages/index/6774/pinkwatching-and-pinkwashing_interpenetration-and- (Accessed 29 April 200).

The Queer Arabs Podcast, 2020. 'Episode 108 [in English]: alQaws!' *The Queer Arabs Podcast* [Online]. Available at: https://thequeerarabs.com/podcast/episode-108-in-english-alqaws/ (Accessed 29 April 2020).

Rancière, J. 2004. *The Politics of Aesthetics.* Translated from French by G. Rockhill. London: Bloomsbury.

Razack, S., 2007. 'Stealing the Pain of Others: Reflections on Canadian Humanitarian Responses.' *The Review of Education, Pedagogy and Cultural Studies* 29: 375–394.

Roy, S., 1999. 'De-Development Revisited: Palestinian Economy and Society Since Oslo.' *Journal of Palestine Studies* 28(3): 64–82.

Schotten, H., and Maikey, H., 2012. 'Queers Resisting Zionism: On Authority and Accountability Beyond Homonationalism.' *Jadaliyya* [Online]. Available at: www.jadaliyya.com/pages/index/7738/queers-resisting-zionism_on-authority-and-accounta (Accessed 25 April 2021).

Shalhoub-Kevorkian, N., 2016. 'The Occupation of the Senses: The Prosthetic and Aesthetic of State Terror.' *The British Journal of Criminology* 57(6): 1279–1300.

Shihade, M., 2015. 'Global Israel: Settler Colonialism, Mobility, and Rupture.' *Borderlands* 14(1): 1–16.

Simpson, A., 2014. *Mohawk Interruptus: Political Life Across the Borders of Settler States.* Durham, NC: Duke University Press.

Smith, A., 2005. *Conquest: Sexual Violence and the American Indian Genocide.* New York: South End Press.

Smith, A., 2010. 'Queer Theory and Native Studies: The Heteronormativity of Settler Colonialism.' *Journal of Lesbian and Gay Studies* 16(1): 41–68.

Taghdisi-Rad, S., 2011. *The Political Economy of Aid in Palestine: Relief from Conflict or Development Delayed?* London: Routledge.

Tartir, A., 2014. 'Criminalising Resistance, Entrenching Neoliberalism: The Fayyadist Paradigm in the Occupied Palestinian West Bank.' PhD thesis, The London School of Economics and Political Science [Online]. Available at: http://etheses.lse.ac.uk/3179/ (Accessed 20 July 2021).

Tobin, R., 2007. 'Eurovision at 50: Post-Wall and Post-Stonewall,' in *A Song for Europe: Popular Music and Politics in the Eurovision Song Contest*, edited by I. Raykoff and R. D. Tobin. Ashgate: Aldershot.

78 *Native Queer Refusal*

Vimalassery, M., Pegues, J. H., and Goldstein, A., 2016. 'Introduction: On Colonial Unknowing.' *Theory and Event* 19(4).

Weber, C., 2015. 'Why is there no Queer International Theory?' *European Journal of International Relations* 21(1): 27–51.

Wolfe, P., 2006. 'Settler Colonialism and the Elimination of the Native.' *Journal of Genocide* 8(4): 387–409.

4 Queering Aesthesis

Introduction

The previous chapter alluded to the role that decolonial queer art plays in mobilising refusals of the settler colonial ga(y)ze. This chapter delves more deeply into how queer aesthetic productions disrupt the sensibilities of hetero-conquest. Pinkwashing exemplifies the normalising of settler colonial violence through the sex/gender system, which simultaneously underlines sensory configurations capturing emotive and affective dimensions of politics. As argued previously, decolonial queering challenges the expansion of settler violence, which functions through making visible, sayable, and audible a modern and pluralistic (gendered and sexed) self, while rendering invisible and inaudible a Palestinian indigene Other that is being marked for the erasure and theft of their pain. A settler sensual regime encroaches onto its native Other via the spectacles fixing the native out of place. The Zionist sensual regime, therefore, confers modes of invisibility/inaudibility/unsayability about Palestinian queerness (Rancière, 2004). That is, queerness vis-à-vis Palestine is either non-existent or only conceived via colonisers' HuManist rescue frame,[1] thereby locking the native within the psycho-political imperatives of failure and misrecognition.

This chapter examines the role Palestinian artistic productions play in articulating forms of resistance to the violence of the Zionist sensual regime. It sheds light on the work of several artists: Nadia Awad's cinematic lens, Alaa Abu Asad's photography and video art, Tariq Knorn's performance art, alQaws's activist/artist musical tracks, and the story of the late dancer Ayman Safiah. Through an engagement with these artists and their work, I unpack the value of a queering aesthesis, which seeks to enunciate a politics of native sense that queers and interrupts the aesthetic-political field of settler colonial encroachment on the native's being. Such politics, I argue, functions on multiple levels: first, it challenges the Zionist configuration of sex and sense, where the projections of sexual pluralism and moral superiority of Israeli humanist values coalesce. Second, it articulates the native's bodily ways of doing, being, and enunciating epistemologies for revival and life. In doing so, it grounds the willingness to challenge the native's own political

DOI: 10.4324/9781003273585-5

80 Queering Aesthesis

imaginary as it succumbs to the imperatives of a settler sensual regime bent on instilling the native's *ghurba* (exile) from her land, (hi)stories, and desires.

Interrupting Settler Structures of Sex/Sense

In the follow up to the killing of Muhammad Abu Khdeir, Haneen and I exchanged some reflections regarding pinkwashing and its functionality through the violence of erasure and dismemberment exercised on the native's being (Field notes, 2014). During the conversation, Haneen shared with me the work of Palestinian American Nadia Awad. *A Demonstration* is a short video shot by Nadia in 2009, focusing on a vigil that thousands of people attended after a shooting at a Tel Aviv gay bar. Haneen reflects on how she 'finds the video very powerful, especially when I watch it now. Just look at the actor who is doing the speech, the speech itself, the audience, and Nadia's cold and distant camera' (Conversation with Haneen, 2014). In the description to the video, which she produced in 2014, Nadia reflected:

> I expected a small candlelit vigil with fifty activists. To my surprise, 10,000 people had gathered in Rabin Square. The vigil was, in fact, a benefit concert where Israeli government officials gave speeches equating the youth bar shooting to the Holocaust and suggesting that Ben Gurion's Zionist vision included LGBT communities. The video I produced from this event is called *A Demonstration*. It focuses on the speech of a young man who appears to have been present at the shooting. However, several local activists told me he was an actor, paid by the Israeli state to represent gay youth at the vigil. Other locals claimed he arrived after the shooting, and some stated he was a relative of a victim. *A Demonstration* questions the ambiguous relationship between public commemorations, mourning and individual memory.
>
> (*A Demonstration*, 2014)

In the film, Nadia's camera wanders among the crowds in Rabin Square gathering to hear a speech projected on a giant screen. The camera catches glimpses of the screen and the emotionally loaded speech runs throughout the film's soundtrack. As the camera zooms in on the speaker (see Figure 4.1), his dramatic expressions come into view, as do the streams of tears on his face. The speech begins lamenting how 'bad this week' has been 'for all of you good people who are here today in Rabin Square' (*A Demonstration*, 2014). Then, the speaker reflects on how the Jewish 'refuge,' in direct reference to the Israeli state, has become 'a slaughterhouse for a despicable murder'(Ibid.). As the speaker bursts into tears, his face blurs slightly and remains blocked from view for a few moments. Through tears, the speaker alludes to Israel's Never Again mission.[2] He quotes a Holocaust poet, who 'found it impossible to recount what happened there' and praises the significance of the work that

Queering Aesthesis 81

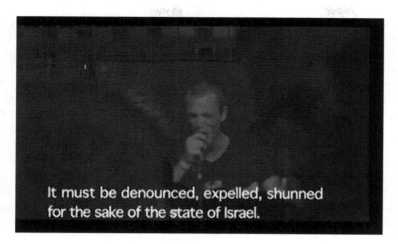

Figure 4.1 A Demonstration
Source: Nadia Awad

he and other members of the Aguda (Israeli National Association for LGBT)[3] undertook. The speaker-on-the-screen then states:

> Your presence here, along with the many who could not come, proves something. We are a nation that really does oppose violence and wants peace. Violence destroys the foundations of Israeli democracy, it must be denounced, expelled, shunned for the sake of the state of Israel.
>
> (Ibid.)

Finally, the speaker, who remains unnamed and unidentified, draws our attention to the 'nice little place called Bar Noar,' which is 'the only place that serves orange juice and salad with mini rainbow flags on one side and Israeli flag on another.' The cinematography of *A Demonstration* imposes a certain sense of distance from the events depicted, preventing the viewer from developing a sense of affinity or empathy towards the speaker or those in the crowd. While the lens captures the event, we are kept at a distance, hovering hesitantly around the crowds and the other cameras that were (presumably) attempting a more proximate depiction. It captures the speaker only on the big screen, giving the viewer the impression of looking at a movie set. Nadia's lens transmits a sense of theatricality that imbues the speech and the speaker; filming the speaker only through his representation renders the viewer aware of this theatrical element. In other words, while the viewer watches what could be described as a representation of a representation, the video reveals the performative character of the aesthetic performance at play

82   *Queering Aesthesis*

(Butler, 1999: 173). Nadia's distant and detached lens accentuates further the distance between viewers and what is conveyed to them on the screen, inhibiting further the emergence of empathetic feelings. In what follows, I argue that Nadia's *A Demonstration* is a visual production that comes from her native exilic positionality vis-à-vis the aesthetic sensual regime that constitutes a decolonial queering lens. Nadia's art-film is a form of decolonial queering aesthesis (Mignolo and Vazquez, 2013) seeking to enunciate a native sense that queers and interrupts the aesthetic-political field of settler encroachment on the native self. Nadia can only enter Palestine while accompanying international delegations. The filming of *A Demonstration*, as Nadia clarifies, took place in 2009 during her first visit to the country as part of a solidarity delegation (Conversation with Nadia, 2015). Nadia views her art-film in relation to what she describes as 'outside-of-time subjecthood' that links to her growing up as a 1948 displaced Palestinian in a US-Christian evangelical context:

> In Florida, I grew up in an evangelical environment. My father is very dark skinned, so everyone thought my father was Black. To such an extent that we had moments—like in Halloween—where the KKK (Ku Klux Klan) would smash our windows. People were trying constantly to identify who you were. So, I always think of Palestinian identity as something outside of time. Because I grew up surrounded by the kind of people who believe that—you know—Jesus is going to come back on a spaceship, and all the Jews have to be back in Israel and we are going to fundraise for them.' Thus, a lot of churches in the south would collect guns to ship to Israel because they are fighting 'a holy war.' There was a lot of isolation and struggle to deal with . . . you are in these communities that need to find out who you *actually* are! And there are other communities where to affirm that you are Palestinian means being a liar because—for them—Palestine 'is not a real place.' So I would get this kind of remark from Jewish-Americans, such as, 'Did your parents tell you that there was "a massacre" that happened? Because that's not true!' . . . and Muhammad Durra?[4] 'Actually *his* father shot him, not the Israeli IDF.' So, it is an interesting subject-position to be encountering strangers throughout your whole life, and then they always ask you a second question, 'Do you actually think that who you claim to be is real?'
>
> (Conversation with Nadia, 2015)

It is in these biographical details that Nadia's 'questioned subjecthood' becomes both a way to experience the globalised mobility[5] of a settler-structuring of sex/sense and a vessel to challenge it from a queer native lens. In *A Demonstration* Nadia synthesises and brings videos together in order to rip apart their meaning and unsettle the aesthetics of these films (Conversation with Nadia, 2015). She 'watch[es] them over and over and over' to remake them anew, giving birth to new visual and audio techniques whose purpose is to undermine the visual and rhetorical logic of such films (Ibid.). She explains her obsession with unsettling grand narratives and mediums of their representation in the media and popular culture:

> In the US there is a whole media culture around a Christian meta-narrative, where those people who used to identify with something, now they have 'seen the light' and transformed into something else . . . After 9/11, people started to appear on news outlets declaring they are 'ex-Muslims.' Some Palestinians flaunted this 'ex-Jihadist' identification, where now 'They believe in the state of Israel.' You know this is all part of a propaganda machine, and it is very ingrained in American culture. It works together with the Christian meta-narrative of resurrection. So, I want to work on a movie that synthesises these narratives together and demonstrate these importance aspects of American culture. Another video I am working on takes these clips on 'missing Middle-Eastern women' and what is behind the veil. For instance, there is a National Geographic film that follows an Afghan woman, who was the subject of this famous photograph—many years ago—known as 'the Afghan girl.' The National Geographic troop goes into Afghanistan 40 years later in order to find her eyes [the photograph was notable because of the girl's startlingly beautiful green eyes]. Finally, as they find her, she is clearly traumatised by the Taliban and the US obliterating her country. She refuses to be photographed but they insist and say they have to do it. Moreover, there is this dramatic music that runs through the whole movie, and so there are so many films (or sic) of this kind . . . I am working on getting these clips together and synthesising them under this theme of hunting and disappearing Middle Eastern women.
>
> (Ibid.)

Nadia's work seeks to reveal what lies at the core of proliferating narratives of becoming and disavowing or what she also defines as a propaganda machine. Those narratives entail the sudden conversion of 'ex-Muslim/Jihadi' after 9/11 or those who want to disclose the reality of 'Muslim women,' such as the National Geographic film, or in the case of *A Demonstration*, those who disclose the reality of 'Israel as a gay haven.' Nadia combines these narratives in order to represent them anew, revealing—and so troubling—the multiple power structures influencing the production of these representations, which are gendered and sexualised. In her co-written piece with Collen Jankovic, she describes the technique of her queer art-films as one that unsettles the aesthetics of narratives and documentaries and 'draws attention to the ways in which they construct truth claims and potentially sympathetic viewing positions' (Awad and Jankovic 2012: 139). Nadia's artistic techniques convey a decolonial aesthesis[6] that reconfigures dominant colonial sensual structures.

84 *Queering Aesthesis*

She reflects on how, while being in Rabin Square, she had to make sure not to let slip she was a Palestinian, to counter a feeling of unsafety because to reveal herself as Palestinian would have been a risk given the 'highly nationalistic Jewish-Zionist sentiment at the event' (Conversation with Nadia, 2015). *A Demonstration*, therefore, relays a native sense of haunting (Gordon, 1997) that emerges from an outside-of-time subject position, excluded from, and potentially threatened by, the non-violence of liberal Jewish democratic values. Nadia's queer lens reveals and undermines the Zionist configuration of sex and sense where the projections of sexual pluralism and moral superiority of Israeli humanist values coalesce. It demonstrates how pinkwashing emerges from the 'histories that cannot rest' (Coddington, 2011: 748), thus exposing and dramatising the aesthetic elements of the reality on screen. In doing so, her cinematic lens bespeaks a native seething presence that meddles (Gordon, 1997) with the spectacles celebrating Israeli-ness as equated to sexual modernity and the negation of violence.

Nadia's work resonates with that of Alaa Abu Asad, who comes from the predominantly Arab city of An-Nasira/Nazareth, located in the north of historic Palestine. I was acquainted with Alaa's work through the conversations I had with Nadia and another artist, fashion designer Omar Khoury, whose work is discussed in Chapter 6. Growing up within the borders of the exclusive Jewish state, Alaa is trapped within a peculiar state of absenteeism. Like the rest of the so-called Israel's Arab minority, Alaa occupies the status of the unrecognised,[7] dismissible,[8] and/or transferable Other:[9]

> I never thought I would be an artist, I thought it was just a hobby. But somehow, I ended up doing it. Being in this peculiar status as an 'Arab Israeli citizen' has pushed me into this place. It meant having to study and gain a degree from an Israeli institute, which I—sometimes— consider to be bad luck. The fact that I graduated from Bezalel Academy of Arts and Design in Jerusalem has influenced my work a lot. It pushed me in a certain direction, influencing how I engage with photography and filmmaking.
>
> (Conversation with Alaa, 2014)

Moreover, Alaa's words echo Nadia's reflections regarding the subject position's influence on the kind of art being pursued.

> All this obsession my work has with cropping and cutting comes from a desire to deconstruct and reconstruct photography. To deconstruct what both photography and the image is about. I feel that one of my duties is to challenge both the act of photography and the viewer. I think my work revolves around this dynamic of passive/active, who has the power and who takes control. This goes in all levels of relationships, including art. For instance, in photography you have the photographed

object and the viewer/photographer. Like those photographers in war, their position is the same as the soldiers. Take, for example, all these reporters of Haaretz.[10] It reflects this power dynamic very much. If you think how the Israeli film industry generates representations of Palestine and Palestinians. They do not just colonise us; they also have the power to tell our story.

(Ibid.)

Alaa aims to unhinge and queer power mechanisms whose functioning reproduces the colonial power machine. The relationship between the photographed object and the viewer/photographer is not a neutral one; rather, photography as an artistic act is caught in a complex web of power relationships.

Think about the relation between the Israeli photographer and the photographed Palestinian. There are moments where Palestinians are photographed without them knowing. There are other moments where the Israeli, who occupies a superior position, imposes the photographing act onto 'its object,' even if it bluntly refuses. Then, there are other cases where Palestinians see themselves as victims and Israelis as saviours. All these three cases demonstrate how un-ethical photography can be within such dynamic, because the Israeli is photographing essentially from a superior position.

(Ibid.)

Alaa's work unravels the power dynamics that lie at the core of a photographic act. Photography is always and already an aesthetic/political act that reifies colonial structures of power. There is no place left for neutral ethics, since it is settler colonialism that determines the relationship between Israeli photographer and Palestinian photographed object. Alaa's words, therefore, espouse Rancière's reflections on art as a form of knowledge, which constructs fictions that 'define variations of sensible intensities, perceptions, and the abilities of bodies' (2004: 35). Alaa gives the example of the Israeli photographer Miki Kratsman, who also happened to be the head of department at Bezalel Institute, where Alaa studied.

He used to be the media photographer for the Israeli newspaper Haaretz. For a long time, he worked in the West Bank and photographed funerals and many other incidents. His current project is to go back to his photo archives, cut each face out and zoom into them enlarging the picture. Then, he posts those photos on Facebook on a public page called 'People I Met.' Next to each photo—and there are hundreds of them—he writes, 'Do you know what happened to the person in photo?' According to me, this is very unethical and reveals the analogy with the photographing act per se.

(Conversation with Alaa, 2015)

86 Queering Aesthesis

Alaa draws on the work of Kratsman to explain the unethical components of art, indicating how the photographic act invades the lives of others to exemplify the hetero-conquest power dynamic. Kratsman's technique of capturing photos of Palestinians, enlarging them through the zoom technique, and publishing them on his Facebook page typifies the superior power position from which Palestinians are viewed, photographed, and probed by Israelis. The dynamic between Palestinian photographed/object and Israeli/photographer recalls the pinkwashing production of rescue-empathy frame discussed in the previous chapter, which is symptomatic of native entrapment within the HuManist (Human/Man) regime of hetero-conquest.

In his final project at Bezalel Institute, called *Photowar Project*, Alaa transports his ideas on photography into an artistic work that challenges both the act of photography and the viewer. In a big wooden frame hung on a white wall (Figure 4.2) Alaa displays the following text:

> What if the colonised has a camera in the hand the same way the coloniser does, and s/he, the colonised, has a chance of using that camera while standing in front of her/his coloniser? Is the perspective the colonised chooses in order to photograph her/his coloniser the same as the coloniser's perspective when s/he often photographs the colonised? Does the same reason behind the photographing act performed by the colonised sit equally with the coloniser's act? And so, is the location

Figure 4.2 PhotoWar Project
Source: Aalaa Abu Asad

where the colonised chooses to stand to photograph her/his coloniser the same as the coloniser's? Will the colonised photograph her/his coloniser, ever, anyway?

(PhotoWar Project)

Alaa's questioning frame shows that anything the colonised can photograph intertwines with the dominant political conditions. In other words, politics and aesthetics intersect, and define each other.

> I chose to frame these rhetorical questions on the wall around the coloniser/ colonised relationship and whether the colonised would ever want, or have the chance, to photograph the coloniser. Of course, given the position of the colonised, they will not do it. How many Palestinians would you see going to photograph Israelis? Almost zero! And why is that? Because they are busy striving for survival. Even if they want to go photograph, they will not do it because they cannot even reach the other side with this fucking wall and all the checkpoints standing in-between. People cannot even gain access to see their families and relatives across the wall! Let alone go and photograph Israeli faces!
> (Conversation with Alaa, 2015)

Alaa's work reveals and disrupts the work of photography as an incubator of the frames that constitute ways of seeing the world. It purposefully captures 'the mandatory framing' through which a photograph yields an interpretation (Butler, 2007: 951).

> I take the photographic act apart in order to test the relation between the witness and the document/image. This work is about what we [the viewers] see and what we are told to see and, at the end, to challenge the viewer's 'naked eye' of seeing and watching.
> (Alaa, Statement for Exhibition, 2015)[11]

Alaa's work challenges what the viewers are made to see in a photograph. It 're-imagine[s]' the image through different acts such as cropping, retouching, changing, etc' (Alaa's portfolio). Its goal is to guide the viewer to see how the framing dictates the mechanics of seeing and watching, thereby forcing the viewer to acknowledge the power relations involved in image production. In a video art depicting a picnic with his family on the beach of the depopulated Palestinian village Alzeeb, in the north of historic Palestine, Alaa films a fisherman. A text runs alongside the image of the fisherman: 'A fisherman in the centre. To the right, what one does not see is the depopulated village'[12] (see Figure 4.3). Alaa's video, which includes footage of the family swimming and picnicking on a summer day, relays the peculiar state of being a 48 Palestinian. Alaa explains how this trip, which has become a summer ritual, matters to him and his family but also

88 Queering Aesthesis

Figure 4.3 Picnic to the Beach
Source: Alaa Abu Asad

encapsulates the weight of being and living as a 48 Palestinian. He relays that a pre-1948 mosque still stands there (Conversation with Alaa, 2014). Similar to Nadia, Alaa's video comes from a native queered positionality whose sense of haunting meddles with the colonial aesthetic logic of viewing and constructing native space. Contra to Kratsman, Alaa's footage exposes the very frame of its imaging, revealing to the viewer the power of photographers as they zoom into an object (fisherman in centre) while purposefully ignoring others (the depopulated village). By making the process of 'imaging the image' visible, Alaa's footage 'exposes and thematises mechanisms of restriction' (Butler, 2007: 952). These artistic works demonstrate how queerness characterises Alaa's lens.

> A lot of people look at my work and ask me in the way I blur imagery whether it is a man or a woman, but that's not the point I aim at. What concerns me more is challenging these frames through which one interprets 'man' and 'woman.' This is all part of the way I want to deal with and address the theme of power in daily relations.
> (Conversation with Alaa, 2015)

Another of Alaa's works, *Masturbate bil Beit*, confronts power frames of sex and sense that constitute reality. This video, which lasts for three and a half minutes and was shot in 2012, captures Alaa filming himself while masturbating at home, as the title indicates in Arabic. The video begins with a written statement on screen declaring that what viewers are about to watch is a 'Bruce LaBruce remake.' Throughout the act of masturbation, a picture of the former Iranian president, Mahmoud Ahmadinejad, hangs on the wall behind him, close to the Iranian flag. While masturbating, Alaa seems to be

Queering Aesthesis 89

holding a picture. When the video ends with Alaa's ejaculation, the picture is revealed to be a photograph of Ahmadinejad.

Alaa explains that this work was influenced by LaBruce's unapologetic approach to homosexual sex where he shows characters beyond prevalent 'gay orthodoxies' (Knight, 2015: n.p.). Similarly, Alaa's video contains a bluntly provocative perversion. *Masturbate bil Beit* uses the Iranian flag and the Iranian president to draw an explicit reference to an Islamic context. However, by reading this reference against the meta-narratives depicting Iran as a country repressing sexuality and persecuting LGBT communities,[13] Alaa's video projects an unapologetic queer-self. The video articulates queerness as embodying the reality of closeted-ness, which hides inside *el beit* (the home), and perversion, which is instead found 'beneath the folds of [Islamic] fundamentalism.'[14] Alaa's video imposes a confrontation with queerness that channels gay identifications as they evolve vis-à-vis perverted, closeted, Islamic Otherness. It shows an explicit scene of masturbation and arousal in response to the very icons that pinkwashing narratives use as representative of the Islamic/Middle Eastern repression of sexuality and homosexuals (i.e., Iran). Simultaneously, Alaa's *Masturbate bil Beit* invites viewers to penetrate the reality of Middle Eastern/Islamic desire, only to reveal attributes of perversion and closeted-ness rather than the urge to come out and/or be saved from homophobia. In such a case, the perversion of the Arab lies in the way it flaunts the very lens of their own representation qua perversion/closeted-ness. As Awad and Jankovic (2012: 141) comment:

> Abu Asad's video unapologetically confronts viewers with the desiring embodiment of an unsanitised, non-normative version of queer Palestinianness, an image that irreverently flies in the face of (primarily Israeli and US) depictions of queer Palestinians who need to be saved from homophobic Arab and Muslim societies. In other words, 'Masturbate bil Beit' defiantly refuses to respond to negative portrayals of Palestinians with a comforting version of queer Palestinian masculinity.

Masturbate bil Beit demonstrates how a queer lens undermines the colonial ga(y)ze and its superior position in relation to an inferior, in-need-of-saving, and colonised Other. It confronts established relations of power and privilege through a redistribution of the aesthetic terms that allows an alternative imagination of the political conditions.

Alaa's work bears further resonance with that of Tarik Knorn's, which reconfigures the aesthetic/political field to challenge the normalising frames of liberal colonialism. I encountered Tarik for the first time during a writing workshop organised by alQaws in Ramallah in the summer of 2013. Coming from Ramallah in the West Bank, Tarik's artistic work revolves mainly around drawings, performances, and paintings. Tarik's interest in art was consolidated after being granted a scholarship to study a degree in fine arts

90   *Queering Aesthesis*

in the United States. Tarik's subject position and the study experience in the US influenced how politics would occupy a central role in his definition of art.

> The courses I took were unstructured. The critique centred on technique, avoiding content, as there was very little attention given to political issues, especially among my peers—a majority of which was white, upper middle-class, straight guys. Coming back home every summer—to Palestine—helped me maintain a certain perspective, as my friends were extremely well-read and well-versed in the importance of activism. I began to focus on how policies affect people's lives in real ways, exactly like gender does. I am constantly reminded of the importance of political literacy, specifically from a Marxist, queer, feminist, anticolonial perspective. And I guess I can never feel fully comfortable identifying as an artist, unless I reach a point where I easily communicate political issues via art. This is hard, since art nowadays is merely decorative and endorses oppressive regimes.
>
> (Conversation with Tarik, 2014)

Tarik defines art as a medium to pose 'questions about various issues, whether in society, politics or economics' (Ibid.). Thus, art ought to 'inspire, engage, [and] open up possibilities for positive social change.'

> I want my art to say 'No! We mustn't accept this, we deserve better as Palestinians, as queers, as women, as working class, as people of colour . . . etc.' Ideally, I hope I can create a propaganda machine that raises awareness and effectively critiques at the socio-economic level.
>
> (Ibid.)

Tarik deems art a tool to refuse the oppressed positionalities of those striving for a better world. This method of saying no as Palestinians and queers comes from the artist's journey in the United States, where the little attention given to politics within the artistic field complements the pinkwashing narratives faced first-hand.

> I was hearing more and more stories about gay Middle Eastern Men who are being rewarded by Western liberal ideology, when the intention was white-washing and normalise colonialism. I responded to them by repeating the argument on 'How are you saving them when your tax money and military is killing them?'
>
> (Ibid.)

Tarik's frustration over those narratives about Middle Eastern gay men serving to whitewash colonialism activates the urge to challenge the consumption of the Other in what the artist identifies as liberal colonialism. For these reasons, during an international dance event at the college, Tarik decided to turn this frustration into an artistic performance.

> There was an end of semester event run by a student organisation, called Dance Alloy, where twenty or so choreographers proposed to create a 3-minute dance routine with a group of dancers, picking a song of their choice. At the time, I was very politically involved and felt very resentful towards the lack of criticism within arts. This happened, in particular, with dance, since international students often become choreographers of those songs that are widely celebrated in their cultures. I was becoming more sensitised to the consumption of the other, and the use of international students' culture to create an illusion of peace and diversity, which legitimises liberal colonialism. Several Western academic institutions exploit culture in ways that are identical to the 19th century model of anthropology, where indigenous subjects were studied and viewed as 'specimens' or 'missing links,' as 'savage, untamed exotic pleasures,' purely for a colonial (white) audience.
>
> (Conversation with Tarik, 2015)

Tarik's observations on liberal colonialism link with the analytical parameters outlined in the previous chapter. The reflections on the consumption of indigenous Other within platforms of diversity and peace resonate with the hegemony of the international ga(y)ze reproducing colonial conquest via peace agendas.[15] For these reasons, Tarik's dance performance at Dance Alloy sought to discomfort the white liberal gaze and its underpinning logics: i.e., unveiling and saving repressed others.

Tarik's choreographed show starts with the entrance on stage of a group of women dressed as belly dancers (Figure 4.4). Splitting into two separate lines, they begin to move rhythmically to the beat of Arabic music. In the middle of these two lines of dancers, cloaked figures sit on their knees at the back of the stage. The cloaked subjects, among them Tarik, come forward and reveal themselves to the audience while dancing to the rhythm of M.I.A.'s song 'Bad Girls.' As Tarik, who is dressed as a belly dancer, starts to dance in the middle, we see two figures on the side of the stage: one with chains around their hands dressed in black lingerie with handcuffs attached and another dancer holding and flaunting a gun around. Tarik suddenly stops dancing and begins performing a series of bodily movements that recall a Palestinian mourning ritual, thus, leading the group into a burial ceremony ritual (Figure 4.5). The dancers furiously beat their hands onto their chests, then onto their knees, shake their heads left and right, resembling Palestinian women wailers. In the last part of the performance, the two dancers at the sides of the stage approach Tarik in an aggressive manner and force him to kneel. One of the dancers, who represents the police, handcuffs Tarik, while the one in military costume holding a gun covers Tarik's face with a plastic bag (Figure 4.6). Starting as a traditional seductive performance with

92 *Queering Aesthesis*

Figure 4.4 Tarik's Dance Show
Source: Tarik

Figure 4.5 Tarik's Dance Show
Source: Tarik

Figure 4.6 Tarik's Dance Show
Source: Tarik

Queering Aesthesis 93

a group of belly dancers, the show moves slowly into a disturbing scene of police and military torture. What begins as a fun dance show turns to bear a strong political message, as Tarik explains:

> I wasn't sure how to include the political element, until I visited a sex shop in New York City and bought three lingerie costumes. One of the military, one of the police, and one of the black leather get up. The first portion I choreographed was a typical Egyptian belly dance routine, placing women at the forefront and allowing a snippet of the seductive temptress to come out to play.
>
> (Conversation with Tarik, 2015)

A moment of unveiling follows the seductive display of the belly dancers, what Tarik describes as 'the queer not cis men' dancing to the rhythm of M.I.A.'s song.

> The liberal gay subjects come out—so to speak—to play, in a sardonic act of unveiling, as the blankets fall to the ground and reveal the fabulousness. What better song to have than Bad Girls by M.I.A.!
>
> (Ibid.)

Tarik chose M.I.A.'s song 'Bad Girls' because its official video-clip offers a typical version of orientalist imagery. It shows Arab men in their traditional dress driving and dancing behind the singer in the desert. The video also includes stereotypical scenes of horse riders in the Arabian desert. The Bad Girls, or 'rebel girls' as the writing on the wall at the beginning of the video shows (*fatayat mutmaridat*), are the ones M.I.A. sings to while they drive stunt cars under their burkas.[16] It is, thus, to the rhythms of M.I.A.'s 'Bad Girls' that women in the Arab desert reveal the rebelliousness under their burkas. The song reiterates stereotypical representations of Arabs as associated with desert culture and burka-wearing women who strive to be bad. It encapsulates an orientalist reproduction of Middle East patriarchal oppression and desert culture that is being challenged by the rhythms of a liberating Western feminism. Following M.I.A. and the American rhythms of her singing for those bad girls, women of Arabia finally reveal badness and *tamarrud* (resistance).

Tarik's performance re-channels the production of orientalist imagery in Western aesthetic productions. Gay Middle Eastern subjects emerge from under their cloaks to unveil all their fabulousness and rebelliousness. At the same time, the performance demonstrates the colonial power relations underlying such acts of unveiling. Celebrating Middle Eastern Bad Girls/ Gays as exotic subjects in need of liberation underlies colonialism. This is where the performance turns into a mourning ritual recalling both indigenes' death and struggle. Performing Palestinian women wailers, Tariq's choreography demonstrates a clear reference to settler colonialism and the gender violence it propagates. Further connection to US imperialism in the region is seen in the last scene where the two dancers representing the military and

94 *Queering Aesthesis*

the police violently attack the gay oriental subject, re-enacting a moment of incarceration and torture. Tarik explains:

> I wanted the audience to make the association between LGBT rhetoric and colonialism. The police and military are always there to maintain the status quo; hence trapping queerness within a limited stereotype, just so it cannot threaten its sovereignty. In essence, they normalise colonialism and imperialism. At the end, I made a reference to incarceration by having one of the enforcers place a shroud on my head and handcuff me—I was thinking of the Iraqi Abu Ghraib and Guantanamo Bay as examples.
>
> (Conversation with Tarik, 2015)

Tarik's reflections describe the utilisation of a dance performance as a tool to confront Western liberal narratives of LGBT communities in the Middle East. This is expressed further by the ways in which the audience reacted to the performances, as Tarek recounts:

> I was intrigued when people's racism intensified after the performance. A lot of people complained it was too political, it was uncomfortable for many. However, I think that this kind of confrontation, this kind of literal illustration connecting our daily practices with politics helps me learn how to deal with such an issue through creative means. And it also inspires debate. I'm not saying it's my job to educate the coloniser. However, if I'm to have a conversation, I'd like to come from a position of strength. Upsetting the often-immutable power dynamic.
>
> (Ibid.)

Tarik's dance performance both confronts and discomforts the colonial (liberal) gaze because it unveils the violence present in the rhetoric of saving and liberating (gay) Middle Eastern subjects, thus upsetting its parameters of tolerance and peace. Echoing the counter-identification work of anti-pinkwashing,[17] such an artistic work creates the ground for decolonial queering aesthesis possibilities, which emerges beyond calls to celebrate diversity and the saviour rationale of LGBT oppressed subjects.

Reclaiming and Healing Native Sensuality

Ghanni a'an al taa'riff launch event took place in an underground Haifa club during the summer of 2013. Although being a West-banker[18] and thus normally never allowed to gain access into what is identified as Israel proper, I was able to attend this event as a result of staying longer than the Israeli one-day permit allowed. I had secured this permit thanks to the international organisation[19] I was working with at that time.

As I walked into the Haifa underground club at 8pm on a Saturday, I saw Haneen, and we started chatting about me making it [being able to attend] and how it felt to be here for the first time in Haifa! 'It feels very

Queering Aesthesis 95

strange—you know—being here,' I said as we both tried to make our way in. At the door, the guard mumbles something in Hebrew to me, and while I stand choked unable to respond Haneen quickly interferes by responding in English: 'why do you have to assume that we should be speaking Hebrew in this space?' she then looks at me and gestures with her head *yalla* come in.

In the midst of darkness and disco-lights, we blended into a group of people who stood chatting and smoking. Haneen introduced me and, as we continued to talk about my experience of being here for the first time, A., a Palestinian from Haifa, joined to comment: 'Wala', welcome to what they call Israel; I feel closeted all the time here, *nahnu mughayabun* we are absented in this state of theirs. *Present-absentees*, that's what they call us!'

The feeling of closetedness that A. expressed was familiar. It did not only relate to my fear of being caught with no valid permit, which governed my whole day, but it also was a consequence of an encounter with an Israeli-Jewish couple with whom my friend and I hitched a ride[20] to arrive at downtown Haifa. I recounted how I had to hide behind my silence during the whole trip, while my friend, who is French, was conversing with them about a trip the couple had recently made to Paris before the conversation, somehow, turned into a commentary regarding some recent news from the US on gay rights restrictions. I recounted how the couple started to boast arrogantly about how progressive this country is, and that what the US is trying to achieve, has long been accomplished here!

My choking silence throughout the trip found its echo among the walls of the emptied houses of the depopulated Arab neighbourhood of Haifa's Wadi Al Salib,[21] which I had visited earlier that day. It was among the ruins of Wadi Al Salib that one could feel the ghostly presence of those who have been forcefully absented in order to create 'this state of theirs,' I thought to myself. A. and I exchanged prolonged looks, filled with silent melancholy, before the voice of Haneen interrupted to announce the launch of *ghanni* and thanking everyone who had contributed to the project. Music and singing commenced and we all had our eyes fixed on the stage.

(Diary notes, Haifa, 2013)

The above ethnographic note was written during the launch event of the first album of alQaws's project *ghanni a'an al taa'riff*, which took place in 2013. I remember hearing the songs for the first time during a ride in Haneen's car. As we drove around Ramallah, listening to the first song of the album, *Manakir* by Haya Zaatry, Haneen explained how alQaws approaches *ghanni* as a smart way to proliferate narratives on sexuality that can reach out, through use of social media, to everyone and everywhere (Field notes, 2013). In a conversation with Ghaith, he reflected on the value of the project in the way it brings together volunteers comprising activists, artists, and singers from across Palestine to share with their wider society the *hikaya* (story) that is not often told within our communities (Conversation with Ghaith, 2015). The untold *hikaya* found within *ghanni*'s musical tracks captures another example of queering aesthesis, the unsettling of the hetero-conquest regime animates the indigenous sense of queer haunting.

96 *Queering Aesthesis*

My encounter with A. in that Haifa club and the surge of emotions in relation to the denial of my entry, our sense of closeted-ness, and absented presence in 'that state of theirs' captures the ghostly presence of an indigene queer sense. *Ghanni's* promotional videos (see Figure 4.7 and Figure 4.8), which preceded the launch of the musical project, centre upon the ghostly,

Figure 4.7 *ghanni's* Promotional Video
Source: Ghanni 3an Ta3rif 01 (2013)

Figure 4.8 *ghanni's* Promotional Video
Source: Ghanni 3an Ta3rif 02 (2013)

Queering Aesthesis   97

queer subject position. Watching those videos, it is possible to observe how an unknown figure, eccentric looking and out of the ordinary, occupies a central role in each one of them. The queer, haunting character of the figure lies in the combination of those possessed qualities, such as strangeness and illusionary presence. Strangeness signifies a non-familiarity, something out of the ordinary that is difficult to pin down; the exceptionality of the figure makes it impossible to categorise according to known and familiar gendered attributes—meaning man and/or woman. It demonstrates how queerness, as Eve Sedgwick describes it, is 'against the strictures of received classifications,' thus, a 'continuing movement . . . troublant . . . and strange' (1993, xii). At the same time, the figure possesses phantasmal qualities that articulate its strangeness. This is shown through its constant reappearance in the videos, despite people's nonchalance and—most importantly—their inability to see the figure. While the video allows the viewer to see how the figure remains invisible to the people they encounter, its illusionary and ghostly presence relays the Palestinian sense of absent-present reality.

In its desperate attempt to draw people's attention by continuous gesturing, the figure reveals to the viewer, who can see its (in)visibility, a desire for acknowledgment from those who continuously ignore it, as if it does not exist. The figure encapsulates a *hikaya* that hovers in Arab space, carrying a desire to open up new discussions about sexuality and gender diversity in Palestinian society through music, which is what alQaws aims to generate with the launch of *ghanni*. It is a collection of the desires of those who fail to ascribe to the regulating structures of gender and sexual familiarity in Palestinian society. At the same time, the openings that *ghanni* aims to activate within Palestinian society encourage an interruption of the settler sensual regime where the violence of Zionist pride in gay rights—the Israeli couple I met—substantiates the necessary flow of Hebrew—both as a language and as a reflection of the Judaisation of land via depopulating Arab villages such as Wadi Al Salib—within the settler state. Haneen's statement interrupted the flow of Hebrew so it gestures towards the world of *ghanni*. Like the three promotional videos pushing to make *ghanni*'s queer stories audible, Haneen's words also gestured towards the *hikaya*, pushing to be seen and heard against the (sensory) will of the occupier. *Ghanni*'s productions capture a queering aesthesis that can be understood further, as I shall demonstrate, through an analysis of the latest production of the same project. The musical tracks entitled *minkom o feekom* ('We are from you and continue to live among you') is a medley of four music tracks that are based on the traditional folk music of Palestine and the wider *Shami* (Syria) region. According to alQaws (2020: n.p.), *minkom o feekom* is:

> A colloquial way for us to say we are an integral part of society, a statement against social denial and colonial narratives isolating Palestinian queers from Palestinian society, and an invitation for our

98 *Queering Aesthesis*

society to engage in a discussion around sexual and gender diversity in Palestine.

In the following, I draw on two tracks—*ala dalouna* (bears several meanings amongst them 'a name of a Canaanite lover' and 'the act of asking for help') and *ya zareef al tool* ('tall handsome man')—to build an account of a queering aesthesis that works for the enunciation of liberatory native sensuality.

Palestinian folk music comes from the indigenous folkloric *turath* (heritage) of the wider region of Greater Syria (*bilad al sham*): Syria, Lebanon, Jordan, and Palestine. In the last century, Zionist settler colonialism and the Palestinian Nakba have contributed to the carving of a distinct form of Palestinian folkloric artifacts ranging from *dabkeh* dance to music and embroidery. Concurrently, and driven by a sense of fascination and reclamation of indigenous Palestinian-*ness*, the logic of replacement and conquest has also operated at the level of cultural production; since the 1930s, settlers have appropriated indigenous cultural productions, such as the *dabkeh* (see Kaschl, 2003). Jewish-Israeli performances of *dabkeh*—it has, for instance, become a mainstay of the Arabised version of the Israeli national anthem 'Hatikvah'[22]—in place of Palestinian native performances, serves to reaffirm the settler presence and native disappearance. It thus comes as no surprise that the Palestinian reclamation and revival of a folkloric *turath* (heritage) has become an integral part of the struggle for freedom and liberation. This process of revival came to prominence during the launch of the Palestinian *thawra* (revolt) following the establishment of the PLO in the mid and late 1970s. The Palestinian folklorist dedication to historicise and document the lyrics of liberation songs reached its zenith with the First Intifada (Barghouthi, 1994). The folk genres of *ataaba, dal'ouna*, and *zareef el tool*, which are poetic forms of orally transmitted melodies usually set around repeated maqam phrases, have gained particular prominence as distinct forms of Palestinian musical *turath* (see Barghouthi, 1980). Characteristic of these musical forms is their malleability to accommodate lyrical alterations within the tradition of oral poetic singing, known as *zajal*.[23]

The nationalisation process of Palestinian *turath* music reveals the relations between ideas of nation and gender. Masculinity comes through as integral to the Palestinian national project in the role of protector, thereby designating a protectee role to women.[24] Weddings, for instance, became a prominent site for nation building and singing, where protest songs were sung as often as wedding songs were sung at protests, if such a distinction could even be made (McDonald, 2013: 4). McDonald's ethnomusicology relates the poetics of masculinity within wedding celebrations as an effect of the nationalist movement's operationalisation of indigenous wedding songs and dances, turning them into acts of engendering resistance and sacrifice to the nation (2010). Here one can understand how the Palestinian National Authority's (PNA) recent use of violence against alQaws's activities in the West Bank[25] relates to the masculinist and heteronormative vision of a free Palestine, which is inscribed in the colonised failure to see beyond the regime

Queering Aesthesis   99

of settler sensual configuration. In contrast to the existential and political conditions of the PNA, alQaws's *turath* music opens the way towards a native sovereign sensuality, allowing her to escape from the grip of the coloniser. Here is an extract from *al dalouna*:

دلعونا
منكم وفيكم بنضلنا هونا
منضلنا هونا بلادك وبلادي حنّوا علينا الوطن حنونا
منكم وفيكم، وبعدو الشارع
مش عارف إحنا فعل مضارع
ما زهق فينا، فينا يصارع
بدل ما يحارب اللي احتلونا
منكم وفيكم، يما ويا يابا
حرام نتشرد ونروح غرابا
حرام يروحوا من الأرض صحابا
في دفا دياركم والله خلونا
منكم وفيكم: إسأل المراية
طلطل ع روحك واسمع الحكاية
فيكم ما زلنا من البداية
كبرنا بوطننا مثل الزيتونا (اللازمة

ala dalouna, ala dalouna
We are from you and we continue to live among you
We remain here, this is my country and your country
Let's be compassionate to one another, our homeland is the land of compassion
We came from you and we continue to live among you
Yet somehow you doubt our presence
Have you not tired from fighting us, instead of fighting our coloniser
Oh mother and father we are from you and deserve to remain with you, so not to disperse and Become estranged from one another
How sorrowful it would be for our land to lose its people
In the warmth of our home, let us remain
We are from you and we continue to live among you: look in the mirror
Reunite your soul, and listen to the story
Since the beginning, we have been here
Like the olive trees we have continued to grow in the homeland

Ala dalouna is one of the most popular types of folkloric songs in Palestine, present at almost every Palestinian wedding celebration. It has four hemistich stanzas, where the first three have similar endings and the fourth usually ends with the long sound 'na⁻,' which is the sound used to perform the *dabkeh*. AlQaws appropriates *ala dalouna* in order to tell the queer *hikaya* (the story) long silenced within nationalist aesthetic productions, leading to societal 'doubtful[ness] [of] our presence.' The singers affirmatively and repetitively

100 Queering Aesthesis

declare the phrase '*minkom o feekom*,' 'we are from you and we continue to live among you,' and that 'like the olive trees we have continued to grow in the homeland.' The adoption of *ala dalouna* comes from the song's significance in multiplying the value of the Palestinian political model of Sumud (steadfastness), offering a liberatory vision of 'fighting our coloniser.' Thus, it brings to life a native grounded knowledge of queering, inviting healing from the sorrows of dispossession captured in native exile from home. It is a call for a queering of the homeland, striving to make heard and felt the urgency for 'the warmth of our home' and a reunion of the soul. AlQaws's queering story turns away from the colonisers' sensual regime—casting the native self away from home—by looking inward to recognise oneself: 'look at [herself] in the mirror.' Here the song offers a reconfiguration of home that is woven into the embodied experiences and modalities of indigenous sensual ways of knowing and feeling in/of place: 'we [are] like the olive trees' that have always been there 'since the beginning.' The narrative of *ala dalouna* (re)maps the sensual and spatial grammars governing native life and obstructing her connection to her roots (Goeman, 2013). It reinvigorates native spatial and bodily topographies, unsettling settler colonial sensual violence that imposes an outside-of-time subject position. *Ala dalouna* conjures Palestinian notion of 'auna' as understood and practised by rural communities who sought to band together and provide mutual aid to one another in the face of Ottoman taxation and oppressive feudal systems and later the British mandate regime of land confiscation to pave the way for the Zionist project (Al-Araj: 38–41). This practice encapsulates indigenous way of life within an organically crafted model of social reciprocity and responsibility, which entailed the establishment of a horizontal social organisational structure where gender equality and anti-hierarchical relations prevail (Ibid.).

alQaws's *ala dalouna* production enact an aesthetic/political reorientation of the native liberatory project away from the hetero-conquest model that subjugates their people in the first place. It recalls Palestinian socioeconomic way of life, whose 'auna' base differs from the subsequent collapse of the term to Western-backed NGO model of volunteerism and humanitarianism that have become predominant under PNA rule (Ibid.). Thus, a queering of *ala dalouna* proposes a conjuring of a native past that unsettles the hegemonic international ga(y)ze and the neo-colonial developmentalism enshrined in the Oslo structure.[26] It further challenges the gendered/sexed schemas of 'authenticity' and 'purity' that underpin nationalist rhetoric. This articulation exemplifies the openings and the yet-to-come future directions (spatio-erotic) enabled by the queering aesthesis reimagining of a native past. This emerges further in *ya zareef al tool*.

اي ظريف الطول وقف تقولك
راير غالع قبر وبالدك أحسنلك
خايف يا ظريف تروح وتتملك
وتعاشر الغير وتنساني أنا

Queering Aesthesis 101

يا ظريف الطول، أسمر و طيفي
غنولك كتير وغنوا عن اونك التعريفي
بس ما حد عرفك زي يي اي ظريفي
بستنآك انا مية ألف لـ سنة

يا ظريف الطول يا سن الضحوك
إيدك بمسكها قدام اماك واباوك
ولو تقول أهلك عني ابعدوك
بهرب بالليل ونعن سنن رانا

O, zareef eT-Tool,
stop so I can tell you
You are going abroad but your country is better for you
I am afraid you will get established there
And find someone else and forget me

O, zareef eT-Tool, with a nice dark skin
They sang for you and sang about who you are (sexuality)
But none of them know you like I do
I shall wait for you a hundred years

O, zareef eT-Tool, with a wide grin
I shall hold your hand in front of your mother and father
If you say that your family has torn us apart
We shall run away at night, and announce our secret

Zarif al tool recounts the story of a Palestinian forced into exile (*ghurba*) and is traditionally sung from a first-person perspective of he who has stayed behind; he laments the condition of exile that has separated the indigene from the homeland. In the second and third stanzas, queer sexuality emerges subtly, yet directly, as the male narrator flirts with the beauty of his tall handsome lover's 'nice dark skin' and 'wide grin,' evoking an amorous relationship or connection: 'none of them knows you like I do.' The singer also daringly points that 'I shall hold your hand in front of your mother and father' and hints at 'run[ning] away at night' to 'announce our secret.'

This is yet another example of queering *turath* songs, which tackles indigenous conditions of *ghurba*/exile while articulating a yearning or desperate waiting for the beloved: 'I am afraid you will get established there . . . and find someone else and forget me.' AlQaws's production thus (re)orients the native's past to accommodate the rhythms of a queer sensuality in a way that draws on—in a specific way—the Palestinian indigenous *zajal* tradition. *Zajal* refers to a traditional form of oral poetry that is semi-improvised to adapt to the context and is usually sung between *zajjalyin* (poets) in the local dialect. AlQaws's *hikaya* brings the listener to confrontation with the queering essence of native's *turath*, revealing malleability qua the stories and desires that *zajal* narrates.

102 *Queering Aesthesis*

Before moving on to conclusion, I want to finally and briefly turn to one more example of queering aesthesis, the case of the late Palestinian dancer Ayman Safiah. In a video production called 'In Your Absence' (Figure 4.9 and Figure 4.10). Safiah performs a whirling dervish dance within the ruins of the depopulated Palestinian village of Kufr Biraim in which his dancing

Figure 4.9 'In Your Absence'
Source: YouTube, www.youtube.com/watch?v=pJhPZ-dAYQk

Figure 4.10 'In Your Absence'
Source: YouTube, www.youtube.com/watch?v=pJhPZ-dAYQk

Queering Aesthesis 103

evokes a phantom figure that seems to continually appear and disappear as we (the viewer) and another dancer in the film search desperately for the phantom-like dervish. Ayman's movement among the ruins of Kufr Biraim alludes to Palestinian refugees—the video closes with the words 'I will be complete, the land says, when the refugees come back'[27] and the sense of ghostly haunting they trigger against the realities within the settler state that are taken for granted (Gordon, 1997). In May 2020, Ayman's body washed ashore close to Atalit, a depopulated Palestinian town south of Haifa (Akil, 2018); he had been swimming with friends when a violent wave swept him away. His friends and family searched for him desperately for days, organising voluntary search teams with hundreds of people, and criticising the lack of help from Israeli emergency services. On reporting the incident to Israeli police, the first response was, as is so often the case, 'Jewish or Arab?' Upon his disappearance, a media campaign was waged in the search for Ayman. Videos and articles were shared around his work and also about the determined spirit he had as someone who never shied away from expressing himself, including transgressive sexuality and love, to perform modern forms of dance that might be frowned upon or discouraged. Despite the challenges that Ayman faced, he expressed in one emotional video a defining moment in his life where his father asks 'Ayman won't you come home?' to which Ayman replies, in that moment, 'I realised that my father understood all along.' Ayman then continues tearfully: 'If I am lucky with one thing in my life, it is the presence of my parents and family' (Makan video, 2020).

The swallowing of Ayman's body into the violent sea recalls a familiar tragedy of Palestinian disintegration. It was the same Mediterranean Sea that became a site of displacement for thousands of Palestinian refugees whose involuntary departure marked their Nakba to this date. Ayman's figure captures this Nakba but also alludes to the determination and hope of a futural return. Ayman's body perished at the violent sea, but his dancing spirit never surrenders; it continued the dance in the midst of Haifa's coast along two other depopulated villages in the south (Kfr Lam and Tantura)[28] until finally reaching the shore of yet another depopulated Palestinian town, Atalit. Ayman whirls and everyone is on the look-out for the phantom figure. By acknowledging and recognising Palestinian refugees' right of return, Ayman's whirling dance shows the native's persistence in the face of settler denial; the very utterance, 'Is he Jew or Arab?' breathes life into death. This life was further celebrated during the funeral of the whirling figure, a joyous celebration marking a moment of recognising the life and unity Ayman's dance ushers into the world around him as thousands came together from across different communities to honour, sing, and join in the dance. His funeral was exceptional in that his body was laid to rest in the Islamic cemetery while the local church opened its doors for people to pay their condolences to the family (Khatib, 2020). This unifying moment stands against the native dismemberment within the structures reproducing

104   *Queering Aesthesis*

colonised misrecognition through the creation of stratified identities and inter-communal conflicts.[29]

Conclusion

At the heart of Zionist settler colonialism lies an aesthetic/political regime that unveils the intertwinement of sex and sense to the continuity of Nakba. Pinkwashing is a crucial site for revealing how a settler sensual regime—mediated by the aesthetic configuration of Israel as a place of gender and sexual pluralism—encroaches onto its native Other. Palestinian artistic productions queer and redistribute the aesthetic terms, allowing an alternative imagination of the political conditions. They generate a queering aesthesis whose interruption of the coloniser's structuring of sex/sense relays decolonial subjects' alt-aesthetic/political possibilities. Nadia Awad's cinematic lens rips apart grand narratives and their representations revealing *A Demonstration* of pinkwashing. Alaa Abu Asad's present-absent location within the Zionist state provokes the production of an unapologetic queer lens that deconstructs the frame of its own narration. Tarik Knorn's performance art brings into view the links between LGBT rhetoric and colonialism, upsetting the sense of comfort of a liberal audience that wants to celebrate diversity. Queering aesthesis capture the labour of unsettling settler configuration of sex and sense and alludes to alternative possibilities to re-exist decolonially. AlQaws's queering tracks complement the political work that the group does in Palestine and internationally, proliferating decolonial queering against the forces maintaining an 'out-of-time' subject position. The group's appropriation of *turath* songs to narrate the queer *hikaya*, long silenced within this same regime, further elucidate the significance of inhabiting a world of decolonial queer erotics. It is a world that celebrates the revival of communities and bodily mappings, which carve the way for the indigene's homecoming. The constant motion and movement of Ayman Safiah's whirling dance embodies indigene homecoming. The circular continuity of this movement not only refuses to submit to the violent temporal bounds of the settler sensual regime, but also captures indigene's will for life through constant folding back *and* towards a reconstructed sense of self/homeland.

Overall, the artistic productions explored in this chapter exemplify native methodologies for life that are inextricably tied to an Indigenous feminist stance and theory of the political (Simpson, 2014). Queering aesthesis, therefore, challenges queer and feminist theorising that reproduces the amnesia of settler colonialism because it lacks a serious engagement with the openings of decolonial knowledge within queer aesthetics. Such openings pertain to the possibilities that the work of decolonial queering activates via typologies of native sovereign sensuality. In doing so, queering aesthesis reveals epistemologies of life inscribed in the refusal to be accommodated to the set of legible conceptual and/or political sensual scripts disabling the continuity of the native's queer resistance.

Notes

1 See discussion in Chapter 3.

2 This is in reference to Israel's founding premise as a safeguard against anti-Semitism. See: www.jpost.com/israel-news/netanyahu-never-again-is-israels-mission-656842 . Israel's definition of antisemitism is mobilised to ward off any criticism of its racist settler colonial premise. Similarly, the Holocaust is invoked by Israeli LGBT to reaffirm an affiliation to the state and its ' Never Again' premise, which protects it from any criticism of the violence that the state has been based on in relation to Palestine.

3 See: http://awiderbridge.org/the-agudah/ (Accessed 24 June 2021).

4 Muhammad Al-Durrah is a Palestinian child who was shot by Israeli occupation forces in Gaza during the Second Intifada. The story of his death went viral because the moment of his shooting was captured on camera. See: www.youtube.com/watch?v=arRgkXDLwlM (Accessed 24 June 2021). And: www.independent.co.uk/news/world/middle-east/the-killing-of-12-year-old-mohammed-al-durrah-in-gaza-became-the-defining-image-of-the-second-8624311.html (Accessed 24 June 2021).

5 See discussion in Chapter 3 in relation to global mobility of Israel.

6 Mignolo and Vazquez explain: 'The first is a concept that now belongs to the sphere of philosophy; the second to language in general, in any language. Thus, if aestheTics is indeed modern/colonial aestheTics and a normativity that colonised the senses, decolonial aestheSis has become the critique and artistic practices that aim to decolonise the senses, that is, to liberate them from the regulations of modern, postmodern, and altermodern aestheTics' (2013: 8).

7 In reference to the unrecognised villages in the Negev. See: Nasara (2012).

8 See Adalah reports on how 'successive Israeli governments regularly enact legislation which excludes, ignores, and discriminates against the Palestinian Arab minority.' www.adalah.org/en/content/view/7771 (Accessed 24 June 2021).

9 In reference to Avigdor Lieberman's infamous proposition of a transfer plan for Israel's Arab minority. Liberman is an Israeli politician who since 2021 serves as finance minister. He also served as Israel's foreign minister (2009–2012; 2013–2015) and defence minister (2016–2018). See: www.theguardian.com/world/2014/mar/25/transfer-arab-israeli-citizens-palestinian-state (Accessed 24 July 2021).

10 *Haaretz* is an Israeli newspaper.

11 See link to the artist's statement for the exhibition 'Image, Imagination rRsurrection' at the Al Ma'mal Foundation for Contemporary Art [Jerusalem]: https://gallery.mailchimp.com/f7198d36a43e6b2c1e6443d6b/files/Image_imagination.pdf?utm_source=almamal+mail+2015&utm_campaign=ec2a0cfae0-August_Newsletter6_25_2015&utm_medium=email&utm_term=0_1ae1d1494e-ec2a0cfae0-282002441&ct=t(July_Newsletter6_25_2015)&mc_cid=ec2a0cfae0&mc_eid=00b0637fdc (Accessed 24 June 2021).

12 This video, entitled 'A Failed Confession Attempt' can be accessed at: http://aboasadalaa.wixsite.com/portfolio/aunts (Accessed 25 June 2021).

13 An article in *The Guardian* reflects on a 'study' that has been conducted by a non-profit organisation based in London on the life of the LGBT community in Iran. The study reveals the level of persecution of LGBT Iranians who live in secrecy. It draws further on the Iranian president denying the existence of 'homosexuals' as a product of Western immorality in his country. See: www.theguardian.com/world/2012/may/17/iran-persecution-gay-community-revealed (Accessed 24 June 2021).

14 Ibid.

15 See discussion in Chapter 3.

106 Queering Aesthesis

16 The burka is a full body cloak that also covers the face of those who wear it. The song's video can be accessed here: www.youtube.com/watch?v=2uYs0gJD-LE (Accessed 24 June 2021).
17 See discussion in Chapter 3.
18 Someone who comes from the 'West Bank' in Occupied Palestine.
19 While I was working with an international organisation in Hebron, I acquired a 1-day permit into Haifa, where Palestinians from the West Bank are usually denied entry.
20 Public transport does not function on Saturdays because of Shabbat. Thus, the norm is to hitchhike with random people.
21 A depopulated Arab neighbourhood in downtown Haifa. A visit to the ruined and emptied houses of Wadi al-Salib attests to the forceful dispossession of Palestinians since the creation of the Israeli state in 1948. The neighbourhood, which overlooks the sea, is juxtaposed with new modern buildings illustrating the slow gentrification processes that are taking over the area. Palestinians classified in Israeli law as 'absent-present' are unable to come back or reclaim their homes in Wadi Al-Salib. For more information, see: www.wrmea.org/2016-january-february/palestinian-homes-abandoned-in-nakba-attest-to-history-of-haifas-wadi-salib-neighborhood.html (Accessed 21 June 2021).
22 See: www.youtube.com/watch?v=ywq1wXU_HZs.
23 The etymology of zajal is related to play and musical entertainment in S. Zuhur (2001).
24 See discussion in Chapter 2.
25 This will be unpacked in Chapter 5.
26 See discussion in Chapter 3.
27 See: Khalil, M. S. 2012 In your Absence. *YouTube*. Available online at: www.youtube.com/watch?v=pJhPZ-dAYQk (Accessed 20 August 2021).
28 See: ___ (2020) Ayman Safiah Swam in the Air like a feather. Fusha. Available online: www.arab48.com/ﻔﺴﺣﺔ/ﺳﺟ/ﺭﻗﺺ/2020/05/27/ﺃﻳﻤﻦ-ﺻﻔﻴﺔ-ﺳﺒﺤ-ﻓﻲ-ﺍﻟﻬﻮﺍﺀ-ﺧﻔﺖﻣ (Accessed 20 August 2020).
29 As Magid Shihade (2021) writes, 'While the Jews became categorised as such (religiously and ethnically nationally), the Palestinians were defined as "Israeli Arabs"—a category that makes them belong fully to neither. It also defined them according to their religious affiliations and created new ones. Thus, as of 1948, they turned from being Palestinians, to become Christians, Muslims, and Druze.'

Bibliography

A Demonstration, 2014. *VIMEO* [Online]. Available at: https://vimeo.com/99671737 (Accessed 24 June 2017).

Ahmed, S., 2010. *The Promise of Happiness*. Durham, NC: Duke University Press.

Akil, M., 2018. 'Atalit: Land and Memory.' *Arab 48*. Available at: www.arab48.com/%D9%85%D8%AD%D9%84%D9%8A%D8%A7%D8%AA/%D8%AF%D8%B1%D8%A7%D8%B3%D8%A7%D8%AA-%D9%88%D8%AA%D9%82%D8%A7%D8%B1%D9%8A%D8%B1/2018/04/16/%D8%B9%D8%AA%-D9%84%D9%8A%D8%AA-%D8%A7%D9%84%D8%A3%D8%B1%D8%B6-%D9%88%D8%A7%D9%84%D8%B0%D8%A7%D9%83%D8%B1%D8%A9- (Accessed 22 June 2021). Source in Arabic.

Al-Araj, B., 2018. *I Have Found My Answers: Thus Spoke the Martyr Basel Al-Araj*. Jerusalem: Ribal Press.

alQaws, 2020. 'New from Singing Sexuality: Minkom O Feekom.' *alQaws News*. Available at: www.alqaws.org/news/New-from-Singing-Sexuality-Minkom-O-Feekom?category_id=0. (Accessed 22 June 2021).

Queering Aesthesis 107

Awad, N., and Jankovic, C., 2012. 'Queer/Palestinian Cinema: A Critical Conversation on Palestinian Queer and Women's Filmmaking.' *Camera Obscura* 27(2): 135–143.

Barghouthi, A., 1980. 'Palestinian Folk Literature: Ya Zareef al-Tool.' *Al-Turath wa al-Mujtama* 13: 7–20.

Barghouthi, A., 1994. 'The Role of Arab Popular Songs in the Palestinian Intifada,' in *Folk Literature in Al Intifada*, edited by A. Barghouthi. Amman: Markiz Ihya' Al Turath Al Arabi. Source in Arabic.

Butler, J., 1999. *Gender Trouble: Feminism and the Subversion of Identity*. New York: Routledge.

Butler, J., 2007. *Frames of War: When Is Life Driveable?* Verso: London.

Coddington, K., 2011. 'Spectral Geographies: Haunting and Everyday State Practices in Colonial and Present-Day Alaska.' *Social & Cultural Geography* 12(7): 743–756.

Daghan, S., 2012, 'Iran's Persecution of Gay Community Revealed.' *The Guardian* [Online]. Available at: www.theguardian.com/world/2012/may/17/iran-persecution-gay-community-revealed (Accessed 22 June 2017).

Dirbas, N., 2019. 'Ayman Safiah: Life Is Dance.' *Al Arabi al Jadeed*. Available at: www.alaraby.co.uk/%D8%A3%D9%8A%D9%85%D9%86-%D8%B5%D9%81%D9%8A%D8%A9-%D8%A7%D9%84%D8%B1%D9%82%D8%B5-%D9%87%D9%88-%D8%A7%D9%84%D8%AD%D9%8A%D8%A7%D8%A9-0?fbclid=IwAR0kTKXG5J-YJg4spqsztVsXGp36eNTJY5ZAeQKIpLXW-8kEXeYiEHOe5N9o (Accessed 22 June 2021). Source in Arabic.

Ghanni 3an Ta3rif 01, 2013. *Youtube*. Available at: www.youtube.com/watch?v=TsyliiaD290 (Accessed 22 June 2021).

Ghanni 3an Ta3rif 02, 2013. *Youtube*. Available at: www.youtube.com/watch?v=yHrrK-AIGEI (Accessed 22 June 2021).

Goeman, M., 2013. *Mark my Words Native Women Mapping our Nation*. Minneapolis: University of Minnesota Press.

Gordon, A., 1997. *Ghostly Matters: Haunting and the Sociological Imagination*. Minneapolis: University of Minnesota Press.

Kaschl, E., 2003. *Dance and Authenticity in Israel and Palestine: Performing the Nation*. Leiden and Boston: Brill.

Khalil, M., 2014. 'In Your Absence.' *Youtube*. Available at: www.youtube.com/watch?v=pJhPZ-dAYQk (Accessed 22 June 2021).

Khatib, I., 2020. 'kufr Yasif: Thousands Participate in Funeral of Ayman Safiah.' *Makan*. Available at: www.makan.org.il/Item/?itemId=60228 (Accessed 22 June 2021). Source in Arabic.

Knight, C., 2015. 'A Philosophy of Homosexuality and Interview with Bruce LaBruce.' *3:4* [Online]. Available at: http://fourthreefilm.com/2015/04/a-philosophy-of-homosexuality-an-interview-with-bruce-labruce/ (Accessed 24 June 2021).

Makan, 2020. 'Ayman Won't You Come Home?' *Facebook Video*. Available at: www.facebook.com/Makan.Digital/videos/646190472602685

Massad, J., 1995. 'Conceiving the Masculine: Gender and Palestinian Nationalism.' *Middle East Journal* 49(3): 467–483.

McDonald, D. A., 2013. *My Voice Is My Weapon: Music, Nationalism, and the Poetics of Palestinian Resistance*. Durham, NC: Duke University Press.

Mignolo, W., and Vazquez, R., 2013. 'Decolonial AestheSis: Colonial Wounds/Decolonial Healings.' *Social Text-Periscope*. Available at: http://socialtextjournal.org/periscope_article/decolonial-aesthesis-colonial-woundsdecolonial-healings/ (Accessed 24 June 2021).

108 Queering Aesthesis

Nasara, M., 2012. 'The Ongoing Judiasation of the Neqab and the Struggle for Recognising the Indigenous Rights of the Arab Bedouin People.' *Settler Colonial Studies* 2(1): 81–107.

Rancière, J., 2004. *The Politics of Aesthetics*. Translated from French by G. Rockhill. London: Bloomsbury.

Shihade, M., 2012. 'Settler Colonialism and Conflict: The Israeli State and Its Palestinian Subjects.' *Settler Colonial Studies* 2(1): 108–123.

Simpson, A., 2014. *Mohawk Interruptus: Political Life Across the Borders of Settler States*. Durham, NC: Duke University Press.

Zuhur, S., 2001. *Colors of Enchantment: Theater, Dance, Music, and the Visual Arts of the Middle East*. Cairo: American University in Cairo Press.

———, 2017. 'The Discriminatory Laws Database.' *Adalah* [Online]. Available at: www.adalah.org/en/content/view/7771 (Accessed 24 June 2021).

———, 2020. 'Ayman Safiah Swam in the Air Like a Feather.' *Fusha*. Available at: www.arab48.com/فسحة/جسد/رقص/2020/05/27/أيمن-صفية-سبح-في-الهواء-لخفته (Accessed 22 June 2021). Source in Arabic.

Part II
Imagining Otherwise

5 Towards Radical Self-Determination

In August 2019, alQaws's activities in the West Bank became the site for violent targeting by the Palestinian National Authority (PNA). An unprecedented direct attack on the group was unleashed through a statement issued by the spokesperson of the PNA police, Louai Irzeqat, in the follow up to alQaws's organising of one of its forums on gender and sexuality known as *Hawamesh*[1] (margins) in the city of Nablus. The statement affirmed the police's intention to ban any alQaws activities, confirming that these activities go against the traditions and high values of Palestinian society with a particular reference to the city of Nablus, which is known for its 'strong familial relations' (Imgur, 2019: n.p.). It further confirmed the need to stop these activities that are 'dividing our society and posing a threat to civil peace,' clarifying that the police will do its role in 'pursuing the organisers of this collective and taking the necessary legal actions against them' (Ibid.). Finally, the statement ends with a call upon citizens to contact the police regarding any person they come to suspect of having connections to the group. Such a statement issued by the PNA marked an escalation of violence against alQaws and queer people in general. AlQaws contextualised this mounting violence in its response:

> This statement comes a week after alQaws held a widely published discussion-based event in Nablus, and three weeks after last month's stabbing of the Palestinian queer teen and alQaws' subsequent organizing around it. Prior to Irzeqat's statement, there had been a wave of unprecedented attacks by dozens of people flocking to alQaws' social media platforms, angered by the announcement of our event in Nablus, considered a sacred 'traditional' Palestinian city. Those hateful messages and posts threatened violence and prosecution, promoted lies about alQaws and our activities, as well as myths about LGBTQ people in general.
>
> (alQaws, 2019: n.p.)

AlQaws's response illuminates the violence, in digital (social media attacks), public (stabbing of a queer teen at the hand of their brother),[2] and finally—with

DOI: 10.4324/9781003273585-7

112 *Towards Radical Self-Determination*

the PNA statement—Institutional spheres which Palestinian queers had to face within the same period in 2019. The summer of 2015 had marked the start of a wave of violence accompanying an unprecedented, heated public debate around homosexuality and queer politics in the local context of Palestine. The debate and violence were epitomised in the follow up to a Palestinian artist's painting of a rainbow flag on six slabs of the side of the Zionist apartheid wall overlooking a refugee camp in the West Bank city of Ramallah. Khaled Jarrar, the artist who took this initiative, stated that his decision to paint the rainbow flag, which came in the context of celebrating the institutionalisation of gay marriage in the US through rainbows going viral on social media, was meant to shed light on the Palestinian plight for freedom amidst ongoing Israeli discrimination and apartheid (Al Shayib, 2015: n.p.). Least expected for Jarrar was to see the reactions this rainbow painting prompted within a group of young men describing themselves as 'heroes of the homeland' who in turn waged a campaign to whitewash and 'cleanse the wall from this shameful garbage' (Ibid.). This public attack complemented the inciteful statements that had been made during the same period by deputy head of the Palestinian Islamic movement in 1948,[3] which had targeted Palestinian queers and alQaws's work using the most derogatory and demeaning terms.

I argue that the summer of 2015 was the catalyst for dynamics of violence and resistance that serve to ground decolonial queering on two interrelated levels: first, it was a moment to assess and critically comprehend the socio-political dimensions of the unfolding violence where re-instantiation of hetero-conquest takes place on various scales. Second, it sheds light on the value of alQaws's work towards radical self-determination whose aim is to reimagine Palestine Otherwise.

On Violence: Internalising Pinkwashing

The PNA statement against alQaws not only marked an unprecedented direct attack at Palestinian queers from Authority, but also became, as alQaws activist Joul Elias warned, 'a valuable catch' for the Zionist state's pinkwashing agenda (2019: n.p.). Zionist utilisation of the event to serve its pinkwashing agenda was quickly revealed in a statement of support that was issued by Fleur Hassan-Nahoum, the deputy Mayor of Jerusalem, a self-proclaimed feminist and Israeli advocate, who stated:

> I would like to officially invite the LGBTQ group from the West Bank to hold their event in #Jerusalem or closer to home in one of the Jewish centers in Judea and Samaria. This should not be happening to you #LGBTQ.
>
> (Fleur Hassan-Nahoum, Twitter statement, 2019)

Nahoum's statement undoubtedly serves to illustrate Elias's point with regards to how this violent event turns into a golden opportunity that serves the Zionist pinkwashing agenda. Indeed, the same dynamic emerged during the summer of 2015 when international coverage of Palestinian whitewashing of Jarrar's rainbow painting collapsed into the very pinkwashing logic of Palestinian homophobia versus Israel as a gay paradise, which Palestinian queer and feminist groups, including alQaws, work to combat.[4] At the same time, Elias's observation could be taken further to argue that the violence epitomised by the PNA statement is, in fact, symptomatic of the internalisation and reproduction of pinkwashing within the colonised psychic and socio-political structures serving, as argued in Chapter 2, the re-instantiation of hetero-conquest.

To argue this way is to challenge some of the debates that have ensued in the wake of violence, including within queer circles themselves, denouncing what is claimed to be alQaws's hyper-focus on combatting pinkwashing and ignoring the 'internal' Palestinian context of homophobia and violence. Such claims were re-echoed in earlier debates and challenges voiced against what was seen as alQaws's hyper-involvement in the politics of fighting Israel internationally[5] rather than concentrating on the necessary internal fight against our society's homophobia (Field notes, 2014). In one instance, Haneen Maikey challenges this internal versus external binarism that enveloped criticisms of alQaws's anti-pinkwashing work by explaining how the violence of pinkwashing functions internally. Pinkwashing is not merely Zionist propaganda (alQaws, 2020: n.p.), it is essentially about the kind of violence within which the colonised are meant to be trapped. In other words, pinkwashing essentially strives to render Palestinian presence and futurity as void of decolonial queer possibilities. Therefore, the only logic that Palestinian queers should be left with is: my father will kill me; Israel is my saviour (Field notes, 2014). Here we can contemplate how the PNA violence on alQaws and Palestinian queers is based on the reproduction of the notion that there is no space/place for queerness in Palestine. In other words, PNA violence is symptomatic of pinkwashing as internalised, capturing colonised entrapment within a politics of national liberation, which succumbs to hetero-patriarchal orientations. These cohere—as I argued in Chapter 2—with the re-instantiation of hetero-conquest. In the PNA statement, there is an emphasis on Nablus as the city that captures the valuable traditions and high morals of Palestinian society, positing the PNA police as the guardian of both Nablus and its untouchable values. Thus, the PNA embodies a colonised internal re-reproduction of sub-identities and societal classifications along moralising grounds that are instrumental for their regulation within the settler state's configuration of Time, Space, and Sex. Colonised reproduction of the geopolitical and hetero-patriarchal boundaries of conquest entwines the need for their subjugation and regulation within the substructures of the settler colonial project. Sexual alienation is key to colonised reproduction within these substructures that 'buoys the powers of colonial governance' (Driskill *et al*, 2011: 19). Alienation, akin to what has been theorised in relation to indigene's sexual orphaning (Zaborskis, 2016),

114   *Towards Radical Self-Determination*

defines the native's entrapment within the psychic social and political structures of shame and oppression.

One of the central aspects to alQaws's work is the production of analysis offering an understanding of the historical processes through which sexual alienation is produced and maintained within the Palestinian context. Following its organisation of a 3-day school titled 'Sexual Politics in the Colonial Context of Palestine,' alQaws released a collection of articles[6] tackling the intersection between the sexual and the political in our context. One of the articles (Badarni, 2015) sheds light on the issue of sexual torture within the Zionist prison system, revealing the silence around it because of the fear of societal stigmatisation, particularly when it comes to interrogators' violation of women's bodies. Badarni's analysis is vital in illuminating how the trauma of settler colonial institutions—i.e., the prison system—induces fear and stigmatisation in relation to native sexuality. In another piece from the same collection, Maikey and Hilal trace the historical production of the Palestinian homosexual 'Israelised agent,' meaning with a connection to Israel (Hilal and Maikey, 2015). They reveal how an image is instilled by the colonisers who aim to break Palestinian resistance via the weaponisation of its moral values.[7] At the same time, Palestinian national political factions allow this weaponisation to take place because they failed to expand and challenge society's 'moral spectrum' beyond what the occupier deemed it to be. In these analyses, alQaws's production of knowledge sits at the intersection of the sexual and the political, precisely for the purpose of shedding light on how the alienation of the sexual from the political has taken place in discursive and material ways. The production of such an analysis in 2015, which marked—as I explained earlier—the unleashing of social violence and public debates, is no surprise. The Arabic analysis alQaws produced and distributed through a collaboration with the local journal, *Mada Al-Carmel*, further provides the necessary historical and contextual reading to comprehend how native sexuality has been locked within the realm of shame and oppression via the disciplinary mechanisms of the settler state and a Palestinian national project that could not encapsulate a sufficiently capacious understanding of the sexual/political.

The violence that was waged by the Authority in 2019 complements that of 2015 where the reproduction of the national figures of 'hero' and 'guardian' come hand in hand with the intensification of native entrapment within 'oppressed, repressed, and shamed sense of reality' (Rifkin, 2012: 28), capturing a colonised internalisation of pinkwashing. This internalisation manifests itself on two interrelated levels: first, it works on actively denying, shaming, and alienating any queer relationality to Palestine locales. This denial is captured in the violence perpetuated by the political representatives within the '67 boundaries'—i.e., the PNA—but also by the political representatives of 1948 communities—Arab MPs in the Knesset—who continuously deny the existence of homosexuality within our society. Second, this denial is intimately linked with the regeneration of the settler state and its institutions,

Towards Radical Self-Determination 115

captured through colonised political systems that subscribe to colonial governmentality. The enforcement of the settler state and its institutional base is not only enabled by official bodies like the PNA in the West Bank and/or Knesset representatives in 1948,[8] but can also be seen in the act of 'cleansing the wall' by the young heroes. In so doing, a politics of resistance at the popular level mirrors the national project's hetero-patriarchal emancipatory vision, which winds up re-instantiating the spatio-sexual boundaries of hetero-conquest: i.e., the apartheid wall being sanitised from queer garbage.

Pinkwashing as internalised functions not only through the violent disallowing of queerness in relation to Palestine but also through its simultaneous enforcement by the coloniser: Israel. This is seen clearly in the PNA statement where the condemnation of alQaws appears within the framing of queers as suspicious and foreign forces, which usually implies connections to the enemy and/or external agendas that are bent on destroying the Palestinian societal fabric. Indeed, this captures the history[9] of Palestinian national politics mobilising fear and the persecution of the native informant (homosexual) figure (Alqaisiya *et al*, 2016). At the same time, further enforcement of queerness in relation to Israel also takes place within local liberal and capitalist circles, whose support for Arab LGBT rights takes place through the provision of funding to Israel's LGBTQ task force: the Aguda. This is the case of the Arab-owned company of Tahinit Al Arz, which sparked debates with regards to this action in July 2020. While the debate was split between those who supported the company's act based on a pro-feminist and pro-equality stance and those who boycotted the company in condemnation of their support for the LGBTQ community, alQaws had its own concerns to voice on the two spectrums of the debate. AlQaws and Palestinian queers had to deal, yet again, with another wave of societal violence and condemnation of queer Palestinians and their sheer presence. Yet this incident unveiled intersecting capitalist and liberal voices whose only version of the Palestinian queer presence tallies with that of Zionist pinkwashing. AlQaws declares in a statement titled 'Tahinit Al Arz Debate: Intersections of Societal, Colonial and Capitalist Violence':

> . . . Societal violence is no less harmful than the violence of the various colonial institutions, among them the Aguda [which] has a long history of arrogant and orientalist projects. These are nothing but a reflection of the larger colonial policies of the Zionist entity, which Palestinian women and queer rights groups call pinkwashing policies . . . whose main aim is to erase Palestinian existence and frame it only within the Zionist saviour logic . . . It may be unusual for private Palestinian companies to support sexual and gender pluralism issues, something that may be seen by many as a positive step. However, this support did not go beyond a symbolic level and remained captive to the interests of capital, far away from investing in community discussion in the most real and constructive manner.
>
> (alQaws statement, 2020: n.p.)

116 *Towards Radical Self-Determination*

Similar dynamics to those encapsulating the Al Arz company debate emerged earlier in the 2015 incident of painting the wall with a rainbow flag and the discussions that followed when alQaws had to face a wave of societal violence and shaming that came hand in hand with the enforcement of queerness in relation to rainbow flags and gay marriages by colonial and capitalist institutions. In an article published in the same 2015 collection, Budour Hasan addressed discussions around homosexuality within our local contexts and how they seem to polarise between homophobic violence and the copy-pasting of global—meaning white, rich, and Western—definitions of gay rights (Hassan, 2015). Pinkwashing as internalised captures the violence of indigenous homophobia that is, at the same time, not to be de-linked from the very mobilisation of settler colonial sexualities (Morgensen, 2011), which both the US and the Zionist entity encapsulate. Morgensen explains the concept of settler sexualities in relation to the US context of naturalising settlement, which queer non-natives enable by virtue of rallying liberation à la citizenship ethos; that is, reproducing the continuity of the settler colonial presence, which, in turn, denies native queer aspirations for decolonisation (Morgensen, 2012). *The New York Times* reporting on the Al Arez company episode (Rasgon, 2020), where voices from the Aguda were centred, while erasing alQaws's position, illustrates the functionality of settler colonial sexualities.[10]

AlQaws's work challenges homophobia within the local Palestinian context by centring the fight against the reproduction of the very sexual-colonial institutions in native imaginings of queerness. In so doing, it mobilises decolonial queering towards Otherwise Imaginings that exceed the 'oppressed, repressed, shamed, and imposed sense' (Rifkin, 2012: 28) of sexual-colonial reality.

Decolonising Desire: Carving Decolonial Queer Consciousness

During a meeting in Ramallah, Ghaith discussed how alQaws, through its work in the field, started to realise that there was a victim mentality present within groups they worked with. Palestinians who struggle to live comfortably with their own sexual orientations grow resentful toward their families and communities, developing what Ghaith calls a 'rejectionist approach.' He expands:

> We discovered through our work in the field that the image 'we are victims' is internalised within so many people we work with. . . . There are lots of people that, once they start recognising their sexual orientation, develop a rejectionist approach toward their society and families. They start viewing themselves as separated from their families and communities, which they perceive as a source of oppression. There is this growing rift, therefore, between them and Palestinian society at large.
> (Conversation with Ghaith, 2014)

Ghaith's reflections identify a problematic factor in recognising sexual identities for some Palestinians. This recognition goes hand in hand with

Towards Radical Self-Determination 117

rejecting one's society and community. Hence, a victimhood mentality starts to emerge. This victimhood mentality emanates from what was discussed at the Sexuality School as 'fantasies that we have, where the coloniser has something to offer us,' which 'neither a group like alQaws or my community can offer' (Field notes, 2015). Against this background of victimhood and a separationist mentality, alQaws undertakes the task of building a decolonial queer consciousness whose aim is to break the internalisation of such a mentality and challenge the individualism that defines an identity politics approach to sexuality.

> [W]ithin the Palestinian context we cannot have an identity politics approach that divorces us from society because we do not live in an individualistic capitalist context. Our land is occupied, it is colonised, and our society is community-based. This is related to our political situation because the coloniser always tries to divide us, separating communities from each other. It's a Zionist strategy of divide and rule, manifested not only in the physical reality of borders and the wall separating Palestinians but also in mentally and emotionally separating us from one another. . . . We cannot build our own 'gay communities' and ghettos like elsewhere. This happened in the West because of capitalism and individualism. Here, we did not have an industrial revolution or whatsoever, so there is always a connection between extended families and communities that is enshrined in our societal structure.
>
> (Conversation with Ghaith, 2014)

Ghaith and other alQaws activists describe the dangers lurking in the adoption of an individualistic framework, which will entail separation and rejection from the community. They explain how individualism reifies the Zionist strategy of divide and rule. Haneen states:

> It is the aim of the coloniser to categorise us into various groups rather than recognise us as one people. Ever since Zionism was established, Palestinians were always seen as either Bedouins, Druze or shepherd herders. This process is part and parcel of negating their identity, their recognisability as a nation.
>
> (Maikey, 2014: n.p.)

AlQaws activists' understanding of Palestinian dismemberment determines the strategies used to challenge it since it entails unpacking the layers of wider Palestinian internal divisions and the production of dichotomies of 'Us versus Them.' Most importantly, alQaws's understanding of these divisions derives from their local work with various groups. As Ghaith explains:

> Since alQaws's spaces bring together various Palestinians from different places, including those '48 Palestinians' [Palestinian residents of what

118 *Towards Radical Self-Determination*

became Israel in 1948 are locally called 48 Palestinians] or 'East Jerusalemite' Palestinians and 'West Bankers,' we started to notice the kind of problematic language emerging between these various groups: one that is divisive and enforces the projections that one group has of another.

(Conversation with Ghaith, 2014)

A growing dichotomy of 'Us versus Them' is noted in relation to projections of sexual freedom and/or oppression between Palestinians who come from the West Bank and those who reside in 48 (Field notes, 2014). The proximity that one group shares with the presumed spaces of sexual freedom or oppression exerts an influence on the ways they describe each other, enforcing a dichotomous logic of 'Us versus Them.' For example, it is quite the norm for Palestinians from the West Bank to assume that more freedom is granted to 48 Palestinians by virtue of them residing in Israel. At the same time, 48 Palestinians would normally assume that coming from the West Bank is synonymous with homophobia and sexual oppression. It is also equally important to emphasise the various categorical hierarchies that exist within each locale.[11] This dichotomous and Manichean logic opposing West Bank victims to 48s sexual freedom contains the violence of internalised pinkwashing at the subjective level. In other words, in the process of being keen on exploring sexual orientation and cementing a gay identification, one can reproduce the frames of recognition that the colonising power uses towards them (liberated gay/oppressed victim, progressive/homophobic). 'One's struggle for sexual freedom' necessarily entails—for some—identifying as 'a victim of society and family' (Field notes, 2015). This victimisation is not necessarily void of the violence and homophobia one faces within their communities, as discussed earlier. At the same time, however, alQaws's work to rebuild decolonial queer consciousness should be seen as key to the labour that the group initiates to counter the violence while revealing its dual functionality both at the subjective and objective scales.

Indeed, central to the violence faced by Palestinian queers is the very concept of freedom and liberation, which, as activists note, has collapsed into reproducing the coloniser's image. Within the process of seeking sexual freedom and/or identifying as a victim, some Palestinians perceive Israel as a space to aspire to and within which sexual freedom can be both desired and exercised. Haneen highlights how:

Palestinians too want to go and visit Tel Aviv's sandy beaches, hug gay men there and consume tourism . . . we also want to be free with this growing concept of freedom that is so absurd.

(Maikey, 2014: n.p.)

The Palestinian reproduction of desires and concepts of sexual freedom reflects both a pinkwashing logic and imaginings of Palestinian sovereignty within the paradigms re-instantiating hetero-conquest. The striving for

Towards Radical Self-Determination 119

closeness to Tel Aviv, where supposed freedom lies, must be situated in relation to the agenda of modernising à la Tel Aviv, activated by the Oslo process. As discussed in Chapter 2, the example of the modern Palestinian Rawabi city, which rises to depict proximity to Tel Aviv, perfectly captures the issue at hand. At the same time, this modernising agenda enforces the reality of spatial enclavisation across Palestine. Desires for Tel Avivian sexual freedom foster this colonial spatial-temporal hierarchy, denoting Palestinian internal fragmentation. When alQaws points out the dangers of the 'Us versus Them' dichotomy, it warns against the consolidation of spatial-temporal colonising hierarchies among Palestinians themselves. Simultaneously, the use of this dichotomy enfolds the web of self-victimisation. To define oneself as a victim of an oppressive society is also a means of seeking proximities to spatial-temporalities of sexual freedom. This proximity and distance translate into a growing rift within Palestinian society, which occurs as LGBT identifications are articulated within discourses of oppression and victimhood. The concept of sexual freedom/identity is also constituted in relation to the idea of happiness that the coloniser's space is meant to encapsulate.

The following ethnographic reflection captures a summary of a discussion I had with Haneen, Ghaith, and other alQaws members and friends at a café in Ramallah.

> Haneen comments on the phenomena of liberal Palestinian LGBT and she pronounces each letter in a French-like manner, thus extending their sound in a campy fashion: *ehll jhay bay tay*. These *ehll jhay bay tay* are the happy ones, as she describes them laughingly. Later, throughout the evening, we use the term Sa'idoun [happy ones] to describe those Palestinian liberal out and about [Happy gays]. In particular, the conversation reflected on some individuals who, having had the chance to travel and live abroad, in America or Europe, are now accepting to talk about their experiences as gay Palestinian men at Zionist-funded initiatives and events.
>
> (Field notes, 2014)

This ethnographic moment is important because it offers a chance to examine alQaws's critique of internalised pinkwashing via *ehll jhay bay tay* (Palestinian gay liberal) striving for happiness. These happy directionalities, which emerge as a result of gay (liberal) identifications, comply with Zionist frames of narrating the life and experience of Palestinian queerness. Happiness orientates gay Palestinians towards 'Tel Aviv [gay] happiness' because happiness and any other discourse on the good life operates within existing structures of power, whereby subjects orient themselves toward happy objects (2010: 29). In other words, as Sara Ahmed argues, to desire happiness also means that happiness is what you get in return for desiring well (Ibid.: 34). This is where the regulatory premise of happiness lies, since it includes a historical distribution of good/bad, happy/wretch that sustains

120 *Towards Radical Self-Determination*

the dominant power structure. For instance, dominant heterosexual frames impose a shared orientation towards certain right paths conducive of social goods, such as marriage and family. Crucial to this discussion is the unmasking of the history of colonialism and empire in enforcing happiness as a social commodity. Frantz Fanon's work (1963) on the 'good habits' of the coloniser that the colonised seek to emulate help to do this.[12] Fanon refers to the internalisation by the colonised (black man) of the colonial order as he seeks acceptance within the civilisational paradigms of the coloniser (white man). In particular, the orientation by the colonised towards the coloniser's spaces creates a need to distance oneself from the 'wretchedness of the colonised.'[13] Similarly, internalised pinkwashing unveils a desire for proximities to Israeli spaces, such as 'its [gay] sandy beaches,' while moving away from the homophobia of Palestinian communities. AlQaws's awareness of the violence that pinkwashing as internalised activates within the psyche and subjecthood of Palestinian queers paves the way to initiate a decolonial queer consciousness where alternative cartographies of self-realisation can be found beyond 'this absurd concept of freedom' and/or 'happiness.' AlQaws creates a space for critique (Martin and Secor, 2014) that combines both topological (absurd concept of freedom) and topographical (internalised colonial geopolitical divisions) spaces.

Activists' use of the term happy ones and the camp sounding *ehll jhay bay tay* (LGBT) recalls an *unhappy queer* positionality that seeks to unsettle dominant paradigms of happiness. According to Sara Ahmed, positive psychology explains happiness as something that promotes flow rather than restraint vis-à-vis the world; yet it fails to take into account how power structures affect this flow. She wonders what happens to those who fail to be 'in flow,' facing the world as 'resistant' or 'alien' by indicating:

> What if to flow in the world is not simply understood as a psychological attribute? What if the world 'houses' some bodies more than others, such that some bodies do not experience the world as resistant? We might need to rewrite happiness by considering how it feels to be stressed by the very forms of life that enable some bodies to flow into space.
>
> (2010: 12)

The questions that Ahmed poses about happiness as 'a flow' resonate with alQaws's work to disrupt gay/happy *ehll jhay bay tay* paradigms through a critical inquiry into those 'bodies that Israel erases and those others it wants to save' (Field notes, 2015). AlQaws's analysis unpacks how this flow of the happy Palestinian *ehll jhay bay tay* is based on the hierarchy that the colonising power creates between various Palestinian bodies/spaces/temporalities.

> On the one hand, there are the bodies that Israel cares to kill and erase— as happens in Gaza. On the other hand, there are those bodies—the

Towards Radical Self-Determination   121

queer bodies—that should be saved. The only Palestinian who is worth saving, therefore, is the one that falls within Israeli exotic fantasies about who the Palestinian queer is.

(Alqaisiya *et al*, 2016: 134)

The happiness that alQaws identifies in internalised pinkwashing on the subjective scale echoes ideals of happiness that recolonise the Palestinian national body when dominated by the notion of 'the happy family,'[14] which demonstrates the re-instantiation of the hetero-colonial order in imaginings of Palestinian liberation. The Authority's statement against alQaws reiterates these sentimental attachments to familial values presumed to stand in contrast to what the group and queerness in Palestine encapsulate. Decolonial queering offers a venue to critically evaluate colonised attachments to the very emancipatory ideals that constitute the continuity of their subjugation.

Building Communities

AlQaws's activation of decolonial queer consciousness entails rejecting the circulation of self-victimising narratives. Muhammad from Yafa, who joined the group in 2007 to organise support networks and counselling services in various spaces throughout Palestine, discusses alQaws's modus operandi, reflecting on its political and ethical stance:

> We are conscious and cautious of this idea of circulating personal narratives of suffering because of sexual orientation . . . You see, I worked as a freelancer with different organisations, and I have seen how personal stories get used in their reports and in order to draw funders. In alQaws, I see how we have a completely different approach. The very idea of using individual stories or circulating them on Facebook or through other means is a red line. At the same time, it reflects alQaws' political and social approach. We are not interested in circulating stories of victimhood. We are aware of how it feeds the expectations of certain institutions and cements grand narratives on the Palestinian LGBT who need saving by Israel. A lot of people continue to try and drag us into this place but, unlike others, we refuse to go there
>
> (Conversation with Muhammad, 2014)

Muhammad explains how the focus of alQaws is to bring out 'a collective story' (Ibid.), rather than investing in the personal narrative of victimhood, an approach that complements alQaws's goal of building communities and agents for social change (Conversation with Ghaith, 2014). Starting from the summer of 2013, the year marking my introduction to alQaws, I could see how the group works on building communities through the creation of spaces for care, safety, and intimate sharing. As I had travelled all the way from Hebron—south of the West Bank—to Ramallah in the north to

122 *Towards Radical Self-Determination*

attend a 3-day workshop organised with DarkMatter,[15] Haneen informed me that a friend of alQaws, G., would gladly host me in her house. G., who would later become a close friend of mine, welcomed me into her house and 'other alQaws members that [she] loves so much and considers her true family' (Field notes, 2013). By spending time in G.'s house, I saw first-hand how the provision of spaces of care capture the material activation of decolonial queer spaces of homing, which 'transcend territorial borders and nation states and a symbolics of national struggle' (Shalhoub-Kevorkian and Ihmoud, 2014: 394).

> At G.'s I met people from many parts of Palestine, heard all kinds of Palestinian dialects and seen beautiful staging of drag, music and poetry performances. I have tasted the joy of cooking and sharing meals with a group of people who felt so familiar to one another. G. would show me how, for tonight, I'd be sleeping in the bed that she usually allocates for Omar, whom she describes as a brother of hers: 'When O. is not around I worry so much . . . This is my real family; I love them so much Walaa and when they are around, I feel whole.' At G.'s you would want to sit in that small veranda and engage in *fadfada*, letting it out, talk all day. She tells me how this, her place, has accommodated the fears and frustrations of many people in the community; 'Those who need an ear always come here *habibti*.'
>
> (Field notes, 2014)

AlQaws's homing spaces foster indigenous queer re-rooting beyond the imposed settler colonial hierarchies and the confines of national-project imagining of a future Palestinian state. Palestinian feminists offer analytics of homing to capture 'returning to our home/land as a space of reconstructing Palestinian socialites and identities, of re-rooting through a radical praxis of love that can give birth to new forms of resistance' (Shalhoub-Kevorkian and Ihmoud, 2014: 394). AlQaws's homing spaces encapsulate indigene's return on multiple levels. A return to one's 'true family' marks an indigene's home-coming within the registers of familiarity and comfort (Marie Fortier, 2003), exceeding heteronormative notions of belonging that Palestinian statist nationalism enforces. Simultaneously, this return to the micro-domestic space of love, familiarity, and joy enfolds the larger activation of an indi-gene's return to the homeland, making room for a reconstructed sense of nationhood with the capacity to rupture the colonial order of Manichean compartmentalising (Fanon, 1967: 109). The love and support that G. holds and provides for those who maintain her sense of wholeness shows how con-sciousness of oneself in relation to the Other is activated within the spaces of be/longing (Bryant, 2015) that decolonial queering encapsulates. To *be* at home is to inhabit a material place that simultaneously animates *longing*; 'To long is to imagine, to pine for or to claim agency as a creative practice' (Ibid.: 263). G.'s is a place where many are made to feel at home through the sense of comfort, safety, and affective affinity that the space transmits. Such energy of love and safety spring from the very subjects, i.e., G. and those who want to unload by talking or performing, and whose gender and sexual orientations yearn to imagine oneself and Palestine differently.

The space for unwinding, sharing, and listening that G.'s house offered also encapsulated the labour of care that tens of volunteers within Al-Khat Listening and Information Hotline service provide to callers in need of information and/or any form of support. R. spoke passionately about the work Al-Khat has been doing for years where she and other volunteers provide the necessary support and advice on sexuality LGBT and gender identity issues for callers and/or online chatters (Field notes, 2014). Haneen also explained that Al-Khat is one of the most sought-after services that alQaws provides: 'We get callers from everywhere in Palestine looking for a safe space to discuss all their doubts and questions on sexuality issues.' She adds that 'People with all sorts of problems call us on Al-Khat, including those who engage in pre-marital sex or only need someone to listen to them' (Conversation with Haneen, 2014). The importance of Al-Khat lies both in the support provided to callers from everywhere in Palestine—including Gaza, where physical presence might be challenged by Zionist policies of blockade—and in being a basis for further support initiatives that draw on the needs and doubts of Al-Khat callers and chatters. Muhammad provides an interesting example, describing how a group of 13 transsexual people who had initially contacted Al-Khat now formed a group meeting for support and consultation, which alQaws facilitates (Conversation with Muhammad, 2014).

AlQaws's homing spaces, whether in a workshop, digital, or private spaces of care exhibit Palestinian identities coming together as part of a collective exercise on what sexuality and decolonisation entail. Reflecting on pinkwashing, alQaws members spoke not only of the Palestinian LGBT internalisation of this logic, but also of the wider Palestinian aspiration for a good life. This good life is also closely related to Israel, for example in the form of tourism permits to 'visit Israel . . . enjoy and consume Israeli products' (Field notes, 2015). Activists provide analysis of the sub-identities that Oslo has cemented, enforcing divisions between the various 'insiders/ outsiders' (Field notes, 2015). These insider/outsider binaries are measured in relation to what could become a visibly recognisable state of Palestine in the West Bank and Gaza, excluding 48 Palestinians and the hundreds of thousands of refugees who live beyond the nation-state's territorial borders.

> Oslo was instrumental to produce sub-identities, classify us into blue and green document holders. We should also look at how, for example, we—Palestinians—are performing the very sub-identities that Israel issued for us. Thus, the very green or blue material ID documents that are supposed to separate and categorise us from one another are also seen in our perception of each other.
>
> (Sexuality School, Field notes, 2015)

124 *Towards Radical Self-Determination*

In another discussion with regards to pinkwashing as internalised and the violence of desiring coloniser's spaces and bodies, G. retorts:

> I would not want to be in a relation with an Israeli woman, even if we share the same sexual orientation. Why would I want to be with those who steal my land and destroy my home on a daily basis?! She is an occupier!
>
> (Field notes, 2013)

As G. spoke, I was thinking of her family house back in Beit Jala where she hosted me once and took me to see the land that belongs to her family. I remembered how on the way there, we had to stop the car by the gate the Zionists have placed to obstruct Palestinian entry. We got out and walked all the way up to where we met up with her brother on beautiful terrain that housed a cave, which the family has turned into a cave-house since an Israeli military order prohibited them from building or expanding in the area. G. explained that the land is under threat of confiscation. 'We have been in court with them for years now, they want this piece of land because of its strategic location, but they haven't understood yet that we won't leave nor give it up. This land is our soul and everything we fight for' (Field notes, 2013). AlQaws's homing spaces trigger a process of remaking of the home from within (Gopinath, 2005: 14). That is, while they provide a homecoming with one's true family—G.'s house in Ramallah—that can be realised away from one's family house—in Beit Jala—they nonetheless do not necessarily entail leaving one's biological family once and for all. Rather, alQaws's homing activates a space for reconstructing the familial and national home, capturing the oneness of indigene's struggle against dispossession.

Decolonial queer homing, therefore, generates a process of 'vigilant awareness' where continuous work and critical thinking is needed to build community and foster self-love against all modes of 'socialisation that . . . perpetuate domination' (Hooks, 2003: 36). Further evidence of alQaws's work on rebuilding the space of the home from within is the research the group has conducted with a plethora of counsellors, social workers, and field researchers about Palestinian families' interactions with their children's diverse gendered and sexual experiences. In March 2021, the group released the research document and followed it with an educational webinar where both research contributors and other psycho-social professionals came together to discuss and reflect on the research and its findings. Throughout the discussion, Asrar Kayyal, one of the people who worked on the research, explains the lens of the psyche of the oppressed that has been deployed to understand the dynamics of the interaction between individuals and their families:

> People who have been subjected to long term oppression deal with pressure in distinct ways. In that within our society we have the

Towards Radical Self-Determination 125

tendency to deal with an overwhelming issue in a black or white manner, and this applies both to the individual with diverse sexual and gender identities and also their parents. While the latter's reaction to their child's sexuality would be: 'now I am being put in a situation where I must choose either my son/daughter's needs or my wider societal belonging,' the individual looking for their parents' support already comes with a preconceived judgment that 'my family is backward and there is no way for them to accept me and therefore, I must leave.'

(alQaws webinar, 2020)

Kayyal explains how alienation emerges at both individual and collective levels:

. . . as a society we have reached a place where it is much easier for one to escape rather than have that deep and tough dialogue that should essentially lead us to understand and alleviate the violence . . . Palestinian societal traditions and values are never static, and we have to start seeing and integrating our cultural dynamism to our own approach of dealing with issues related to gender and sexual diversity.

(Ibid.)

Through this research, alQaws assumes the activist-educator role who is initiating 'dialogical actions' for social change (Freire, 2000: 180). That is, by bringing reflections from the research done in the field with individuals and their lived realities, alQaws activist-researchers not only transmit knowledge about the lived realities of subjects but also initiate 'that deep and tough dialogue' demanding new world-articulation 'through words, work and action-reflection' (Freire in Coelho Pena *et al*, 2018: 13). Haneen comments at the beginning of the webinar that the value of this research derives from many years of working closely and intimately with other individuals, encapsulating all the conversations we had with them but also with 'ourselves too.' She draws on her own experience with her family and the changes she has faced on a personal level. The *collaborative*—with psycho-social workers—and *real*—individual's experiences—dimensions of the research show alQaws's ability to establish a living reciprocity between self/other, child/parent, family/society, and client/therapist challenging the violent psychology of dismemberment and alienation that Kayyal discussed earlier. Kayyal further comments on how

By not letting go of its national identity, alQaws functions as an alternative space from which one's healthy recognition in relation to who they are can take place while leading them then to take that experience and what they have learnt back to their familial homes and relations.

(alQaws webinar, 2020)

126 *Towards Radical Self-Determination*

Kayyal's point captures the decolonisation of the space of the home from within, where indigene's return to oneself embeds a return to one's family, home, and Palestine as a whole. Such a return requires the capacity for 'unrelenting resistance' (alQaws news, 2019b) leading the pathway to a decolonial world that is yet to come.

Revolutionary Pathways

AlQaws's work centres the relationship between the question of liberation and tackling gender and sexual violence and mechanisms of its reproduction among Palestinians. Speaking about the Haifa-based bimonthly discussion forums on gender and sexuality in Palestine, known as *Hawamesh*, Haneen refers me to an alQaws article on the Arabic website *Qadita* about 'gender violence in social media,'[16] which sums up a few ideas from the analysis that the discussion forum offered regarding the intersection of gender and sexual violence within our context. The writer(s), identified as Louise Louise, reveal(s) how 'fighting patriarchy in our society as a human feminist cause is one of the major pillars upon which our queer struggle is based' (2014: n.p.). The piece adds further, 'To connect our struggle with women's oppression in our society is a necessity to understand violence on a deeper, more comprehensive level' (Ibid.). Reflecting on the violent comments that circulate in the streets or a Facebook post about a 'man who wears tights,' thus passing like 'a woman,' Louise's article critically examines the viral spread of gender violence in the realm of both social media and daily interactions within 'our schools, streets and homes' (Ibid.). It explains how gender violence persists in Palestinian society, drawing the necessary connection between queer politics and the patriarchy of Palestinian society that alQaws's work reveals. In addition, the piece addresses the 'common misconception' that follows violence towards those assumed to be gay because they look more feminine or those assumed to be lesbian because they appear or act manly. Instead, the piece reveals 'the complexity of sexual identities that do not necessarily rely on gender performances' (Ibid.).

Through the *Hawamesh* forum and the analytical perceptions, in the written and conversational format it propagates, alQaws channels dis-identifications to gender hierarchies and their reproduction in Palestine. Louise's article demonstrates how the question of gender and its regulation within Palestinian society stands at the core of what alQaws does, demonstrating further the queerness of the group's positionality. In fact, alQaws challenges the concept of (un)manly roles and behaviours versus (un)womanly ones, tracing how patriarchy activates this gender hierarchy, which is loaded with violence. Identifying this violence leads alQaws to question its regulatory premises, elaborating an analysis that challenges the compulsory order of sex/gender/desire (Butler, 1999: 9).

AlQaws's *Hawamesh* platform and Louise's article show the group's early-on framing of its queer politics in relation to a Palestinian feminist standpoint. According to alQaws, the violence that both Palestinian women and queers face ought to be read in relation to one another. This urge to connect the two struggles together becomes particularly manifest alongside the increasing amount of violence that Palestinian queers and women are subjected to. The year 2019 marked not only the persecution of a gay boy but also of a young Palestinian woman at the hand of her family. In a Facebook post, alQaws provides their reflections on such painful events:

> The news about the killing of Israa Gharib stirs sadness and pain as well as anger and the urge to overthrow and change the patriarchal system in which we live. The system which legitimated the killing of Israa is the same one that allowed a brother to stab his brother because of his sexual orientation/gender identity. This patriarchal system justifies killing and attacking women and queers and harming them on a daily basis . . . Oppressing us, controlling our bodies, lives and killing our dreams . . . our work is an essential fight against patriarchy and masculinity that plagues our society. We aspire for a more just society for women, queer people and for all Palestinians.
>
> (alQaws Facebook post, 2019)

The call to overthrow the masculinist patriarchy of our society comes hand in hand with the need to re-signify the limits within the vision of a Palestinian collective identity where violence against non-conforming individuals becomes sanctioned for the needs of the wider collective (Louise, 2014: n.p.). AlQaws confronts the dichotomous logic in Palestinian nationalism that prioritises the liberation struggle, while other issues—including gender violence—should only be addressed after liberation is achieved (Conversation with Ghaith, 2014). In this regard, activists explain the criticism that the group faces as it tries to raise awareness of the intersectionality of these struggles, stressing the heteronormative structure that define liberation. Ghaith and Haneen stress:

> Not only do homosexuals continue to be branded as Israelised and collaborators. Rather, the mere fact of talking of the intersectionality of struggles and/or trying to break the hierarchy of struggles (national freedom first, women/sexuality struggles afterwards) is judged as a divergence from the main [priority] national/collective struggle for liberation.
>
> (Field notes, 2015)

AlQaws's spaces not only challenge the hierarchy within which national priorities are construed, but most importantly, show how within this hierarchisation we witness the recolonisation of native bodies and lands by comprador native elites.[17] In an online conversation I had with Haneen Maikey we both discussed how violence against gender and sexually diverse people

128 *Towards Radical Self-Determination*

and the presence of a group like alQaws intimately links with the increased wider repression of social/political forces within Palestinian society that threaten the status quo. In June 2021 after a PNA killing of a famous Palestinian opponent from the South of Hebron, Nizar Banat, protests waged against the Authority started to spiral all over Palestine. Within these protests, the PNA's violent targeting of women and queer activists reached a peak. Protestors' bodies, primarily women, were not only violated, harassed, and violently beaten in the streets but also their personal belongings, including phones, were stolen for the purpose of launching defamation campaigns. AlQaws was quick to issue a statement against the violence of the Authority that resonated with the group's own experience of violence.

> Escalating violence and repression, such as the gender violence that we witnessed yesterday, is an essential core to the existence of the Palestinian Authority and every repressive patriarchal authority. The PNA therefore will harness any tools for its survival and to protect itself, its institutions, and its political and capitalist interests. We at alQaws have lived this violence and experienced it first-hand when the Authority attacked us and used our work with gay and trans people as a tool to gain societal legitimacy and popular support, especially at times when popular resentment escalates towards it, such as any discussion related to division, administrative corruption, or collusion with colonialism or others. The defamation campaign launched by the Authority since yesterday seeks to achieve two goals: the first is to deter and intimidate social groups—primarily women—from taking to the streets and continuing to protest, and the second is to distract from the main event and the growing popular demand to confront and hold the Authority accountable. It must be said that the Authority succeeded in creating a state of fear among activists, with its actions from yesterday, and even endangered the lives of Palestinian women. This fear is legitimate and natural when faced with such a repressive Authority, but on the other hand, it is important to say out loud that this fear will not dissuade the popular masses, particularly women, transgender people, homosexuals, and anyone who challenges gender roles and norms from confronting oppression and continuing to shake the foundations of the Authority until it collapses.
>
> (alQaws news, 2021)

In another *Hawamesh* meeting, alQaws's new director, Haneen Sadir, discusses the role played by Palestinian political parties and leadership in sanctioning violence against queer people for the purpose of regaining the legitimacy that it has lost in the eyes of the masses through the activation of the Authority's role as guardians of morality and civil peace. The Authority seeks to capitalise on moral panics within society to regain legitimacy. Yet alQaws fights against gender and sexual violence to make room for difference

Towards Radical Self-Determination 129

within Palestinian collective identity. In doing so, they activate a politics of decolonial queering that 'works on, with and against' (Muñoz, 1999: 12) a national self-determination project, which has become abstracted from indigene's struggle against hetero-conquest. In this struggle, alQaws relies a lot on visual and aesthetic modalities whose circulation within the public sphere seeks to redefine dominant hetero-sexist norms within Palestinian society.

One early example of alQaws's circulation of queer glimpses within the city space is the graffiti (Figure 5.1) that activists created during the summer of 2014 along the route to Ramallah city centre. The graffiti comprises writing that translates from Arabic as 'Queer passed through here' and close to it one sees two kissing faces of the same sex/gender. As we walk together by the graffiti, one alQaws affiliate from Ramallah expresses the happiness they feel as they walk by this graffiti and see it daily en route to work: 'it's like queering up the city a little bit (chuckles) and a reminder to everyone in the city and also ourselves that we *do* exist' (Field notes, 2014). Similarly, Muhammad considers the graffiti as part of these interventions that alQaws slowly enables and 'can be thought of as a way of spreading queer glimpses here and there' (Conversation with Muhammad, 2015). The capacity of alQaws to introduce these queer glimpses underlies a call for 'widening discussions on gender and sexuality across Palestine' (Conversation with Haneen, 2014). The utilisation of graffiti as a medium per se bears significant

Figure 5.1 Graffiti 'Queers passed through here'
Source: alQaws graffiti (2013).

130 *Towards Radical Self-Determination*

political/aesthetic value. It reflects the group's ability to both manipulate a long political history of graffiti-making that has been utilised to serve a masculinist aesthetic/political value system. Activists joke about how the statement 'Queers passed through here' resonates a lot with the famous slogan of Palestinian political factions, i.e., Fatah passed through here. AlQaws redeploys the very terms through which the Palestinian national movement would express liberation in masculinist terms. In doing so, it provokes queer re-signification of liberation in both discursive and material ways. 'Queers' replaces 'Fateh' not only to break the silence around a queer revolutionary presence but also to show in visual terms indigene's sexual desires that challenge the gendered binarism found within the representational conventions of the national movement like woman-land and masculine-fighters. By encouraging emotions of happiness and affinity to the city space for those subjects who are made to affirm that 'we *do* exist,' the graffiti unmasks decolonial queering both within the public/city space and internally within those bodies transmitting affinities to the meanings on the wall.

Further circulation of queer interventions within the public space happens through activist's design and distribution of pedagogic posters and short educational videos. During 2017, alQaws launched a social media campaign titled 'Difference Never Justifies Violence.'[18] The campaign, which was conducted in partnership with '7amleh: the Arab Centre for Social Media Advancement,' produced three educational videos along with the production of posters and a plethora of experience narratives that alQaws collated from queer individuals from many parts of Palestine. In the first two videos, one sees activists from alQaws performing conversations among a group of friends who are sharing their experiences of violence in the home sphere, school, and the street. Speaking in a simple and local Palestinian dialect, the friends debunk some of the wider societal myths that queer individuals face in relation to their gendered and sexual expressions, revealing how the perpetuation of these myths contributes to the continuity of violence. For example, in Video 1 (Figure 5.2) activists speak about the violence that queers, and especially transwomen, are facing because it is thought they have 'been molested' as children and/or that they propagate diseases. Furthermore, they share common perceptions in the house sphere among the family where it is believed that to be gay is to be a Zionist collaborator or an agent of the West. The friends respond to all these misconceptions by saying LGBT's have always been present in our society 'even before the Nakba and British Mandate.' The third video (Figure 5.3) uses animation focusing on two figures and the verbal harassment they face as they walk in the street from commentators who wonder 'if this is a boy or a girl' to another who would 'want to set this one straight.' As the comments and jokes are heard, we see violent slapping and punching of the figures until they disappear. The campaign sheds light on how violence functions through the verbal utilisation of words such as *shadh* (pervert) and homo (from homosexual) to justify the violence against queer subjects while it introduces a dictionary

Towards Radical Self-Determination 131

Figure 5.2 Myths about Sexual and Gender Diversity in Palestine
Source: alQaws (2017a)

Figure 5.3 Verbal Violence is Not Different From Physical Violence
Source: alQaws (2017b)

of Arabic glossary terms including *mithliyah* (for homosexuality) and *mutahawwil* (transgender). The production of pedagogic and linguistic tools that are meant to counter violence continued in alQaws's 2019 campaign titled: 'Did You Know,' which activists from various universities distributed

132 *Towards Radical Self-Determination*

its flyers within the university campuses (alQaws news, 2019a). The flyers[19] included statements such as: 'Did you know that not every male is a man and not every female is a woman and that gender and sexuality are not interchangeable?' 'Did you know that that our gender identities are not solely hetero or homo?' 'Did you know that patriarchal violence impacts us all regardless of how we identify?' 'Did you know that our gender and sexual identity is much more complex than what our clothes/bodily gestures may relay?'

AlQaws's visual and written production of materials, which infiltrate public and digital space to spark debates and challenge society's perception on gender and sexuality, demonstrate activists' systematic determination to take the matter of violence into their own hands, thereby showing their capacity to act as agents for change.

> LGBTQs in Palestine are not victims waiting to be saved; in fact, young and old LGBTQ activists are leading this first-of-its-kind, anti-violence video campaign to build a stronger Palestinian society that celebrates all forms of diversity.
>
> (alQaws news, 2017: n.p.)

Part and parcel of alQaws's work to claim their agency in the face of violence is their strategic partnering with other civil society organisations, a step that has become vital in responding to forms of violence on a macro-scale. In the follow up to the PNA statement, alQaws mobilised its position as a legally established civil society organisation to work on enforcing human rights like other civil society organisations within the context of Oslo-shaped Palestine. AlQaws utilises this legal framework to serve its own interest of being a legitimate institution like any other. Here alQaws smartly navigates itself infra-politically (Scott, 1990). It performs a politics of legitimate advocacy à la institutional base that aligns with the dominant framework of power, while maintaining its location within 'the subordinate discourse [which] takes place beyond the perceptual field of the dominator' (Lugones, 2000: 177). Being a legally registered NGO, alQaws utilises its affiliate position within the Palestinian Human Rights Organisation Council who would, in the follow up to the PNA police violence, issue a strong statement of condemnation citing the illegality of the PNA police action.

> The PNA-police statement violates the provisions of the amended Basic Law and the relevant Palestinian Legislation and international conventions to which the State of Palestine acceded without reservations in many respects including the characteristics of the human rights system and its indivisible universality, the principle of equality and non-discrimination. The Palestinian police is liable to adhere to the constitutional and legal frameworks under which it enacts its responsibility

Towards Radical Self-Determination 133

for law enforcement and the maintenance of security and protection for all citizens.

(Al-Haq, 2019)

Another statement was also released by alQaws, in collaboration with other civil society signatories, similarly raising a concern for the contravening nature of the PNA police statement but also emphasising a concern with regards to the larger incitement that has been mounting at the hands of people with institutional backgrounds.

> We strongly condemn the participation of people from media, human rights, cultural and psychological backgrounds in the wave of incitement and abuse, which is in violation of Palestinian law. . . . We believe that the natural right of the alQaws Foundation is to conduct its activities and complete its work that seeks to expand societal dialogue, as it has demonstrated over the past years through its contribution to the progress of our society and its containment of pluralism and difference: a fundamental human right guaranteed in Palestinian law and international human rights treaties. The Palestinian police and official bodies must protect citizens without discrimination and provide them with security and safety as stipulated by law. . . . We are all keen on enhancing stability in the Palestinian social fabric as well as expecting the rule of law and rights and freedoms in the State of Palestine.
>
> (Statement, 2019)

At first, it appears that alQaws positions itself on the side of the rule of law, thus aligning its statement to the values upheld by the PNA for the maintenance of civil peace. However, alQaws is enacting a performative shift (Yurchak, 2003). That is, it aligns strategically with those terms to reorient their meanings, which have been emptied of significance by the Authority's ritualised speech. The PNA, in fact, has increasingly used 'law and civil peace' as tools to justify its very oppression against those who threaten the status quo within the Oslo framework. This fact became crystal clear for the Palestinian masses in the aftermath of the PNA killing of the opposition figure Nizar Banat. Following his death, the PNA prime minister's increasing reference to freedom of speech translated, in practice, into more repressive mechanisms against political opponents and protestors.

While the counterstatements issued by civil society partners functioned as a means to make the PNA police withdraw its inciteful statement against alQaws, the mobilisations the group continued to build from the bottom-up activated Otherwise Imaginings to dominant discourse. This has been shown in the work the group continues to do in mobilising Palestinian uprisings. In the follow up to the wave of mass protests—known as the May 2021 uprising—that erupted all over Palestine against the Zionist eviction policies of Palestinian families in Jerusalem, alQaws activists were

134 *Towards Radical Self-Determination*

at the forefront of organising and leading the fight against Zionist settler dispossession policies. Omar Al-Khatib, who was among those brutally beaten and arrested by the Zionist police forces (see Figure 5.4), situates the recent liberatory events within a larger cumulative work that Palestinians, including those in alQaws, have been leading against the settler colonial institutions and those semi-structures—i.e., the PNA—that subjugates Palestinians (Mansour, 2021: n.p.). Omar reflects particularly on how pinkwashing has been weaponised in the recent queer solidarity protests with Palestine, which has been faced with Zionist response of, 'you are like the stupid Turkey that is running around happily for Thanksgiving' (Ibid.). Omar further reflects:

> This kind of discourse is an excellent example of Zionist pinkwashing policies, which our coloniser employs to tell queer Palestinians that we must hate our society because it will slaughter us. In doing so, we are left with more fragmentation and no hope or prospect for societal change, because our only protector is supposedly the criminal colonial entity named Israel. This is why we cannot conceive of any Palestinian uprising where forms of struggle are separated from one another. We must be honest with ourselves and see the indivisibility of our liberation.
>
> (Ibid.)

Figure 5.4 Zionist Police Force Arrest Omar Al-Khatib
Source: Palestine Online, 2021

Omar presents other examples that explain how our movement for liberation should be cautious in re-enforcing gendered and sexual violence that groups like alQaws work to combat.

> For example, celebrating the ability to challenge and confront colonialism with strength and steadfastness sometimes comes hand in hand with reinforcing discourses that celebrate hyper-masculinity and reproduce a masculine hierarchy that elevates the personality of the young Man/ Hero. This is something we, as women and queer people, pay the price for . . . Our role in alQaws lies in emphasizing the concept of indivisible liberation, and the permanent link between struggles, the road is long and not easy, and there is more than one front, but our breath is long, and our resistance continues.
>
> (Ibid.)

Indeed, Omar's insights were important to centre some of the problems that emerged in the follow up to continued Palestinian protests, this time against PNA political persecution, which, as discussed earlier, unleashed violence against women and queer people's bodies. The alQaws's *Hawamesh* event titled 'Oppression from Colonisers and Palestinian Authority: Feminist and Queer Reflections on the Uprising,' brought together activists from alQaws and other feminist grassroots organising to centre the questions that the feminist queer perspective offers with regards to resistance and the violence unleashed by Zionist settler occupiers and the PNA Security Forces. Shada, from the Tala'at feminist grassroots movement, comments on how the feminist and queer presence in the uprising has shown that

> We are part and parcel of the struggle for liberation of Palestine and we refuse to sit idly outside of the core questions around which our being revolves. . . . We stand at the heart of countering violence that is being perpetuated by settler colonials and their subordinate regimes . . . This is not just about liberation of land and homeland, but the redefinition of liberation to include our bodies as entwined to the question of land. This a moment to think of the kind of future imaginings of decolonisation we strive for.
>
> (alQaws Hawamesh webinar, 2021: n.p.)

Muhammad from alQaws shares reflections from queer people's experiences in the protests and the kind of power dynamics in the public sphere, which resonated with what happens in the domestic space. He explains:

> We have seen first-hand how the street space reproduces some of the patriarchal and hetero-sexist violence that we are familiar with and here violence comes in the form of an angry look, or the kind of slogans picked for the demonstration or the domination of Men. This is where

136 *Towards Radical Self-Determination*

some of us sometimes felt held back and had some doubts whether to step out and if we did, we might have felt a need for a compromise by not being too visible and/or go with the flow in order to protect oneself. At the same time there was a sense of hope rising within these spaces because we felt the need to be part of that wider defiant and united collective . . . what pushed us also was seeing the level of people's defiance and capacity to push back against violence and re-claim the streets and spaces of cities like Lyddh. Also, seeing our own friends and people we know standing defiantly in the demonstrations was a push for the rest of us to join in and be part of this moment of dreaming liberation

(Ibid.)

Throughout the conversation, activists discussed the emotions of despair and hopelessness the colonial institution seeks to plant within the colonised psyche precisely through the internal violence that the indigene must face from each other. The PNA security personnel embody the functioning of this internally directed violence, which as the third speaker from Tala'at Razan states, 'aims to kill any sense of hope and continuity that the uprising held.' Razan explains how demoralising the protestors was a strategic way to re-entrench the psychology of dismemberment that the Zionist entity and its comprador class have activated within Palestinians.

PNA utilisation of words such as '*hishik bishik*,' a phrase which carries demoralising connotations, to describe protestors in Ramallah is meant to activate a sense of distanciation between the Ramallah protests and those in other parts of Palestine i.e., Hebron.

(Ibid.)

Palestinian political fragmentation is re-enforced through a moralising discourse that works to produce the PNA as the legitimate and only guardian of Palestinian moral values but also as the only channel through which the fantasy of Palestinian irreconcilable difference (Ramallah versus Hebron) can be contained. Activists discussed the emotional weight of despair, fear, and hopelessness that all these violent mechanisms attempt to plant within the protestors to disrupt their mobilising. At the same time, they collectively reflected on the necessity to continue the fight by strategising differently and creatively each time[20] and by finding the needed strength and joy within our collectives that can maintain our sense of hopefulness and defiance (alQaws Hawamesh webinar, 2021). A 'Rallying Cry for Queer Liberation' is the call that alQaws launched for the protests that brought queer Palestinians and allies together to reclaim their place on the path for liberation. The first 'Rallying Cry for Queer Liberation' took place in July 2020 following on from a previous gathering organised in 2019 to protest violence, and another 'Rallying Cry for Queer Liberation' was launched in September 2021. These protests, which took place in Sahit Al Asir in the city of Haifa, are a clear manifestation of the growing power and increased visibility that activists are proclaiming in the face of pain, violence, and fragmentation. The 2020 protest was particularly significant in countering the violence that Palestinian queers have been facing for years and which reached a peak in 2019. In her speech at the demo, Hanen Maikey declares:

> We've come to Haifa, from all over Palestine, to protest the suppression of our activities and events—from Jaffa to Nablus to Ramallah! Your persecution only fuels us to create larger, louder spaces for queer life in Palestine. . . . We've come to put an end to the Israeli occupation's attempts to exploit our pain and 'pinkwash' our struggle. Over the past two decades, the colonial propaganda of pinkwashing, although persistent and well-funded, hasn't been able to erase us! If anything, the failures of pinkwashing have only emphasised that queer liberation necessitates the liberation of Palestine and all Palestinians.
>
> (alQaws article, 2020: n.p.)

In the second Queer Rally for Liberation, which took inspiration from the Palestinian uprising of May 2021, the new director of alQaws, Haneen Sadir, declares:

> We came to shout NO to the patriarchy that is oppressing our children and women. We came to shout against the settler colonialism that works on fragmenting us, alienating us from our society, and families. This coloniser that works on planting despair in our hearts, negating us from a society that could embrace us. We came to shout against Capitalism and the individualism that dismembers communal support systems.
>
> (alQaws leader speech, 2021)

These rallies reflected activists' capacity to mobilise support and build coalitions with different grassroots collections, including the Tala'at feminist organising, the Haifa Youth Movement, and others present at the rally and who also supported it with promotional material and videos circulating on social media. Activists circulated posters for the rally in various places in Palestine, echoing 'our call for liberation across the whole of Palestine and beyond the geographic boundaries that separate us' (Hirak and alQaws video, 2021). In one of the videos from the protest, the call for *thawra Did al Istimar* (revolt in the face of the coloniser) heightens as protestors pass near the Israeli state police. Some of the protestors grab on a Goblet Drum and the dom tak rhythm generates the dance of joy and shouts for freedom, marching along with the upheld signs of Handala, Palestinian keffiyeh, and rainbow-Palestine flags. The increasing media and public attention towards the rally can be seen in the amount of local media coverage that it gathered from various media outlets. In an interview with Omar Al-Khatib in the local newspaper of Al Madina, vital questions were raised and answered.

138 *Towards Radical Self-Determination*

REPORTER: You link your call for a queer rally for liberation with the recent uprising that shook Palestinian streets, what is the connection between the two?

O. AL-K: Perhaps the main question here is with regards to how gender and sexuality issues matter to the liberation of Palestine. The answer is simple: these issues define what justice and liberation mean in our context and how it can be achieved. . . . Palestinian queer and trans people have lived in this land for so long and have experienced the impact of settler colonial violence on our bodies and lives. We, like the rest of our people, have lived this uprising and been part of it and that is why, in the spirit of this wider uprising, we aim to continue the struggle from three interrelated points: first, this latest uprising has shown a level of unity and interdependence among Palestinians everywhere which is what our queer struggle aims at, while also emphasising the need to integrate a gender/sexuality lens within that wider striving for unity. Second, the uprising has made us confront many questions with regards to our relationship with the public sphere where a lot of violence and exclusion unfortunately takes place against queer subjects. Third, alQaws calls for this protest as an attempt to restore the movement and bring back that spirit of defiance to the street, especially now in moments where people might feel fatigued and exhausted

(Al Madina, 2021: 8)

The words of Omar are revealing of the role that alQaws organising plays in highlighting the relation between queerness and decolonisation in Palestine. The alQaws-led 'Rallying Cry for Liberation' is both an extension of and a basis from which the Palestinian path for liberation continues. Through activists' reclamation of the streets of Haifa—but also of other Palestinian spaces and digital spheres through the distribution of analysis, videos, and posters—Palestinian queers create a counter-space (Fraser, 1990) that challenges dominant structures of hetero-conquest. In creating this counter-space, activists enable the subjectivation of decolonial queer movement, which, as Muhammad describes, encapsulates how we can see ourselves, our dreams, and our aspirations in the moment of liberation (alQaws Hawamesh webinar, 2021).

Conclusion

In early May 2021, Zionist settler colonial policies of oppression were being met with heightened Palestinian resistance across the whole of Palestine. *Min al mayya lil mayya* (from the Jordan River to the Mediterranean Sea) Palestinians rose in unity for the Unity Intifada. A call for a general strike was launched on the 18 May 2021 via the Dignity and Hope Manifesto, declaring the need to write a new chapter of unity, to challenge the prison system to which Palestinians have been forcefully relegated by Zionism and

Towards Radical Self-Determination 139

the political elites serving the interests of the coloniser (Open Letter, 2021: n.p.). Considering these events, alQaws issued an online source reflecting on this moment of uprising and how 'queer liberation is fundamentally tied to the dream of Palestinian liberation.'

> Queer liberation is fundamentally tied to the dreams of Palestinian liberation: self-determination, dignity, and the end of all systems of oppression. . . . Queer liberation is a political approach to sexuality and gender, rooted in the rejection of heteronormativity and patriarchy, which is the basis of every system of oppression—including Israeli settler colonialism. . . . Queer liberatory politics assert that we, as queer and trans Palestinians, are an integral part of our society and our struggle. . . . Israeli settler colonialism, and tactics such as 'pinkwashing' weaponise our queer experiences to place us in opposition to our own society and communities. Our answer to pinkwashing is to say that liberation is indivisible, and that there will be a place for all of us at the rendezvous of victory.
>
> (alQaws article, 2021: n.p.)

AlQaws's vision of queer liberatory politics that is tied to Palestinian self-determination reflects the decolonial queering ability to encapsulate a revolutionary agency whose aspiration for change derives from the firm belief that 'revolutionaries must dream; if their imagination dwells on the injustice of how things stay, they do not simply dwell in what stays' (Ahmed, 2010: 196). Central to the effort to imagine oneself, society, and Palestine Otherwise is the labour of countering violence from within and from without. Decolonial queering activates a process of careful examination of the forces maintaining native entrapment within the system of colonial compartmentalisation. In identifying and challenging pinkwashing as internalised, alQaws channels the will to detach from the 'crushing objecthood' (Fanon, 1967: 109), sealing the native away from her own self, her story, and place. To strive for a modality of being beyond the logic 'my father wants to kill me/Israel is a democracy' signifies activists' awareness of violence and the mechanisms of its reproduction on multiple psycho-political scales. AlQaws's homing spaces generate self and a wider Palestinian sense of home-(be) coming away from the confines of hetero-conquest as reinstantiated in Palestinian visions for liberation and homemaking à la 'happy family' notion. Decolonial queering, therefore, is the labour of 'excavation' of a desire to be/long that has to do with *a radical self-possession*; enabling an articulation of self-determination at the intersection of the individual and the collective (Alexander, 2005: 307). Activists' circulation of queer glimpses and revolutionary protests within the public sphere captures the decolonial queering effort to make room for 'opening a life' (Ahmed, 2010: 20) towards a reconstructed sense of self/nation, allowing consciousness of the bodies that 'make [us] question!' (Fanon, 1967: 232). AlQaws's queer liberatory

140 *Towards Radical Self-Determination*

politics encapsulate resurgence against the hetero-patriarchal forces whose suppression of indigene's own differences serves to re-instantiate the colonial logic of Manichean delirium. This openness to 'shades of meanings' (Fanon, 1963: 146) does not collapse into the timeless humanism of colonial emancipation, as Fanon warned. Rather, it emerges to articulate and practice a difference that is rooted in the fight against the regime, of Time, Space, and Desire, maintaining colonised subjection on multiple scales.

Notes

1 *Hawamesh*, the Arabic word for 'margins,' is 'a monthly discussion forum about issues related to sexual and gender diversity in Palestinian society. Its aim is to fill the void in the mainstream discourse—including rhetoric of local queer organizing and sexuality activism—in order to disrupt and broaden its domain.' See alQaws 2015: www.alqaws.org/news/New-Hawamesh-Meeting-The-Attack-on-LGBTs-in-Palestine-A-Crises-in-Discourse-Or-a-Culture-of-Exclusion-?category_id=13 (Accessed 27 August 2021).

2 News Report, 2019. "The stabbing of a person in Tumra over sexual orientation" *PALSAWA* [Online] Available at: https://palsawa.com/post/217377/%D8%B7%D8%B9%D9%86-%D8%B4%D8%AE%D8%B5-%D9%85%D9%86-%D8%B7%D9%85%D8%B1%D8%A9-%D8%B9%D9%84%D9%89-%D8%AE%D9%84%D9%81%D9%8A%D8%A9-%D9%85%D9%8A%D9%88%D9%84%D9%87-%D8%A7%D9%84%D8%AC%D9%86%D8%B3%D9%8A%D8%A9 (Accessed 10 September 2020). Source in Arabic.

3 The southern branch of the Islamic movement runs for elections in the Israeli parliament (Knesset) under the name United Arab List, whose current leader, Mansour Abbas, has become the first party of Palestinian citizens of Israel to agree to join a governing coalition with the new Israeli government led by right-wing nationalist Neftali Benet. See: www.aljazeera.com/news/2021/6/5/dangerous-palestinians-on-mansour-abbas-joining-israeli-govt.

4 An article in *The Guardian* describes how 'gay Palestinians tend to be secretive about their social lives and some have crossed into Israel to live safely.' The article was republished from the Associated Press website, which had erroneously claimed that homosexuality in Palestine is banned by law. While a subsequent correction to this flawed information was issued by the same source on the 13 August, it is interesting to contemplate how pinkwashing underpins the approach of western reporters to this issue. Associated Press in Ramallah, 2019. 'Palestinian Protestors Whitewash Rainbow Flag from West Bank Barrier' *The Guardian* [Online] Available at: www.theguardian.com/world/2015/jun/30/palestinian-protesters-whitewash-rainbow-flag-west-bank-barrier?CMP=gu_com (Accessed 10 September 2021).

5 This also resonates with the critique that Atshan (2020), see discussion in Chapter 3, voices against the group.

6 This production happened in collaboration with *Jadal: the Journal of Mada Al-Carmel*. The articles came out on 10 December 2015. See: www.alqaws.org/articles/-Jadal-Publishes-New-Articles-about-Sexual-Politics-in-Palestine-?category_id=0.

7 Pre-marital sex and homosexual acts became a target for Isqat operations.

8 See: Sokol, S., 2020. 'Homosexuality "almost nonexistent in Arab Society", Joint List MK says.' *Times of Israel* [Online]. Available at: www.timesofisrael.com/homosexuality-almost-nonexistent-in-arab-society-joint-list-mk-says/ (Accessed 10 September 2021).

Towards Radical Self-Determination 141

9 See discussion in Chapter 2.
10 AlQaws responds to the *New York Times* reporting: 'We told the *New York Times* that we would be happy to participate in a piece that centres Palestinian queers and the movement we have helped build. Instead, the NYT chose to erase Palestinian queer organisations and interview Zionist Israeli gay organisation "Aguda." NYT's erasure of 2 decades of queer anti-colonial organizing in Palestine is unacceptable. . . . When will the NYT start centring Palestinian queer voices rather than that of our coloniser?' (alQaws Facebook post, 2020).
11 This was manifested in the PNA statement. With its reference to the particularity of the environment and traditions of Nablus, the PNA relies on and reproduces these categorisations among Palestinian locales.
12 He also calls it epidermalisation of the inferiority dynamic (Fanon, 1963: 13).
13 Fanon describes this as the urge to alienate oneself from one's 'fellow Negro' (1986: 58).
14 See discussion in Chapter 2.
15 See discussion in Chapter 3.
16 Louise, L., 2014. 'Gender Violence in Social Media' (in Arabic), *Qadita*. Available at: www.qadita.net/featured/luis/ (Accessed 5 January 2021).
17 See my conversation with Haneen for the Decolonizing Sexualities Network: www.youtube.com/watch?v=Excm5nDvrFw.
18 See webpage: www.alqaws.org/7amleh/English.
19 Can be accessed here: http://alqaws.org/news/alQaws-Distributes-Thousands-of-Flyers-on-University-Campuses?category_id=0 (Accessed 5 January 2021).
20 Through organisational tactics that pertain to the spaces where the demonstration can be held. For example, by demonstrating in other spots that are less knowable to the occupier, we can challenge their capacity to contain the demonstration.

Bibliography

Al-Haq, 2019. 'Statement Issued by Human Rights Organization Council 2019.' *Al-Haq Facebook Post* [Online]. Available at: www.facebook.com/alhaqorganization/photos/pcb.3478326918851443/3478326212184847 (Accessed 19 June 2020).
Ahmed, S., 2010. *The Promise of Happiness*. Durham, NC: Duke University Press.
Alexander, J., 2005. *Pedagogies of Crossing: Meditations on Feminism, Sexual Politics, Memory and the Sacred*. Durham, NC: Duke University Press.
Al Madina, 2021, September. *Al Mithliyoun wa al shari' wa al habba* [Queers and the Uprising]. *Al Madina*. Source in Arabic.
Alqaisiya, W., Hilal, G., and Maikey, M., 2016. 'Dismantling the Homosexual Image in Palestine,' in *Decolonizing Sexualities: Transnational Perspectives, Critical Interventions*, edited by S. Bakshi, S. Jivraj, and S. Posocco. London: Counterpress.
alQaws, 2017a. 'Myths About Sexual & Gender Diversity in Palestine.' *Youtube*. Available at: www.youtube.com/watch?v=2Kl4l-yKbUw (Accessed 19 June 2020).
alQaws, 2017b. 'Verbal Violence Is Not Different from Physical Violence.' *Youtube*. Available at: www.youtube.com/watch?v=jNkL6OkpRRo (Accessed 19 June 2020).
alQaws, 2019. *Facebook Post About Israa Gharib* [Online]. Available at: https://m.facebook.com/AlQawsorg/posts/2603633123026721?locale2=hi_IN (Accessed 19 June 2020).

142 *Towards Radical Self-Determination*

alQaws, 2020. 'Analysis Paper.' *alQaws for Sexual and Gender Diversity in Palestinian Society*. Available at: www.alqaws.org/articles/Beyond-Propaganda-Pinkwashing-as-Colonial-Violence?category_id=0&fbclid=IwAR0ba1z3ydkTUxJnGy97gBzcAqIKP6O7NbcA29F0_qKh2Kar8eend74Bx_s (Accessed 29 April 2020).

alQaws, 2021. 'Recording from Protest.' *Facebook*. Available at: www.facebook.com/watch/live/?ref=watch_permalink&v=4802722736418752 (Accessed 19 June 2020).

alQaws Article, 2019. 'alQaws Response to the PA Police Statement.' *alQaws* [Online]. Available at: http://alqaws.org/articles/AlQaws-response-to-the-PA-police-statment?category_id=0 (Accessed 10 September 2021).

alQaws Article, 2020. 'alQaws' Speech at the "Rallying Cry for Queer Liberation in Haifa.' *alQaws* [Online]. Available at: www.alqaws.org/siteEn/print?id=333&type=2 (Accessed 19 June 2021).

alQaws Facebook Post, 2020. [Online]. Available at: www.facebook.com/AlQawsorg/photos/a.817740694949315/3350397188350307/ (Accessed 10 September 2021).

alQaws Graffiti, 2013. 'Queers Passed Through Here.' *Facebook Photo*. Available at: www.facebook.com/AlQawsorg/photos/a.586867441369976.1073741828.550374051685982/588879291168791/?type=3&theater (Accessed 19 June 2020).

alQaws Hawamesh, 2021. 'Oppression from Colonisers and Palestinian Authority: Feminist and Queer Reflections on the Uprising.' *alQaws Instagram* [Online]. Available at: www.instagram.com/p/CRUOIk-JpLZ/ (Accessed 19 June 2020).

alQaws Leader Speech at Rallying Cry for Liberation, 2021. *alQaws Facebook Video* [Online]. Available at: www.facebook.com/AlQawsorg/videos/3069420223291826 (Accessed 19 June 2020).

alQaws News, 2015. 'New Hawamesh Meeting: The Attack on LGBTs in Palestine: A Crisis in Discourse, or a Culture of Exclusion.' *alQaws* [Online]. Available at: www.alqaws.org/news/New-Hawamesh-Meeting-The-Attack-on-LGBTs-in-Palestine-A-Crises-in-Discourse-Or-a-Culture-of-Exclusion-?category_id=13 (Accessed 10 September 2021).

alQaws News, 2017. 'Difference Never Justifies Violence—New Social Media Campaign.' *alQaws* [Online]. Available at: http://alqaws.org/news/Difference-never-justifies-violence-New-Social-Media-Campaign?category_id=0 (Accessed 19 June 2021).

alQaws News, 2019a. '"Did You Know" Posters from alQaws Roam University Campuses.' *alQaws* [Online]. Available at: http://alqaws.org/%D8%A7%D8%AE%D8%A8%D8%A7%D8%B1%D9%86%D8%A7/-%D8%A8%D8%AA%D8%B9%D8%B1%D9%81%D9%8A-%D8%A5%D9%86%D9%88-%D9%85%D9%86%D8%B4%D9%88%D8%B1-%D9%84%D9%-84%D9%82%D9%88%D8%B3-%D9%81%D9%8A-%D8%A7%D9%84%D8%AC%D8%A7%D9%85%D8%B9%D8%A7%D8%AA?category_id=0 (Accessed 19 June 2021).

alQaws News, 2019b. 'Unrelenting Resistance: alQaws Annual Report 2019.' *alQaws* [Online]. Available at: www.alqaws.org/news/Unrelenting-Resistance-alQaws-Annual-Report-2019?category_id=0 (Accessed 19 June 2021).

alQaws News, 2020. 'Tahinat Al Arz Discussion: Violence Through Societal, Settler Colonial and Capitalist Forms.' *alQaws* [Online]. Available at: http://alqaws.org/%D8%A7%D8%AE%D8%A8%D8%A7%D8%B1%D9%86%D8-%A7/%D9%86%D9%82%D8%A7%D8%B4-%D8%B7%D8%AD%

Towards Radical Self-Determination 143

D9%8A%D9%86%D8%A9-%D8%A7%D9%84%D8%A3%D8%B1 %D8%B2-%D8%B9%D9%86%D9%81-%D8%A7%D9%84%D9% 85%D8%AC%D8%AA%D9%85%D8%B9-%D9%88%D8%A7%D9 %84%D8%A7%D8%B3%D8%AA%D8%B9%D9%85%D8%A7%D 8%B1-%D9%88%D8%B1%D8%A3%D8%B3-%D8%A7%D9%84%- D9%85%D8%A7%D9%84 (Accessed 10 September 2020). Source in Arabic.

alQawsNews,2021.'PNASuppressionandDefamationofProtestors:APredictablePatri-archalAttempttoSlamProtests.'*alQaws*[Online].Availableat:http://alqaws.org/%D-8%A7%D8%AE%D8%A8%D8%A7%D8%B1%D9%86%D8%A7/%D9%8 2%D9%85%D8%B9-%D9%88%D8%AA%D8%B4%D9%87%D9%8A%D 8%B1-%D8%A7%D9%84%D8%B3%D9%84%D8%B7%D8%A9-%D9%8- 5%D8%AD%D8%A7%D9%88%D9%84%D8%A9-%D8%B0%D9%83% D9%88%D8%B1%D9%8A%D8%A9-%D9%88%D9%85%D8%AA%D9 %88%D9%82%D8%B9%D8%A9-%D9%84%D8%B1%D8%AF%D8%B9- %D8%A7%D9%84%D8%B4%D8%A7%D8%B1%D8%B9?category_id=0 (Accessed 19 June 2020). Source in Arabic.

alQaws Webinar, 2020. 'Palestinian Families Interactions with Their Children's Diverse Gendered and Sexual Experiences.' *alQaws* [Online] Available at: www.facebook. com/AlQawsorg/videos/156509489682783 (Accessed 10 September 2021).

Al Shayib, Y., 2015. 'Rainbow on the Walla by Artist Khalid Jarrar Stirs Controversy, Young Men Whitewash it at Night.' *Al Ayyam* [Online]. Available at: www.al-ayyam.ps/ar_page.php?id=f7dd039y259903545Yf7dd039 (Accessed 10 September 2021).

Associated Press in Ramallah, 2019. 'Palestinian Protestors Whitewash Rainbow Flag from West Bank Barrier.' *The Guardian* [Online]. Available at: www.theguardian.com/world/2015/jun/30/palestinian-protesters-whitewash-rainbow-flag-west-bank-barrier?CMP=gu_com (Accessed 10 September 2020).

Ayyob, A. 2019. 'alQaws Group: PA Police Statement Is a Very Valuable Catch to Israel.' *Vice Media Group* [Online]. Available at: www.vice.com/ar/article/ wjw5vy/%D9%85%D8%A4%D8%B3%D8%B3%D 8%A9-%D8%A7%D9%84%D9%82%D9%88%D8%B3- %D8%A8%D9%8A%D8%A7%D9%86-%D8%A7%D9%84%D8%B4 %D9%91%D8%B1%D8%B7%D8%A9-%D8%A7%D9%84%D9%81 %D9%84%D8%B3%D8%B7%D9%8A%D9%86%D9%8A%D8%A9- %D8%B5%D9%8A%D8%AF-%D8%AB%D9%85%D9%8A%D9%86- %D8%AC%D8%AF%D8%A7%D9%8B-%D9%84%D8%A5%D8%B3%D 8%B1%D8%A7%D8%A6%D9%8A%D9%84 (Accessed 10 September 2020). Source in Arabic.

Badarni, H., 2015. 'Beyond the Israeli Prison's Rods: Between the Sexual and the Political.' *Jadal* [Online]. Available at: https://mada-research.org/wp-content/uploads/2015/11/JDL24-2-Hadil.pdf (Accessed 10 September 2020). Source in Arabic.

Bryant, J., 2015. 'The Meaning of Queer Home, Home Cultures.' *The Journal of Architecture, Design and Domestic Space* 12(3): 261–289.

Butler, J., 1999. *Gender Trouble: Feminism and the Subversion of Identity*. New York: Routledge.

Coelho Pena, A., Rezende Nunes, M. F., and Karamer, S., 2018. 'Human Formation, World Vision, Dialogue and Education: The Present Relevance of Paulo Freire and Martin Buber.' *Educação em Revista* 34: 1–18.

144 Towards Radical Self-Determination

Decolonizing Sexuality Network, 2021. 'Haneen Maikey and Alqaisiya—Decolonial Café Panel 1.' *Youtube* [Online]. Available at: www.youtube.com/watch?v=Excm-5nDvrFw (Accessed 19 June 2020).

Driskill, Q. L. Finley, C., Joseph Gilley, B., and Morgensen, S., (eds.), 2011. *Queer Indigenous Studies: Critical Interventions in Theory, Politics and Literature*. Arizona: Arizona University Press.

Fanon, F., 1967. *Black Skin, White Masks*. London: Pluto Press.

Fanon, F., 1963. *The Wretched of the Earth*. New York: Grove Press.

Fleur Hassan-Nahoum, 2019. 'Twitter Statement.' *Twitter* [Online]. Available at: https://twitter.com/FleurHassanN/status/1163175502397489159?web=1&wdL OR=c3AC5F109-5F11-4D4D-8A5D-D658097F92A6 (Accessed 10 September 2020).

Fortier, A. M., 2003. 'Making Home: Queer Migrations and Motions of Attachment,' in *Uprootings/Regroundings: Questions of Home and Migration*, edited by S. Ahmed, C. Castañeda, A. M. Fortier, and M. Sheller. Oxford: Berg Publishers.

Fraser, N., 1990. 'Rethinking the Public Sphere: A Contribution to the Critique of Actually Existing Democracy.' *Social Text* 25(6): 56–80.

Freire, P., 2000. *Pedagogy of the Oppressed*. New York: Continuum.

Gopinath, G., 2005. *Impossible Desires: Queer Diasporas and South Asian Public Cultures*. Durham, NC: Duke University Press.

Hassan, B., 2015. 'Homosexuality and Equality Discourse: A Critical View on Gay Marriage.' *Jadal* [Online]. Available at: https://mada-research.org/wp-content/uploads/2015/11/JDL24-3-Budoor.pdf (Accessed 10 September 2020). Source in Arabic.

Hilal, Ghaith, and Maikey, H., 2015. 'Reconstructing the Homosexual Image in Palestinian Society.' *Jadal* [Online]. Available at: https://mada-research.org/wp-content/uploads/2015/11/JDL24-6-HaninGhayth.pdfc (Accessed 10 September 2020). Source in Arabic.

Hirak, Haifa, and alQaws, 2019. 'Promotional Video: Rallying Cry for Liberation.' *alQaws Facebook Video* [Online]. Available at: www.facebook.com/watch/?v=180349874195902 (Accessed 19 June 2021).

Hooks, B., 2003. *Teaching Community: A Pedagogy of Hope*. New York: Routledge.

Ibrahim, A., 2021. '"Laughable, Naïve": Palestinian Party Move to Join Israel Govt.' *Al Jazeera* [Online]. Available at: www.aljazeera.com/news/2021/6/5/dangerous-palestinians-on-mansour-abbas-joining-israeli-govt (Accessed 10 September 2020).

Imgur, 2019. [Online]. Available at: https://imgur.com/jhmh1nd (Accessed 10 September 2020).

Louise, L., 2014. 'On Gender Violence in Social Media.' *alQaws* [Online]. Available at: www.alqaws.org/%D9%85%D9%82%D8%A7%D9%84%D8%A7% D8%AA/%D8%A7%D9%84%D8%B9%D9%86%D9%81-%D8%A7 %D9%84%D8%AC%D9%86%D8%AF%D8%B1%D9%8A-%D9% 81%D9%8A-%D9%88%D8%B3%D8%A7%D8%A6%D9%84-%D8%A7 %D9%84%D8%AA%D9%88%D8%A7%D8%B5%D9%84-%D8%A7%D9% 84%D8%A7%D8%AC%D8%AA%D9%85%D8%A7%D8%B9%D9%8A?ca tegory_id=0 (Accessed 19 June 2020). Source in Arabic.

Lugones, M., 2000. 'Multiculturalism and Publicity.' *Hypatia* 15(3): 175–181.

Maikey, H., 2014. 'Signposts from alQaws: A Decade of Building a Queer Palestinian Discourse.' *Fuse Magazine* [Online]. Available at: http://fusemagazine.org/2013/04/36-2_maike (Accessed 19 June 2020).

Makhtalafnash, 2017. *alQaws/7amleh* [Online]. Available at: www.alqaws. org/7amleh/English (Accessed 19 June 2020).

Mansour, N., 2021. 'On the Concept of Indivisible Liberation.' *AlJumhuriyya* [Online]. Available at: www.aljumhuriya.net/ar/content/%D9%85%D9%81% D9%87%D9%88%D9%85-%D8%A7%D9%84%D8%AA%D8%AD%D8% B1%D8%B1-%D8%A7%D9%84%D8%B0%D9%8A-%D9%84%D8%A7-%D9%8A%D8%AA%D8%AC%D8%B2%D8%A3?fbclid=IwAR0hCHjg1gs iMQoeMRQLBzwbsIkAEWljnAf_y_V710Umko44XYoZILvxj3Y (Accessed 19 June 2020). Source in Arabic.

Martin,L. and Secor, A., 2014. 'Towards a post-mathematical topology,' *Progress in Human Geography*, 38 (3), pp. 420–438.

Morgensen, S., 2012. 'Theorising Gender, Sexuality and Settler Colonialism: An Introduction.' *Settler Colonial Studies* 2(2): 2–22.

Morgensen, S., 2011. *Spaces Between Us: Queer Settler Colonialism and Indigenous Decolonization*. Minneapolis: University of Minnesota Press.

Muñoz, J., 1999. *Disidentifications: Queer of Color and the Performance of Identity*. Minneapolis: University of Minnesota Press.

Palestine Online, 2021. 'Palestinian Youth Omar Al Khatib.' *Twitter*. Available at: www. trendsmap.com/twitter/tweet/1389995668358500353 (Accessed 19 June 2020).

Rasgon, A., 2020. 'The Tahini War: The Food at the Centre of an Arab Gay Rights Battle.' *The New York Times* [Online]. Available at: www.nytimes.com/2020/07/15/ world/middleeast/tahini-gay-israel-boycott.html (Accessed 10 September 2020).

News Report, 2019. 'The Stabbing of a Person in Tumra Over Sexual Orientation.' *PALSAWA* [Online]. Available at: https://palsawa.com/post/217377/%D8% B7%D8%B9%D9%86-%D8%B4%D8%AE%D8%B5-%D9%85%D9%86-% D8%B7%D9%85%D8%B1%D8%A9-%D8%B9%D9%84%D9%89-%D8% AE%D9%84%D9%81%D9%8A%D8%A9-%D9%85%D9%8A% D9%88%D9%84%D9%87-%D8%A7%D9%84%D8%AC%D9%86%D8%B 3%D9%8A%D8%A9 (Accessed 10 September 2020). Source in Arabic.

Open Letter, 2021. 'The Manifesto of Dignity and Hope.' *Mondoweiss*. Available at: https://mondoweiss.net/2021/05/the-manifesto-of-dignity-and-hope/ (Accessed 10 September 2020).

Rifkin, M., 2012. *Erotics of Sovereignty*. Minneapolis: University of Minnesota Press.

Scott, J., 1990. *Domination and the Arts of Resistance: Hidden Transcripts*. New Haven: Yale University Press.

Shalhoub-Kevorkian, N., and Ihmoud, S., 2014. 'Exiled at Home: Writing Return and the Palestinian Home.' *Biography* 37(2): 377–397.

Sokol, S., 2020. '"Homosexuality Almost Nonexistent in Arab Society" Joint List MK Says.' *Times of Israel* [Online]. Available at: www.timesofisrael.com/homosexuality-almost-nonexistent-in-arab-society-joint-list-mk-says/ (Accessed 10 September 2020).

Yurchak, A., 2003. 'Soviet Hegemony of Form: Everything Was Forever Until It Was No More.' *Comparative Studies in Society and History* 45(3): 480–510.

Zaborskis, M., 2016. 'Sexual Orphanings.' *GLQ* 22(4): 605–628.

———, 2019. 'Statement Regarding the Recent Wave of Attack Against alQaws.' *alQaws* [Online]. Available at: https://docs.google.com/document/d/1449oJrSO-xjxGKww0Bhj-8l9zm4eFahh_El1dnolt-dY/edit?fbclid=IwAR11PsHxPa55GjJm qQZOCyZPsGG7zEMuMfP0zcJUlbVld6e-_mqGTZE0gM (Accessed 19 June 2020).

6 Futural Imaginaries

This chapter examines the role that aesthetics play in distributing futural imaginaries of decolonial queering. Futural imaginaries comprise conceptions of subjectivities and the space and time of sociality that remain obscured within prevalent understandings of what Palestinian freedom entails. My main aim is to navigate the role Palestinian queer artistic productions play in making possible other possible worlds beyond 'the prison house of the here and now' (Muñoz, 2009: 1). The chapter is divided into three main sections. The first examines the production of comics within alQaws's spaces and the personal reflections on them of activists to show the value of visualising and narrating the psychological and affectual landscapes of Palestinian queer experiences. In so doing, it describes the necessary role of the emotive and affective to crafting alternate conceptions of Palestinian selfhood, going beyond the strictures of hetero-conquest. The second section draws on Tarik Knorn's satirical drawings and their role in provoking a political message, which is grounded in decolonising sexuality within the Oslo context. The artist's call for a decolonial anti-capitalist consciousness is further revealed through performance art engaging passers-by in active confrontation with 'La La Land' hyper-consumption reality. The next section explores Omar Ibin Dina's *zey al tashrifat* to reveal the role of fashion design in queering processes of male- and state-making, thus opening up room for other fabrications to predominant gendered and sexual scripts of Palestine's futural imaginaries. The conclusion reflects on the role of Palestinian aesthetics in channelling Otherwise decolonial worlds.

Tarwiha Comics

In May 2018, alQaws launched a series of comics, titled *tarwiha*, featuring the lives and stories of four queer characters living different sexual and gender experiences. Through *tarwiha*, which in Arabic carries the double meaning of 'unwinding' and 'end of the school day,' the group aims to 'address the diversity of sexual and gender experiences in schools, choosing to highlight them through an exciting visual storytelling medium that can reach parents, teachers, and, most importantly, students' (alQaws, 2018a: n.p.).

DOI: 10.4324/9781003273585-8

In the launch event for the release of the *tarwiha* book, Omar Al-Khatib discussed how the comics emerge to relay an organic connection to alQaws's artistic capacities given the fact that they have been designed by the activist, Haitham Haddad, from the group (alQaws, 2018b: n.p.). Omar then reflected on the value of tackling young queer experiences through such a creative medium and in the local Palestinian dialect since there are hardly any local comics produced that shed light on these issues (Ibid.). In what follows I draw on alQaws's comics and some of the narrative-responses they prompted from activists to show the significance of centring the psychological and emotional experiences of Palestinian queers to Otherwise Imaginings of Palestinian selfhood.

The series, which alQaws released in a website of its own,[1] revolves around the lives of four characters: Majd, Sari, Rasha, and Rani, whose after-school-*tarwiha* stories are divided into three seasons with eight episodes in each. The visual aspect of the comic relays the significance of a queer visual text that strives to suspend sexual and gender identities and mechanisms of their construction within the local Palestinian context. This is manifest in the ways some of the characters occupy the realm of 'proper' gendered representation as a short-haired 'boy,' Rani, or as long-haired and feminine looking 'girl,' Rasha, while the appearance of others, Majd and Sari, unsettle some of these visual assumptions through the non-normative style of their hair and ways of dressing. During the launch event Omar discussed the issue that alQaws faced regarding the dangerous trope of representation, which might risk cementing certain preconceived norms with regards to how 'queer people look like' in our society (alQaws, 2018b: n.p.). At the same time, we do need to contemplate how the *tarwiha* comic functions as a visual medium that challenges the sex/gender system by revealing the elements of performativity within the construction of gendered identities. In an episode entitled *qawalib bidha taksir*, meaning 'Moulds We Should Break,' each of the character's struggles with the assumptions made about their gendered/sexed identities reveal the forms of violence encountered when failing to perform 'properly.' Sari's mother complains sadly that she has not given birth to a 'real man' (Figure 6.1). In Figure 6.2, Majd is being picked on by a child in the supermarket who wonders 'are you a boy or a girl?' And as we see Rani reflecting on a conversation with 'queen' self-identified Sari that he feels different from other men, we then see Rasha saying to Majd 'Yes but try to convince them that although I do pass [contrary to Majd] as a 'proper girl' I happen to like girls, too!' (Figure 6.3). In the final panel we see Majd wondering 'when are we going to break all these moulds?' as they stand in front of various templates each carrying the name of a certain gendered classification including homo, Bi, *zalmeh* (Arabic for a masculine man), *mara* (woman), *nawa'im* (Arabic for sissy), and *hasan sabi* (Arabic for tomboy) (see Figure 6.4).

Majd's rhetorical question and the overall theme of the comic's episode capture their purpose regarding the disruption of socially codified definitions of gendered and sexed bodies, challenging innate and/or natural conceptions

148 *Futural Imaginaries*

Figure 6.1 Sari's Mother Complains Sadly That She Has Not Given Birth to a 'Real Man'

Source: Tarwiha (2019a)

of these categories. The visual representation of the characters disrupts the logic of either/or identifications upon which gender identity is conceived. We see this manifest in characters' responses to these assumptions, such as when Majd comments 'I am neither boy nor girl,' and when Rasha, in her proper girly-dress, proclaims that she 'likes girls too!' In doing so, the comic invites its readers/viewers to confront their own moulds regarding gendered/sexed identities based on the visual cues provided for them. This is crucial to contemplate in relation to the comic's educational purpose with regards to these issues and how they exemplify a queer pedagogic platform,

Figure 6.2 A Child Wonders 'Are You a Boy or a Girl?'
Source: Ibid.

challenging teachers' and students' compulsive needs to assign gender and sexuality within those unnecessary frames, just as Majd observes. Simultaneously, it forces readers to reflect on the violence inherent to the hierarchical structure embedding these classifications, in the way Majd and Rasha contemplate in one of the panels. Through these characters and their daily interactions with their surroundings, the comic unfolds queer 'orientations' of bodies and spaces whereby failure to follow the prescribed gendered lines goes hand in hand with a feeling of being 'out of place' (Ahmed, 2006: 107). In one episode, tackling the theme of loneliness, we see characters struggle to be part of wider social spaces because of how they only 'extend to certain bodies' (Ibid.: 11). While Sari gets altogether excluded from an invite

Figure 6.3 Rasha Says to Majd 'Yes But Try to Convince Them That Although I Do Pass (Contrary to Majd) as a 'Proper Girl' I Happen to Like Girls, Too!'

Source: Ibid.

to a peer's birthday party, Rasha, who has been invited, feels extremely out of place when she does attend the party (Figure 6.5). The comic shows the violent heterosexual spatial structures, whether at home, in the school, or amongst peers that extend familiarity and comfort solely for those bodies conforming with the gendered expectation of these spaces. In one episode we see how the teacher explains the teenage phase through the feelings of 'love and attraction that one feels for the opposite sex' (Figure 6.6). In another, we see Rani being confronted with homophobic and sexist comments from family members at home (Figure 6.7). The characters and their interactions with these violent structures reveal disorientations and necessary failure to extend those spaces and the gender conformity they prescribe. Rasha responds to

Futural Imaginaries 151

Figure 6.4 Majd Wonders 'When Are We Going to Break All These Moulds?'
Source: Ibid.

the teacher's assumption regarding opposite-sex attraction by asking 'or perhaps they could be attracted to the same sex?' (Figure 6.8).

Rasha's response articulate a queer failure to prescribed gendered lines, thereby instructing an urge and a desire for another direction. It gestures towards the 'yet-to-be inhabited places' (Ahmed, 2006: 12), creating potential for bodies and desires while freeing constraints on the imagination. The comic bridges the gap between the real and fantastical, centring the role of fantasy in dealing with oppressive structures. For example, following feeling out of place during the birthday party, we see a panel with Rasha joyfully shouting, 'I like girls and I have a girlfriend called Nada, I care less about being part of this space' (Figure 6.9). In a previous panel, we see Rasha

152 *Futural Imaginaries*

Figure 6.5 Rasha Feels Out of Place
Source: Tarwiha (2019b)

wondering 'whether she would ever find a girl who could love her' (Figure 6.10), which throws into question whether Rasha has a girlfriend as she claims later and/or whether the whole proclamation, i.e., the panel, is a work of Rasha's imagination with a repressive situation. The comic's disruption of clear distinctions between fantasy and reality encapsulates queer striving for unrestricted imagination and Palestinian queer desiring of Other worlds, beyond what José Muñoz calls the present reality of 'the here and now' (2009: 1). Such disruption to what is authentic and/or imagined comes hand in hand with the comic's capacity to challenge constructions of time and space through forcing a non-linear modality of narration. This is manifest in how one can approach the narrative of each episode of the comic through a circular reading mode entailed by 'a certain amount of anticipation' and

Futural Imaginaries 153

Figure 6.6 Teacher Explains Love
Source: Tarwiha (2019c)

154 *Futural Imaginaries*

Figure 6.7 Rani Confronted With Homophobic and Sexist Comments From Family Members at Home

Source: Tariwha (2019d)

a 'a continual weaving back and forth as the reader first "skips over" the gutter to look at the next panel, and then mentally goes into the gutter to fill in the actions, events, or transitions that took place in the gap between the panels' (Postema, 2013: 66). Through constant weaving back and forth the comic disrupts distinctions between words and images, time and space, thus challenging repro-time by 'encouraging a more complicated meshworked construction of time and space that forces readers outside of the linear chronological model of narrative making' (Manchester, 2017: 19).

The *tarwiha* comic encapsulates a disorientation (Ahmed, 2006) beyond present reality and fixity of meaning within the parameters of repro-time, which is symptomatic of imagining a Palestinian futurity through the

Futural Imaginaries 155

Figure 6.8 Rasha Responds to Teacher's Heterosexual Assumptions
Source: Tarwiha (2019c).

hetero-patriarchal model of giving birth to revolutionary masculinised agents.[2] *Tarwiha*'s stories gesture to the *then and there of queer (Palestinian) futurity* (Muñoz, 2009). To map a desire for queer futurity is not only about desiring—in semi-abstracted forms—a 'better world or freedom' (Ibid.: 30) of the imagination. The potential for Other worlds and directions beyond 'the prison house of the here and now' comprises a desire for 'more immediately better relations with the social' (Ibid.: 30). This is manifest through the role that *tarwiha* plays in circulating everyday affect including emotions, feelings, desires, and impulses that shape queer Palestinian orientations towards oneself and the world around them. Through the stories and day-to-day lives of the four characters we see how they interact with a wide array of feelings ranging from love, attraction, joy, and pleasure to frustration, anger, guilt, and loneliness amongst others. These emotions, impulses, and desires are situated within the social context in which they evolve, interact, and/or 'produce the very surfaces and boundaries that allow the individual and the social to be delineated as if they are objects' (Ahmed, 2006: 10). In other words, emotions and feelings cannot be understood in either the individual or the social. Rather, the 'affective dimensions of ordinary life' are always already situated in relation to socio-political configurations (Cvetkovich, 2012: 11).

In one episode, focusing on 'our emotions,' we see the characters dealing with the web of complex emotions ranging from feelings of guilt in relation to friends and families to expressing self-love and hate, as well as fear and boldness, all at once. A panel then appears with the statement, 'Our emotions do not come from nowhere;' we see Rani standing with a huge hat that contains a list of the surrounding relating to our emotions such as: our friends, families, traditions, etc. (Figure 6.11). In another episode, focusing on self-hate, we see a manifestation of the connection between the personal and the geopolitical. Characters struggle to accept their own image

Figure 6.9 Rasha Announces: 'I Like Girls and I Have a Girlfriend Called Nada, I Care Less About Being Part of This Space'

Source: Tarwiha (2019b)

and overtly 'gay look,' which emerges in relation to society and friends' homophobic perceptions of them but also triggers a realisation regarding the extent of self-hate within Palestinian society at large. In one of the panels, we see Rasha recalling Palestinian self-hate against a background of two images, one of Rasha's mother, who is complaining, 'Ah from these women!' And in the other background image we see her father, complaining, 'We Arabs are backward' (Figure 6.12).

Tarwiha's characters situate self-hate in relation to homophobia in wider Palestinian society showing how it interlinks with women's internalisation of the shame and violence enacted upon them by hetero-patriarchy, which cannot be disavowed from the orientalist logic (progressive/backward)

Futural Imaginaries 157

Figure 6.10 Rasha Wonders Whether She Will Ever Find a Lover
Source: Ibid.

that the colonised man inherits and reproduces. This recalls the native's entrapment within the psychic, social, and political structures of shame and oppression that I discussed in the previous chapter. *Tarwiha*'s images, therefore, put into aesthetic, colourful terms the undisputed connection between the psycho-personal and the geopolitical, revealing in that process the role of a queer emotionality in reclaiming native bodies and Otherwise worlds. In one of the panels, we see the statement, 'I do not want to turn any of my emotions off, I want to live them all' (Figure 6.13). The mobilisation of a queer affective space sits at the core of what the *tarwiha* comic signifies in relation to a space of 'unwinding' that the comic connotes, as well as the very *tarwiha* responses it provokes through activists' narrations of their own affectual experiences, reflections, and personal memories. Following

Figure 6.11 Rani Says Our Emotions Do Not Come From Nowhere
Source: Tarwiha (2019e)

the issue of the comic, alQaws launched cooperation with the online platform Jeem.me[3] where activists shared their reflections on the comic's episodes and their content. In a piece entitled 'On Rage,' M reflects in beautiful poetic prose:

> In days my rage is not supressed; my arm rises, and a star falls from the sky, my tongue pounces and a heart is broken. In days I am storm struck, I swallow the thunder and roar to loved ones. Anger was sometimes a look, sometimes a slap, sometimes a hiss, but always regretful. My family afraid of my angry voice, and I am fearful of their hardship.
> I was born in a gale. My grandmother is Nakba-afflicted, and I am too. The wall grew old, and the Nakba remains. The wall grew old, and

Futural Imaginaries 159

Figure 6.12 Raha's Mother Complains: 'Ah From These Women;' Rasha's Father Complains: 'We Arabs Are Backward'
Source: Tarwiha (2019f)

the memory still calls our names through the creases of the stones. I was born in Jerusalem, amid over consumed metaphors of olives, steadfastness, and resistance. But resistance, at least in my opinion, was being glued to the sofa, flicking between the wailing of television over the martyrs, and 'Rotana' and the singing of Najwa Karam. My child's mind understood life is complicated. My country that I love, was not loved by the world, and therefore did not love me back, and it transpires that it did not love either women or womanlike. At school, I walked head bowed and hunched back. I took the slaps laughing, secretly wishing for supernatural powers or ruthlessness.

Figure 6.13 We Do Not Want to Turn Our Emotions Off
Source: Tarwiha (2019e)

    I grew and rage grew in me. No medication, no psychotherapy, no meditation are salvation to my depression. Nothing extinguishes my flame. This is a well-known story: a hunched-back walk with rifles in his eyes. In the vastness of the universe, I am scattered. In endless traumas I am scattered. My being has become a mere reaction.
    I was probably on a bus, or a rooftop, or maybe howling when I read the news: a brother stabbed his brother. I thought our kitchen knives were for fruit and the occupier—forgetting the slayed women's livers, gutted, and gouged for tenuous motives, and nothing roars from them but an echo. It happened like inhaling happens before exhaling and drinking water to quench the thirst, normal, repetitive without notice or hesitation.

Futural Imaginaries 161

In my *ghurba* (alienation), I am aware, and I am not aware. I carry my anger like an equation with no solution and carry love on my palms as well. In my solitude, I suppress shouting and fall silent. I wish I am a rifle and have my share of bullets. My dreams die in my eyelashes. I complain the leaving and I complain the staying. I tell my friends that our sorrowfulness is waning. On TV, an old man says, after patience is relief. My grandmother replies, after patience is the grave.

(M, 2020: n.p.)

Rage saturates the text and reveals itself in the narrator's bodily domain, i.e., arm and tongue expressions, as well as in the psychological attributes extending to other forms of negative affects like fear, defeat, and depression. Central to how the author makes sense of this rage is their understanding of their 'Nakba-afflicted' genealogy. Hate instructs the logic of conquest and reproduces Palestinian disintegration through the re-instantiation of hetero-conquest, the narrator asserts, 'my country was not loved by the world and did not love women nor women-like ones.' Such affective responses relay the inherent connection between internalised senses of grief/loss/depression, etc. and institutionalised processes of native dispossession (Rifkin, 2012). They further show the continuity of Palestinian Nakba through the violence being directed at queer people; the narrator refers to the incident of a brother killing their own brother and links it to wider devaluing of women's lives. In going back to memories of growing up in Jerusalem, the narrator distils predominant perceptions about resistance and shows the complexity of growing up in relation to the spectacle of martyrdom and the need for dancing and singing. The narrator's anger accompanies the feeling of exile and alienation carried along with them, whether when they leave or when they stay put in Palestine. Such leaving, which could be real, metaphorical, or both at the same time, does not alleviate the feeling of *ghurba*, meaning alienation, that they equally have when deciding to stay put. *Ghurba* is an irredeemable feeling of loss, which relates to native stuck-ness within the realm of death. 'My grandmother replies: after patience is the grave.' At the same time, the narrator relays a sense of hope when saying to their friends that 'our suffering will stop.' The overwhelmingly depressive tone of the *ghurba* afflicted text and narrator informs the desire for a queer native return, underlining the need to recognise and recover from the trauma of hetero-conquest instilling native alienation through internally directed violence against queer and women subjects. *Tarwiha* comic historicises sensory experiences of bodily and emotional pain that trigger new ways to conceptualise relations to oneself, community, and the homeland. In a response titled 'On Loneliness,' Muhammad Abu-Rumailah reflects:

. . . In adolescence, as I became aware of how society perceives different sexual orientations, I began to build my own assumptions about how my family might have reacted to mine, even without directly discussing the

162 *Futural Imaginaries*

issue with them. I would bring up the matter indirectly to suss out my mother's and brother's reaction. I think I was waiting to hear a certain response that would make me feel hopeful. And frankly, at times, the discussion was fruitful to a certain extent. But in general, these conversations were exhausting, and I had no one to talk to or to help guide me. And here I began a phase of isolation. I thought to myself that it would be better to avoid facing this draining topic. Better to wait for my family to change their perceptions first. During this phase, Rani's phrase, from the comics, 'There is nothing better than sitting alone' became my favourite slogan.

But this isolation, unfortunately, did not push me to turn to finding supportive people. I had no idea that such people existed in the first place, and in general, I had not had many friends in my life up to that point. By chance, I found online spaces where people with similar experiences conversed. These conversations took place only in English. During that time, I was completely isolated from Arabic, because it was the language that did not help me with words that would comfort me. I was thinking that my comfort came from the terms that I was being exposed to and that most people would use to describe their identity through terms such as gay/trans/queer/genderqueer etc. However, later I would realise that these words are not the ones that would help me understand my situation. What truly helped me was learning words that described how I felt, like sadness, jealousy, anger, shame. When I could understand what I was feeling, I felt less lonely.

I was 19 years old and at university when I began to understand the importance of having friends with whom I could talk about what I went through and felt. I was spending time with a group of friends I met at the university, and in the same year I also joined an alQaws youth group, after seeing an advertisement on Facebook. When I became part of this group, I understood how lonely I had been for all the years that passed. And here I started to find a space where I was no longer isolated, and it was enough to compensate me for my loneliness within my family. The loneliness in the house increased when my older sister got married and left the house, since she had been the closest to me at home. Sometimes I felt angry that she left me, but now I understand that she too was fighting her own battles. We all have our own battles to fight.

. . . When I built walls between me and my family, the pain might have reduced slightly, but I did not reduce the resulting harm because my walls also prevented me from receiving love from my family. I tried to find this love in other relationships. Yet the constant feeling of abandonment by the people who were closest to me continued to haunt me throughout my constant search for love. Majd's question "will I ever find a girl who loves me, and I love her?" resonated with me. . . . There is a constant fear that we will lose the people we love the most. This fear started pushing me to repeat the same patterns and cling to unhealthy and harmful relationships.

Relationships get more complicated when you are trying to explore and understand yourself and your gender identity. . . . I think for now, I just need to take a deep breath. Because these questions will remain with me, and a large part my future is determined by how I define myself today, and who I want to be tomorrow. These are big questions, whose answers can be left for another day. What matters at this moment, is that I have the confidence to decide . . . that I want to seek a life that is full of a sense of purpose and passion, and, I hope, a day will arrive for me to feel less lonely, whether when with myself or amongst people.

(2020: n.p.)

In another response, titled, 'On Guilt,' Omar Al-Khatib writes:

People close to me know very well of my dire financial situation, which I complain about constantly. Strangely, a few months ago I increased this burden and bought my mother a tumble dryer as a gift on Mother's Day. A gift that I will pay for in instalments for a whole year, something that none of those with negative bank accounts like mine should do. I was as happy with the gift as my mother was, until the awakening moment came with the joke of a good friend who remarked, 'You just want to win over your mum.'

For many years, my mother did not know about my sexual and emotional orientations, or at least we did not face it or talk about it. Denial and avoidance of talking about the subject have stained our relationship with a few clashes here and there about my gender expression, and strange comments and questions about which of my queer friends visited the family home. In the last year, there was no choice but confrontation. The event was not quiet or traditional with the revelation of a conversation on my phone, my disclosure to the family directly, or a sibling or family member spilling the dangerous secret. The issue exploded in the face of society and my family through my work in alQaws and my activism with the group. The matter reached my family's ears through word of mouth, and there was no longer a way to deny it and escape. Some intense conversations with my mother went by relatively smoothly, though plenty of challenges rose along the way. The greatest pain for me and my family was the violence that they had to endure from wider societal circles.

For many years we have lived with institutions—chief among them the family—that stigmatise us. I plunged into a painful and cruel cycle of guilt that stemmed from believing I was the cause of my family's misery and scandal. Intense moments of crying and a desire to self-harm accompanied my constant feeling of self-loathing, all in relation to the sin I have committed, which seems to have been my desire to survive and live. My work has never been separated from my personal life because it is about an issue that I live with, and it has always been a

164 *Futural Imaginaries*

source for learning about myself, a blessing that many are deprived of, perhaps. Being on the comics team was a means for me to contemplate the structures of oppression that manifest themselves in the feelings we experience every day, and the most pressing issue for me was guilt. I realised the extent to which this feeling accompanies me in my life and controls my actions, decisions, paths, and relationships. I constantly strive to compensate my parents for their pain 'because of me,' draining myself to maintain social relationships and a level of idealism in academic and professional realms.

As people born into hetero-nuclear families in the accursed capitalism, this feeling is implanted in us and grows with us from very early stages, mainly because we feel the contradiction and dissatisfaction with the violation of our families that provided us with care and support in childhood, especially in cases where the family is put in a difficult social position in relation to us as Women Gay and Trans. Back to the dryer and my friend, after a not so easy period of deep thinking, I decide that I no longer want to win anybody over. I want to confront my feeling of guilt and the fact that I bear the responsibility for how others feel about me. Guilt is not just a personal feeling, it is also a public one.

(Al-Khatib, 2020: n.p.)

These responses relay activists' autobiographical reflections on the crucial role played by emotions in shaping who they are and the struggles they undertake on a day-to-day basis. The comics resonate with activists' experiences of the web of emotions through which they undergo processes of queer native becoming, which is not arrived at through the liberal LGBT frameworks of identity visibility (Georgis, 2013). Muhammad's reflection shows how encountering predominant terms within the queer English vocabulary fell short of enabling an understanding of the situation, rather it was when being able to understand 'what I was *feeling*' that meant Muhammad 'felt less lonely.' Both narratives reflect on the need to face up to the loneliness and guilt that queer subjects feel vis-à-vis the self and their families because of their sexual and gender orientation. When stating that 'guilt is not just a personal feeling,' Omar captures the entwinement of the political/public within the personal sphere. That is, to feel guilty is not one's own but always embeds others whose situatedness within socio-political structures of defeat, oppression, and violence play a constitutive role in forming native guilt and/or loneliness in the first place. Omar's understanding of guilt in relation to those structures of oppression that 'stigmatise us' helps to show colonised internalisation of the fear and stigma in relation to the sexual, recalling what was discussed in the previous chapter as colonised entrapment within the psycho-political structures of sexual alienation. As argued previously, native sexual alienation also underpins native failure to expand and challenge society's moral spectrum beyond what the coloniser deemed it to be. This further reveals colonised reproduction within settler colonial governmental structures, illuminating how structural feelings of loneliness inscribe internal Palestinian disintegration. Here we can contemplate how activists rewriting guilt and loneliness invests in the possibility to see beyond the compulsory paradigms consolidating the colonised sense of defeat. In doing so they enable Otherwise Imaginings to the senses of failure, disintegration, and stigma that have become an inherent constitutive of colonised performative subjecthood.

The comic's characters and daily struggles are a medium for activists to write native queer emotionality in aesthetic terms, which then triggers reflections through these personal narrations interacting with the comic's content. This back-and-forth movement between the comic's and activists' personal narratives highlights the political potential of a queer aesthetic medium. Both the comic and the narratives challenge Palestinian definitions of selfhood as abstracted from queer native emotionality and the kinship systems they strive for and work towards. The comic relays the story of four queer friends and their *tarwiha* time, which becomes a means to finally find someone with whom to vent out and be together through loneliness, guilt, and the other emotions they collectively share. In a similar vein, activists' reflections show the importance of being part of alQaws's spaces where they became less isolated and take their feelings seriously in the process of recognising and transforming oneself, community, and the homeland. Omar wants to confront the guilt he feels towards his family by recognising the wider societal structures that activate such a feeling. Muhammad embraces Arabic, rather than English, to reflect on the feeling of loneliness which leads him to confidently assert the value of living a purposeful and a passionate life. The *tarwiha* comic involves activists in a journey down the lane of personal memories and day-to-day lived experience to locate the legibility of queer affective relations to meanings of selfhood on micro and macro scales. To create these spaces to share and understand these feelings is a means to 'dream together of a different reality' as Tamir Khalfo reflects in 'On Emotions':

> We readers of the comics, old and young, are encouraged to dream too and to dare think about our feelings and share them with our social surroundings. 'Can we change social structures? Our path can be successful and exciting too.' (Quotes from the comics). alQaws strives to build a place for queer women to meet and contribute to challenging the various patriarchal and capitalist structures blocking our ability to dream. *tarwiha* is a space to think collectively of our emotions and to utilise them as a productive engine for political organising, giving legibility for these affective relations in the larger struggle. There is an urgent need to confront and understand our emotions so that we can survive and sustain ourselves. We also need to channel these emotions within productive activist spaces that are ultimately shaping our larger movement.
>
> (2020: n.p.)

166 *Futural Imaginaries*

The comic, and the response that ensued through activists' affectual narratives, unfolds a queer native emotionality against structures of native *ghurba*. Native queer emotionality enables forms of socio-political organising and modalities of being and relating that are neither reducible nor substantively recognisable within the administrative networks of settler colonial and neo-colonial state logics (Rifkin, 2012). *Tarwiha* is a space that makes the affective narrations of queer native subjects seen, felt, and co-shared towards the 'not-yet-inhabited elsewhere' (Ahmed, 2006: 12). Developing further the exploration of the 'not-yet,' the next section examines the artistic work of Tarik Knorn, focusing on how satirical drawings and performance art gesture towards another form of sociality.

Tarik's Satire and Performance Art

As discussed in Chapter 4, my first encounter with Tarik took place at the writing workshop that alQaws organised in the summer of 2013. When we started conversing a couple of years later, I learnt of his art page on Facebook, named 'Knorn Art,' which I began to follow more regularly in order to remain updated about his art posts. It was one of those posts, consisting of a collection of drawings on the lines of political satire, that sparked a conversation between us about Tarik's growing interest in political cartoons. As he explained, the interest came from 'being influenced by the Palestinian culture of political satire as produced by our famous political caricaturist Naji Al-Ali' (Conversation with Tarik, 2015). Tarik's drawings (see Figure 6.14 and Figure 6.15) illustrate ongoing conversations between a hyper-sexualised figure—called '*???*'—throughout the collection and a black cat, '*Pusspuss*' in colloquial Palestinian. Inquiring about the role of the cat in the drawings, Tarik replied:

> I absolutely love what cats symbolise in popular culture. They are perceived as sassy, vain, spoiled, regal, feminine, megalomaniac divas and they always demand to be taken seriously. Those are qualities that describe to the letter the notoriously apolitical Ramallah-elite. However, I decided to make the cat very politically literate and snarky, directing the hyper-sexualised and apolitical liberal—who I called ???—on the path to revolution using protest chants. I like people whose minds and personalities clash oxymoronically with how they appear visually and physically. I love when a sharp mind catches you off guard. It's a turn on. Cats were also used in Internet Memes as a symbol for Slacktivists and ivory tower intellectuals. There's a lot to work with here, and each comic has its own dynamic and its own campaign.
>
> (Conversation with Tarik, 2015)

What Tarik achieves by the cat figure in these drawings is twofold. First, the cat challenges the viewer's expectations of what it ought to

Futural Imaginaries 167

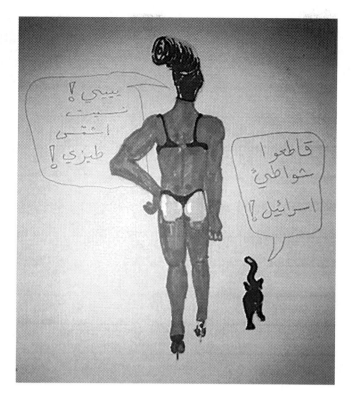

Figure 6.14 *Pusspuss* and *???* on the Beach
Source: Artist

represent. Tarik turns what the cat symbolises for 'slacktivists' or 'ivory tower intellectuals' to a politically literate and snarky figure. The cat is a 'turn on' because it exhibits 'a failure' to identify with its own image. Further, the cat resembles 'Il Grillo Parlante' (The Talking Cricket) of Carlo Collodi's Pinocchio. As 'Il Grillo Parlanta' admonishes Pinocchio who prefers not to face his responsibilities, so the cat voices those concerns and worries that 'the hyper-sexualised apolitical/liberal Ramallah elite' suppresses.

The cat bears a resemblance to Naji Al-Ali's Handala figure, which appears in almost all Naji's cartoons. For the Palestinian cartoonist, who was assassinated in London in 1987 because of his highly provocative and political work, Handala represented the faceless refugee child whose constant presence confronted Zionists' denial of Palestinian refugees' right of return. Handala also spoke truth against those Arab and Palestinian political structures that failed to stand up for and protect their people. Naji explained that

168 *Futural Imaginaries*

Figure 6.15 *Pusspuss* and ??? Before Bed
Source: Artist

Handala is the 10-year-old refugee child whose hands are 'clasped behind his back as a sign of rejection at a time when solutions are presented to us the American way.'[4] Therefore, Tarik's employment of the cat appears to resonate with Naji's Handala, as both deliver politically provocative messages. However, what makes *pusspuss* differ from Handala is the clear investment in the erotic dimension that, as Tarik claims, 'catches you off guard.' While delivering a political/satirical message, the cat also functions as a 'turn on,' which echoes the cartoon's overall purpose in tackling the politics of sexuality within the Oslo context in Palestine.

Figure 6.14 presents ??? in a swimsuit and red heels, as they appear to be walking with an effeminate gait, complaining in Palestinian dialect, 'Oh, I forgot to tan my ass!' Walking alongside '???' there is *pusspuss* who comments, 'Boycott Israeli beaches!' In one of our exchanges, Tarik discusses how he drew this satirical cartoon in order to stress the relevance of the Israeli boycott to queer politics. He tried to highlight 'how Israeli pinkwashing is a

Futural Imaginaries 169

serious issue that needs to be added into our anti-colonial resistance tactics' (Conversation with Tarik, 2015). He also added that:

> The main aim is not only to refer to pinkwashing and the need for boycott, but to also talk about the need to become more involved and mobilised politically as there's a hateful exclusion of the political and historical among liberals, and that seriously harms our resistance.
>
> (Ibid.)

The importance of Tarik's statement, which urges those who uphold a liberal agenda to address 'the hateful exclusion of the political and historical' dimensions, resonates with the idea of internalised pinkwashing, as explored in the previous chapter. Tarik's statement captures a critique of those Palestinian liberal elites whose sidestepping of politics and history has meant naturalising and normalising the settler colonial power regime. In the previous chapter I mapped how alQaws's effort to tackle internalised pinkwashing is one way of addressing Palestinian re-instantiation of hetero-conquest. Tarik's cartoon and the message behind it make a similar critique. In fact, the cartoon unmasks how such desire for a full-body tan, which could be seemingly interpreted as personal, is in fact based on a political stance that is situated within the Oslo political structure of normalising the settler colonial entity. Tarik's drawing offers an artistic depiction of how Palestinian queer desiring of 'a full-body tan at Israeli beaches' reproduces the pinkwashing logic, symptomatic—as argued in the previous chapter—of native attachment to paradigms of freedom and happiness that the coloniser is said to offer. Through calling for a boycott, *pusspuss* addresses and challenges those personal desires and aspirations of the liberal LGBT whose normalising of the coloniser's space and conceptions of freedom suppresses decolonial revolutionary consciousness.

Figure 6.15 presents another conversation between ??? and *pusspuss*. *Pusspuss* defiantly declares, 'I do not recognise the state of Israel;' ??? then replies, '*pusspuss*! We agreed no politics before tucking into bed!' In this case, the cat articulates a political statement that challenges and refutes the liberal 'peace-building model' of Oslo, which recognised the existence of the state of Israel. The response of ??? expresses instead what Tarik also describes as the 'disdain of some LGBTQ groups for the political dimensions of sexuality' (Conversation with Tarik, 2015). On the one hand, Tarik satirises the problematic aspects of a single-issue approach, where 'tucking into bed' means 'no politics.' This single-issue approach to sexuality dismisses the relevance of politics, thus, the value of upholding the decolonial framework. It resonates with the critiques that alQaws faces from within queer groups who, as discussed in the previous chapter, do not see the relevance of talking politics within the movement.

This cartoon also highlights a much-needed 'link between the nation-state's projects and sexuality' (Conversation with Tarik, 2015). Tarik's satire addresses the debate about the well-drawn distinction between the sexual and political dimensions, as respectively relegated to the private domain.

170 Futural Imaginaries

The exchange between *???* and *pusspuss*, therefore, not only challenges the delinking of politics from sexuality but also brings to light the very dimension of the sexual that lies at the premise of the political (i.e., the nation-state project). In particular, the transsexuality of *???* is a striking confrontation with the hetero-patriarchal premise of the nation-state.[5] *???*'s transsexuality complements the cartoon's political message, articulated via *pusspuss*'s rejection of recognising Israel. Tarik's ability to unite those two elements into a context of intimacy confronts us with imaginings—gendered as signified by *???* and geopolitical as signified by *pusspuss*—beyond the reproduction of hetero-patriarchy. While Tarik's comics aim to provoke what he calls the liberal Ramallah elite, so his artistic performance, organised in the same city, delivers a more direct criticism of such elitism.

Whideh wataniyeh (National Loneliness) was an artistic performance staged as part of the Khalil Sakakini Cultural Centre Festival for Video and Performance Art in the summer of 2013. The place where the performance took place and to whom it was directed is important. Tarik emphasises the relevance of performing at a local level within spaces that are accessible to a local Palestinian audience. This view of performing art for a local audience challenges exclusive performances, which Tarik describes as 'the colonial white gaze.' Tarik explains:

> Performances and film screenings outside conventional venues are important as they tend to be more accessible, we need to realise that our audience shouldn't be international and white. There's a time when we need to stop giving the position of audience member to the coloniser.
>
> (Conversation with Tarik, 2015)

Tarik's *whideh wataniyeh* goes beyond a critique of the colonial white gaze, as discussed in relation to Tarik's performance in Chapter 4, and instead moves towards queer Imaginings of an Otherwise for Palestine. The title of the performance plays on the famous Palestinian slogan *whideh wataniyeh*, meaning national unity. As the word *whideh* in Arabic can also signify loneliness, Tarik uses it to indicate the latter meaning (loneliness) rather than the former (unity). From 'unity' to 'loneliness,' the performance took place in one of the streets of Ramallah, adjacent to a Coca-Cola billboard, and Tarik's words help us understand the importance of performing in such a space.

> How challenging it is to penetrate public space, especially with the implementation of neoliberal policies [in Ramallah], where everything is privatised and rendered inaccessible for the sake of profit maximisation and stifling uprisings.
>
> (Conversation with Tarik, 2015)

In *whideh wataniyeh*, Tarik and the other performers come out as walking Coke bottles wearing a *sheikh abayah* or garment, with red ribbons tied

Futural Imaginaries   171

around their waists. Those ribbons stand for the red sticker on the bottle of Coca-Cola representing the brand name. Dressed in costumes resembling Coca-Cola bottles, the performers stand in the street and serve the drink to passers-by. However, as people start drinking, the performers begin to bleed. While serving, the performers hold needles in their hands and, as they start puncturing the squibs[6] attached to their bodies, their simulated bleeding begins. Do note that the performance took place during Ramadan,[7] a month when Coca-Cola is commonly served during Iftar (when people break their fast). During the month, the consumption of Coca-Cola increases significantly in the local context of Palestine, and the performance tries to underline the connections between religion and consumerism, whose relationship transpires also from the Facebook description of the event.

> We've witnessed a matrimonial occasion. In this glorious wedding season, we will celebrate a love consummated between religion and consumerism. Let there be a spectacle, and let that spectacle be a cleansing, sponsored of course by none other than Coca-Cola. While enjoying the show, we—the performers—hope that you reflect on this, but also feel free to interact with us.
>
> (Event Facebook page, 2013)

Inviting people to drink Coca-Cola, Tarik explains how they addressed the passers-by, 'as a loving host, please drink ... May your fast cleanse you ... Ramadan Mubarak'[8] (Conversation with Tarik, 2015). However, as people started sipping their Coca-Cola, black blood gushes out of the performers' clothing, staining the white *abayah* (garment) (see Figure 6.16, Figure 6.17, and Figure 6.18). People's reactions ranged from extreme horror to being incredibly entertained, and—most importantly—'people were able to draw the connection between commodity consumption and a blackening stain on the soul. So to speak, capitalism is killing us' (Conversation with Tarik, 2015). Tarik recounted people's diverse reactions, at times urging others to 'Stop drinking Coke!' or shouting, 'They are dying, we are killing them!' Others preferred to keep drinking and said, 'Let's see what happens to them' (Ibid.).

Tarik further explains how the message 'let us decolonise from hyper-consumption during this holy month' was conveyed to people passing by as the performers started to approach people and ask if they could also paint their faces. People were then face-painted with the message, 'Thank you for ridding us of capitalism and hyper-consumption, now it's our turn to help you cleanse,' which means 'once they go home, they will wash off the face painting' (Conversation with Tarik, 2015). After the performance, a passer-by commented on the relevance of such performance:

> Corporations are really hijacking public spaces inside the city. They introduce products and brands that the masses do not need, they suck

172 *Futural Imaginaries*

Figure 6.16 whideh watanyeh Performance
Source: Artist

them into a vortex that is not relevant to their lifestyle. They distract them and make one live the fantasy that Palestine is free, that life is normal.

(Conversation with Tarik, 2015)

Such allusions to the normality of life in Palestine shown in the city of Ramallah—the hub of the Palestinian Authority's power, with a growing focus on the discourse of development—turns our attention towards the Palestinian trajectory of the recognition of statehood.[9] Being from Ramallah, Tarik elaborates on the particularity of the city, whereby:

Futural Imaginaries 173

Figure 6.17 whideh watanyeh Performance
Source: Artist

> Unlike other West Bank cities [it] is extremely sheltered and full of business entrepreneurs, who have somehow found a way to profit from the Israeli occupation in exchange for legitimizing settler colonialism and institutionalised hyper-consumption, putting oppressive limitations on mobility both physical and class related. Segregated in a classic divide and conquer strategy, Ramallah has become a paradox, a La-La-Land that feeds and nurtures the Israeli occupation.
>
> (Ibid.)

Tarik's employment of the Coca-Cola theme for 'a national loneliness' performance calls for a questioning of those practices that normalise Israeli settler colonialism, boosting individualism, and accepting the fragmented reality following Oslo via the consolidation of the power of the PNA. Thus,

174 *Futural Imaginaries*

Figure 6.18 whideh watanyeh Performance
Source: Artist

Coca-Cola symbolises the adoption of a modernising agenda aimed at normalising the Oslo reality and Israeli colonialism via consumerist practices, which are part of a larger capitalist and settler colonial structure. What is particularly striking about Coca-Cola is its inherent connection to the logic of capitalist enjoyment, which is said never to quench one's thirst. Like capitalism, Coca-Cola is a drink that triggers an endless circuit of hysterical consumption/drinking that never fully ends (Zizek, 2017). The need to enjoy hyper-consumption resonates with the 'La La Land' that Ramallah represents. The Coca-Cola billboard captures the modernising outlook of the city, whose spatial transformation to host PNA elite capitalist aspirations through 'the Economic Peace paradigm' sustains the continuity of Palestinian Nakba.[10] People imagine and practice their lives within paradigms of a modernising futural trajectory that reproduces their Nakba. The political relevance of drinking Coca-Cola lies in that endless cycle of enjoyment that

Futural Imaginaries 175

seems to make life normal; yet it only does so through a misrecognition of how the fantasy of capitalist enjoyment is based on native suffering. Tarik's performance uncovers the commodification of enjoyment as that which is 'killing us.' It confronts the viewer with the reality behind modernising (PNA) agendas. The performance questions the failure of such an illusory sheltered life, urging people to 'stop drinking.' Showing Coca-Cola's fatal effect on bodies, which intensifies as people 'drink more,' the performance stages dramatic moments of self-flagellation. The performance alludes to the need to combat and confront Palestinian enjoyment—meaning, the libidinal attachment—to Coca-Cola, since Coca-Cola stands for the embracing of a modernising agenda that relies on native's suffering.

It is against the backdrop of such analyses that it is possible to capture how significant Tarik's comics and performance are in addressing the linkages between decolonisation and desire. The *whideh wataniyeh* performance makes visible the misrecognition symptomatic of what Sara Ahmed (2010) calls 'the promise of happiness' at the heart of desiring Coca-Cola—a signifier of the PNA modernising agenda—in the 'La La Land' of Ramallah. To reveal Coca-Cola as that element that is 'killing us' is a call to recognise the reality of wretchedness at the heart of the modernising vision of Palestinian statist reality. Acts of self-flagellation recall the queering figure, also discussed in the previous chapter, who is 'willing to be stressed,' as opposed to flowing happily in a world experienced as 'easy' (Ahmed, 2010: 169). In such a scenario, a resistance to the 'distribution of the sensible' (Rancière, 2004: 7) is called for. If the PNA via its colonial authority orders and distributes the fantasy of a Palestinian happily 'flowing' (Ahmed, 2010: 12), which means happiness becomes associated with neo-colonial market economy, Tarik's performance calls for a modification of the aesthetic-politico field of possibility within the public space of the city. It asserts a need to cleanse and decolonise by interrupting hyper-consumerist urges. People's enjoyment and flow in the 'La La Land' of Ramallah is halted because the artistic performance pushes them to recognise the harms within neoliberal policies and PNA visions of statehood-futurity. The performance challenges this reality of native misrecognition (Fanon, 1967) through a sensory (bodily visuals) experience that unveils the suicidal effect of those visions.

Tarik's art unsettles practices that perpetuate Israeli colonialism by questioning mundane desires and actions, such as 'tanning your bottom' or 'drinking Coca-Cola.' Both cartoons and performance allude to the necessity to outline the historical and political dimensions of Palestinians' desires in order to activate a decolonial, queer consciousness. In this vein, the cat *pusspuss* functions as the voice of queer 'utopianism' in the face of 'the here and now' of 'pragmatic gay [liberal] agendas' (Muñoz, 2009: 10). It redirects attention towards an interruption of LGBT 'flow' within the spaces of the coloniser: Israeli beaches. The performance, instead, discloses the problematic aspects of a modernising agenda, whose fantasies of enjoyment perpetuate the structural continuity of hetero-conquest. Having examined how

176 *Futural Imaginaries*

Tarik's artistic works confronts this reality of misrecognition, the following discussion explores how the work of Fashion Design troubles the fantasy of male- and state-making in Palestine.

Omar's Fashion Design

I first met Omar, self-identified as Omar Ibin Dina, at G.'s house in the summer of 2013. My encounter with Omar's work took place in the summer of the following year, July 2014, when I visited his *zey al tashrifat*, or Ceremonial Uniform, exhibition in Birzeit University Museum.[11] Walking into the exhibition, I was met at the entrance by a big poster describing the work and its emergence as:

> A response to the Palestinian National Authority's statehood bid and frenzied campaign to acquire the status of full member of the United Nations. As a collection of garments, accessories, samples, techniques and texts, The Ceremonial Uniform is an imagined system of dress for male officials in this would-be Palestinian state.
>
> (Field notes, 2014)

Inside *zey al tashrifat*, it was possible to make sense of each stage of the work by looking at the panels on the walls. Those provided the viewer with images, ethnographic material, and other collected resources that all contributed to the development of the work. Accessing this material, as well as the designer's initial sketches and ideas, helped the viewer to further engage with the manifold themes the exhibition revealed. *Zey al tashrifat* is a manifestation of fashion designed and presented to imagine beyond its local contexts' ideals of male- and state-making. Omar turns fashion into a tool that challenges hetero-patriarchal ideals of sexuality and the political project of state-making in Palestine, thus exposing the performativity of gender and nation-state building.

Inside *zey al tashrifat* we are faced with an enormous square-shaped shirt with two, ultra-large, rectangular sleeves hanging down from the ceiling (Figure 6.19). The design recalls Palestinian women's traditional dress known as *thawb*. However, far from being a woman's *thawb*, the imprints on the shirt carry the talismans after which it was named as The Talismanic Shirt (Figure 6.20). The talismans include slogans, speeches, icons, and emblems that have come to signify the Palestinian National Authority and its political trajectory of state building. The designer's sketchbook offers a glimpse of the material that inspired The Talismanic Shirt. For instance, the panels on the wall contain a large piece of paper with multiple copies of the PNA official emblem: an eagle. Adjacent to the PNA symbol lies a newspaper extract of the speech at the UN of the PNA president, Mahmoud Abbas. Another emblem of Palestinian statehood—the flag—lies close to the UN symbol and the famous 194 resolution, which, following a long campaign, granted

Futural Imaginaries 177

Figure 6.19 The Talismanic Shirt
Source: Author

Figure 6.20 The Talismanic Shirt
Source: Author

178 *Futural Imaginaries*

non-member observer status to the PNA within the United Nations. An old copy of what the designer identifies as the Seven Solomonic[12] Talismans is juxtaposed with repeated PNA slogans and imagery of machine-guns. The Talismanic Shirt departs from the common reliance on 'sacred texts, numerology, symbolism and geometry to protect from evil' (Field notes, 2014). Rather, it comprises:

> Symbols of the nation, logos, weapons, clichés, and Yasser Arafat's declaration of state speech in 1988 and his United Nations address to the General Assembly in 1974, as well as Mahmoud Abbas's United Nations speech in 2011 and 2012.
>
> (Ibid.)

Omar transforms the PNA's repeated 'clichés' into mythic talismans in order to trouble what the designer describes as the 'Palestinian political establishment and what it stands for' (Conversation with Omar, 2014). Omar explains that what constitutes the symbolic power of talismans, thus making them legitimate, is their investment in repetition.

> Letters, mantras, symbols, and hollow rituals are repeated to create something . . . an identity, yet nobody knows what it means. Repetition is important and clever because it becomes numbing after a while. It is powerful like magic; you see it in the way the talismans are folded and written.
>
> (Ibid.)

The Talismanic Shirt lays out the repetitive dimension upon which the Palestinian political establishment relies to legitimise its statehood project. Omar's design offers an understanding of the concept of repetition vis-à-vis power, unveiling the logic of performativity (Butler, 1999). Repetition is required to re-enact a set of meanings that are reliant upon a 'mundane and ritualised form of their legitimation' (Ibid.: 178). The Talismanic Shirt captures how those symbols of the nation, logos, weapons, and clichés function in the same manner. It is their 'numbing' and empty reiteration that establishes the legitimacy and dominance of the nation-state project of the Palestinian political establishment. At the same time, this repetition allows us to reveal the contingent foundations of these symbols of the nation-state and their tenuous premise.

In the Talismanic and Slogans section of the exhibition, we also find footwear, what the designer identifies as PLO clogs. The clogs also possess a talismanic character, since Palestine Liberation Organisation letters and mottos cover them, such as National Unity (*wihdeh wataniyeh*), National Mobilisation (*ta'bi'a qawmiya*), and Freedom (*hurriya*). However, the clogs offer a direct reference to the settler colonial regime, as the stilts' decoration mirrors the shape of the concrete slabs of the Israeli apartheid wall (Figure 6.21 and Figure 6.22). The panels adjacent to the clogs explain the processes of their

Futural Imaginaries 179

Figure 6.21 The PLO Clogs
Source: Author

creation. Images of the PLO mottos juxtaposed with an image of the apartheid wall demonstrate to the viewer how the combination of both inspires the creation of the clogs (Field notes, 2014). Discussing the PLO clogs and what they try to express, Omar indicates how the PLO's 'need to survive' encouraged their metamorphosis into a neo-colonial authority.

> You can wear the clogs, but you cannot walk on them. According to the idea of such institution [PLO], we need to have a state to be free, we need to be part of the UN, the very institution that handed over Palestine to the coloniser, we need to have a uniform in order to have an accepted identity. It is all groundless rubbish. . . . We should rethink the structure rather than being obsessed with owning it. Palestine, as a concept, is far stronger and far more progressive than what these politicians are trying to do.
> (Conversation with Omar, 2014)

Omar's design renders those clogs un-walkable and, in the process, he reveals their groundlessness. Performativity theory critiques the 'ground'

180 *Futural Imaginaries*

Figure 6.22 The PLO Clogs
Source: Author

upon which identities stand, allowing us to see the 'stylised repetition' of power configurations (Butler, 1999: 179). The PLO clogs reveal an obsession with solidifying an identity whose possibilities are conditioned by the very oppressive power structures delineating Palestinian Nakba. Both PLO clogs and The Talismanic Shirt are designs for the to-be-male-state officials of Palestine, revealing the construction of those masculine agents through the PNA's 'deadening clichés' and how the strive for nation-statism relies on—rather than challenges—the colonial logic of governmentality.

In the final part of the exhibition, titled The Real and The Imaginary, we see a collection of Palestinian traditional garments hanging in the room (Figure 6.23). We read on the panels that *real* garments, worn by Palestinians over the last hundred years and obtained from the museum and family of the designer, are merged with *imaginary* ones (Field notes, 2014). These garments constitute the final outfits worn in the portraits of two figures hung on the background wall, identified as Abu Saleh and Abu Zuhair (Figure 6.24).

The merging of 'real and imaginary' garments throws the viewer into crisis, as those lines distinguishing what is 'real' from what is 'imaginary' are completely blurred. This same process also empowers the viewers since it

Futural Imaginaries 181

Figure 6.23 Real and Imagined Garments
Source: author

forces them to question the very terrains of what is taken to be 'real.' Omar's designs put into question the reality of Palestinian nation-state male-making and force the viewer to imagine a different 'reality,' an Otherwise. During our conversation, Omar refers to 'a history of Palestinian visual art, which builds on a national legacy making an icon of the woman in her peasant dress to imagine and define Palestine politically and culturally' (Ibid.). This process, which was mentioned in Chapter 2, reveals the instrumentality of art in cementing national imaginings of Palestine vis-à-vis gendered origin stories of the woman/land in her peasant dress. Omar's fashion design unsettles the aesthetic/political dimensions of such past constructions in order to reimagine the present and the future. In the two portraits on the wall, identified on the panels as 'Western portraiture,' we see Abu Saleh and Abu Zuhair dressed in their ceremonial uniform. The two figures, seated in a very official manner, recall images of past Ottoman Sultans. The note on the panel describes these portraits as 'a statement of mockery and derision of the inept Palestinian political establishment and its obsession with European modes of government and nation-state building' (Field notes, 2014). The usage of portraiture evokes the long history of portrait production in the late period of the

182 *Futural Imaginaries*

Figure 6.24 Abu Salah and Abu Zuhair Portraits
Source: Author

Ottoman Empire, alluding further to the 'European obsession.' This period also witnessed the launch of numerous reforms—called Tanzimat—whose aim was to trigger a civilisational turn, warding-off foreign and domestic perceptions of Arab East 'backwardness' (Sheehi, 2016: 15). It is important to note that this period, which marked the ushering in of 'modernity,' brought in civil strife, corruption, and exploitation of the peasant class at the hands of a newly emerging elite class (see Abu-Manneh, 1990; Doumani, 1992). While the portraits and the posture of the two figures invoke state-making qua Europe, other elements recall the role of dress in gender configurations. Both figures wear striking colourful heels (Figure 6.25 and Figure 6.26). Their costumes are also colourful and overly accessorised like the background against which they are sitting. Such explicit emphasis on decoration and colour echoes the designer's desire to deconstruct dress and its role in recreating the female body within the contours of hetero-patriarchy. As Omar comments:

> Why do women wear skirts and men trousers? Why is there so much colour and embroidery in their [women] dresses, and practically none in men's dress?
>
> (Conversation with Omar, 2014)

Futural Imaginaries 183

Figure 6.25 Abu Salah
Source: Designer

Such reflection reminds us of Shelagh Weir's examination of Palestinian women's clothing pre-1948, which was 'far more diverse and richly ornamented than men's' (1989: 74). Weir locates the reason for such differentiation in how the design of women's dresses was used to indicate the different stages of womanhood, including their sexual marital status, and to display

184 *Futural Imaginaries*

Figure 6.26 Abu Zuhair
Source: Designer

Futural Imaginaries 185

family and village status (Ibid.). Omar's designs engage with and reimagine a history of dress making and wearing in Palestine not only through using bright colours but also through the striking incorporation of the heels. Far from being an act of supposed 'emasculation,' Omar explains that the heels 'state what the other fabricated garments do not say. Masculinity has an obsession with the body and how to control it, like all social-political practices based on patriarchy' (Field notes, 2014). To demonstrate masculinity's obsession to control the body reveals the contingency within the structure of dress and male-making. The heels, therefore, reveal 'discontinuity' (Butler, 1999: 179) in the picture, which identifies the figures of two males. The names, Abu Saleh and Abu Zuhair, where 'Abu' in Arabic is particularly used to denote 'father of,' resonate with the privileged role of the masculine in passing Palestinian identity from father to son.[13] By revealing disunity in the picture of the identified 'males,' the heels dramatise the fabrication at work in the 'reality' of dress, male, and state inscription.

The designs reveal the fantasy at the heart of dress in order to trouble processes of male- and state-making. Omar's designs destabilise naturalised knowledge, invested in a myth of 'realness' and originality of the dress, the male and/or the state. They also lay out the possibility of reconfiguring dress in other ways, and thus reimagining other forms of past and futural conceptions of gender and Palestinian self-determination. Omar's renaming of himself as Omar Ibin Dina (son of Dina, who is his mother) captures what his designs do in queering the logic of patrilineality and allowing other possible narrations on both familial and national spheres. Simultaneously, the dresses dare to see and imagine what the PNA authority does not enable. In this regard, people's reaction to the exhibition attests further to how such work destabilises the status quo. In our conversation, Omar stressed how Hassan Al Batal, a journalist from *al Ayyam* who is an 'old school PLO and Fatah apologist,' wrote a critical piece saying that 'I should limit my work to art and not go into politics' (Conversation with Omar, 2014). Omar also recounted how some PNA affiliates felt offended by the designs as they made them 'look stupid' (Ibid.) commenting:

> These men put on their western suits and do look like idiots. In fact, they think my uniform is a joke. I think the uniform is far more serious than what these men are doing because *every stitch is made with conscious decision and a knowledge of its origin.* Whereas these men dress up because this is the way things are. This is power, so you want a dress there you are, it is—in a way—a joke but a far more serious one.
>
> (Ibid., Omar's emphasis)

Omar's 'serious joke' underlies a significant connection between the satirical and the political. The presumed 'emasculation of Palestinian politicians' seen at the heart of *zey al tashrifat* should not be dismissed as a joke. Rather, we need to engage seriously with how these designs gesture towards other

186　*Futural Imaginaries*

possible futures for Palestine by revealing the talismanic character at the heart of present male- and state-making 'reality.' Such a critique of the present and the future takes place via a simultaneous questioning of indigene's relation to the past, which is figured through the lens of hetero-patriarchal romanticising of the image of the woman/land in her peasant-ornamented dress. By dismantling the 'myth of originality' in dresses designed in the past, Omar's designs shake 'the story of origin' (Butler, 1999: 46) upon which current validation of hetero-patriarchy stands. Most importantly, the dresses evoke an engagement with the past in its 'performative force' (Muñoz, 2009: 21), enabling possibilities to imagine Other gendered fabrications. Thus, *zey al tashrifat* offers ways of redoing and reimagining the past in order to 'critique the present and help us [re]envision the future' (Muñoz, 1999: 34).

This is seen in particular through the designer's sharing of archival ethnographic material that help explain the process of design making. In the Sexuality and Talismans section, pictures documenting the making of pottery in Palestine are used to explain how an armour was made using local craft traditions. In the background we see a picture of two women, Sarah Shibly and her daughter Najwa, 'who made and decorated pottery jars for storing water and oil' (Field notes, 2014). Underneath the picture we read how Sarah and Najwa 'were well-known for the craft and women used to come to them from the entire area to have their pottery decorated' (Ibid.). Furthermore, a reflection on the relationship between the processes of pottery and identity making is posted for the viewer to read.

> The nature and process of pottery is metaphorical in that it changes from the malleable clay to the unrelenting and fragile ceramic upon exposure to extreme conditions (heat) used to create armour. The metaphor is taken further by comparing identity to protection. Protective as it is, it remains fragile as well as unrelenting. When challenged, it repels or breaks. The protected thus becomes undermined, in peril or independent of protection.
>
> (Ibid.)

Omar's reliance on pottery to create an armour that is presumed to reinforce a protective role in masculine identity comes hand in hand with the revelation of the malleable essence of this object. The process of armour making, therefore, unveils those lost archives, demonstrating the centrality of women's crafts and fabric materials to Palestinian selfhood past and present. By doing so, it brings to the fore the possibility of excavating the past for other gender formations, exposing those contradictions, as well as the breakability of what is often perceived as fixed and eternal. The viewer sees the outcome of what the designer calls The Suspended Armour, which, as the panels describe, was removed from the final outfit because 'it did not fit aesthetically' (Field notes, 2014). The armour, instead, is left to hang on a broken, faceless mannequin (see Figure 6.27). Leaving out the armour from the final outfit but choosing to share it with the viewer through a

Futural Imaginaries 187

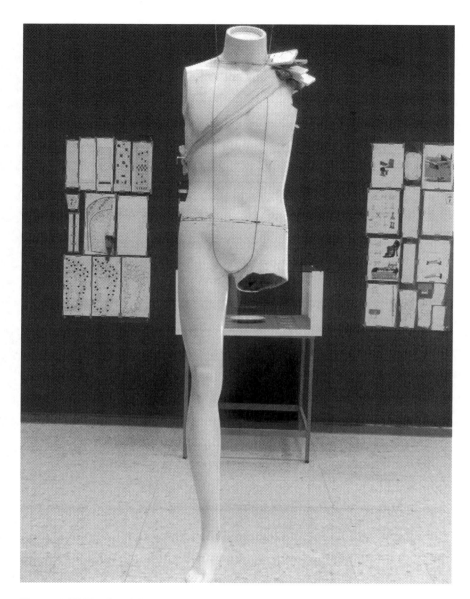

Figure 6.27 Faceless Mannequin
Source: Author

broken mannequin alludes to the necessity of failure to embody a masculinist protective role and identity. It also recalls the many Palestinian bodies that have been broken by the settler colonial machine and demonstrates a native queered positionality in relation to a violent hetero-conquest regime.

188 *Futural Imaginaries*

In our conversation, Omar explained that the two models wearing the final outfit, identified as Abu Salah and Abu Zuhair, are, in reality, two queer Palestinian Syrian refugees who have been doubly displaced from Palestine to Syria and then from Syria to Lebanon where they are now based. *Zey al tashrifat*, therefore, stems from the reality of bodies and dis-identifications to statist, gendered, and dress configurations that buttress the continuity of native's Nakba.

Conclusion

The artistic productions explored in this chapter underline decolonial queering's quest for Otherwise Imaginings in Palestine. Queer artistic productions challenge how Palestinian political trajectory succumbed to institutional and geopolitical boundaries sustaining Nakba and offer alternative cartographies to remap native selfhood and the meanings of the politics of liberation. AlQaws's *tarwiha* narratives reveal the role of queer native affect against structures of *ghurba*. The comics provide a pedagogic platform distilling predominant conceptions on gender and sexuality through the fictive characters' lives and daily struggles. Fiction, at the same time, captures reality as the comics also enable activists to voice their personal narratives and affectual stories enfolding 'the complex entwinement of unacknowledged survivals, unofficial aspirations, and the persistence of pain' (Rifkin, 2012: 31). These affectual narratives not only open the self to forms of identification beyond predominant LGBT identity cues but also trigger spaces for collective sharing and healing from the 'political and economic processes of recolonisation' (Alexander, 2005: 39).

Tarik Knorn's satirical drawings and performance art engage the historical and political dimensions of quotidian desiring of Israeli beaches and consumerist goods, activating a decolonial consciousness that urges for imagining beyond 'La La Land.' In a similar vein, Omar Ibin Dina's *zey al tashrifat* reveals the talismanic process underlining male- and state-making reality while excavating other past and present fabrics that foster a future against the oppressive power structures delineating Palestinian Nakba. *Zey al tashrifat's* blurring of the distinction between what is taken to be imagined versus real is akin to what the *tarwiha* comics do in relation to the real and fantastical and captures the overall process of creative artistic endeavours. Decolonial art queers the very distinction between the real and imagined by making sense of native subjectivity and decolonisation processes on multiple entwined scales. The artistic productions explored in this chapter, from ceremonial fabrics to performing *wihdeh wataniyeh*, reveal that what is taken to be 'real' is in fact made up of 'repeated institutionalised acts of figuration, which create and sustain the material conditions in which peoplehood can be signified and lived' (Rifkin, 2012: 264). In doing so, queering artistic productions not only distil the binarism between what is real and imagined but also open the way for affective, symbolic, and material possibilities that

Futural Imaginaries 189

allow a critical re-evaluation of the spatial, temporal, and relational delimitations of liberatory political imaginings.

Notes

1 http://alqaws.org/tarwiha/ (Accessed 9 June 2021).
2 See discussion in Chapter 2.
3 Jeem is a website that produces knowledge as well as critical and cultural content about gender, sex, and sexuality that challenges and transcends the prevalent discourse of the mainstream media see: https://jeem.me/en/about-us.
4 See: http://muftah.org/understanding-politics-in-the-arab-world-through-naji-al-alis-cartoons/#.WJ2sitLc7IU (Accessed 9 June 2021).
5 See discussion in Chapter 2.
6 Squibs are little nylon bags of black ink taped on random parts of bodies. They are usually used to simulate bleeding by being punctured with a needle or by attaching to it self-detonating fireworks to mimic getting shot.
7 Holy Muslim month which requires fasting all day.
8 An official way of greeting those who fast during Ramadan.
9 See discussion in Chapter 2.
10 Ibid.
11 Birzeit University is located in the town of Birzeit, adjacent to Ramallah.
12 King Solomon's seal in Kabalah Jewish tradition is believed to provide protection, eternity, and well-being. See: www.kabalatalisman.com/king-solomon (Accessed 24 June 2021).
13 See discussion in Chapter 2.

Bibliography

Abu-Manneh, B., 1990. 'Jerusalem in the Tanzimat Period: The New Ottoman Administration and the Notables.' *Die Welt Des Islams* 30(1/4): 1–44.

Abu-Rumailah, M., 2020. 'On Loneliness.' *Jeem*. Available at: https://jeem.me/jadal/%D8%B9%D9%86-%D8%A7%D9%84%D9%88%D8%AD%D8%AF%D8%A9 (Accessed 22 December 2021). Source in Arabic.

Ahmed, S., 2010. *The Promise of Happiness*. Durham, NC: Duke University Press.

Ahmed, S., 2006. *Queer Phenomenology: Orientations, Objects, Others*. Durham, NC: Duke University Press.

Alexander, J., 2005. *Pedagogies of Crossing: Meditations on Feminism, Sexual Politics, Memory and the Sacred*. Durham, NC: Duke University Press.

Al-Khatib, O., 2020. 'On Guilt.' *Jeem*. Available at: https://jeem.me/jadal/%D8%B9%D9%86-%D8%A7%D9%84%D8%B0%D9%86%D8%A8 (Accessed 22 December 2021).

alQaws, 2018. 'Tarwiha Comic Book Release and Discussion in Jerusalem.' *alQaws Articles*. Available at: www.alqaws.org/siteEn/print?id=253&type=2 (Accessed 22 December 2021).

alQaws's tarwiha, 2019. Available at: http://alqaws.org/tarwiha/ (Accessed 22 December 2021).

Butler, J., 1999. *Gender Trouble: Feminism and the Subversion of Identity*. New York: Routledge.

Cvetkovich, A., 2012. *Depression: A Public Feeling*. Durham, NC: Duke University Press.

190 *Futural Imaginaries*

Doumani, B., 1992. 'Rediscovering Ottoman Palestine: Writing Palestinians into History.' *Journal of Palestine Studies* 21(2): 5–28.

Fanon, F., 1967. *Black Skin, White Masks*. London: Pluto Press.

Georgis, D., 2013. 'Thinking Past Pride: Queer Arab Shame in Baree Mista3jil.' *International Journal of Middle East Studies* 45(2): 233–251.

Khalafo, T., 2020. 'On Emotions.' *Jeem*. Available at: https://jeem.me/jadal/%D8%B9%D9%86-%D8%A7%D9%84%D9%85%D8%B4%D8%A7%D8%B9%D8%B1 (Accessed 22 December 2021). Source in Arabic.

M., 2020. 'On Rage.' *Jeem*. Available at: https://jeem.me/jadal/%D8%B9%D9%86-%D8%A7%D9%84%D8%BA%D8%B6%D8%A8 (Accessed 22 December 2021). Source in Arabic.

Manchester, A., 2017. 'Teaching Critical Looking: Pedagogical Approaches to Using Comics as Queer Theory.' *SANE JOURNAL: Sequential Art Narrative in Education* 2(2): Article 2.

Muñoz, J., 1999. *Disidentifications: Queer of Color and the Performance of Identity*. Minneapolis: University of Minnesota Press.

Muñoz, J., 2009. *Cruising Utopia: The Then and There of Queer Futurity*. New York: New York University Press.

Postema, B., 2013. *Narrative Structure in Comics: Making Sense of Fragments*. Toronrto: IRT.

Rancière, J., 2004. *The Politics of Aesthetics*. London: Bloomsbury.

Rifkin, R., 2012. *The Erotics of Sovereignty: Queer Native Writing in the Era of Self-Determination*. Minneapolis: University of Minnesota Press.

Sheehi, S., 2016. *The Arab Imago: A Social History of Portrait Photography, 1860–1910*. Princeton: Princeton University Press.

Tarwiha, 2019a. 'Moulds We Should Break.' *alQaws*. Available at: http://alqaws.org/tarwiha/article/32 (Accessed 22 December 2021).

Tarwiha, 2019b. 'On Loneliness.' *alQaws*. Available at: http://alqaws.org/tarwiha/article/35 (Accessed 22 December 2021).

Tarwiha, 2019c. 'Episode No. 5.' *alQaws*. Available at: http://alqaws.org/tarwiha/article/16 (Accessed 22 December 2021).

Tarwiha, 2019d. 'Episode No. 6.' *alQaws*. Available at: http://alqaws.org/tarwiha/article/48 (Accessed 22 December 2021).

Tarwiha, 2019e. 'Episode No. 8.' *alQaws*. Available at: http://alqaws.org/tarwiha/article/50 (Accessed 22 December 2021).

Tarwiha, 2019f. 'Episode No. 4.' *alQaws*. Available at: http://alqaws.org/tarwiha/article/46 (Accessed 22 December 2021).

The Zizek/ChomskyTimes, 2017. 'Slavoj Zizek on Ideology, Desire and Coca-Cola.' *Youtube*. Available at: www.youtube.com/watch?v=0kgifOXhEak (Accessed 22 December 2021).

Weir, A., 1989. *Palestinian Costume*. London: The British Museum.

7 Conclusion
Decolonial Queer Beginnings

This book sets out to offer an understanding of Palestine and Palestinian queer politics that derive from weaving queer into native positionality and the struggle for decolonisation. In doing so, I engage critically with conventional analytical frameworks on queer politics. These analyses are somewhat problematic because they reproduce the silences that queer theory carries (Meghani and Saeed, 2019) when absenting or not fully engaging with a settler colonial framework and/or a native grounded knowledge of queering. Contrary to this, to centre settler colonialism has meant seriously engaging with indigenous feminist insights to ground Palestinian Nakba within the structural continuity of hetero-conquest. As such, the book's approach has diverged from previous analyses in two major ways: First, it has challenged the type of racism that has been drawn upon to engage queerness in the Palestinian context. That is, xenophobic and homophobic policies against minority communities did not seem sufficient to capture the particularity of settler colonial violence and systematic policies of minoritisation, demonisation, and absentation of the native Palestinian Other. This, in turn, links to the second aspect that conventional literature on Palestinian queerness has missed regarding the centrality of the national question for the indigenes of the world. Some of the analytical frameworks—including within leftists' circles in the West—aiming to trump the nation and challenge queer identifications with it fail to account for how queerness à la nationhood is being articulated for those who remain under the thumb of the settler colonial present.

Decolonial queering is a framework to situate native grounded knowledge for queering as decolonising. It captures the transgressive possibilities that such an entwinement enables not only in the fight against perpetual exile and the Nakba structure but also in ushering a politics of homing, re-rooting and self-determination beyond the re-instantiation of hetero-conquest. In what follows, I chart three intertwined theses on decolonial queering and map them in relation to personal reflections, conversations conducted within activist spaces, as well as present political events. I also point out to areas where future research could be carried out.

DOI: 10.4324/9781003273585-9

192   *Conclusion*

First: Sexuality and Social Formations in the Settler Colony

Decolonial queering begins with the need to centre sexuality as a lens to understand settler colonial conquest. Taking sexuality as a site of analysis means challenging predominant accounts, including within native feminist and anti-imperialist circles, that dismiss the relevance of sexuality and queer politics to native and anti-colonial struggles. The workspaces and productions of the activist/artist provide a rich ground for comprehending how queerness in Palestine challenges and navigates the structures of space, time, and sex of hetero-conquest. Hetero-conquest entails processes of dispossessing the native Other, as well as regulating their lives and bodies within the institutionalised socio-political parameters of the settler state. Such a process remakes indigenous people into non and/or citizens (both at the same time) and manages them within the dictated boundaries of the sovereign settler state. Laws, such as 'Citizenship and Entry into Israel' and Israel's basic definition as Jewish along with absentee property laws,[1] are examples of the institutional foundation of the settler state bent on Judaizing Palestine while regulating Palestinian communities along the sexual, temporal, and spatial bounds of the settler colony. In other words, these laws, which every Zionist government has promoted, put native people in colonially allocated reserves to systematically kill their sense of being a people.

Furthermore, there is the quotidian management of life, which derives from the way socio-economic dynamics are shaped in the settler colony. I write these words while sitting in the Hebron south enclave of the West Bank, a town called Al-Thahriah, that Zionist colonialism has systematically transformed from a self-sustaining Palestinian economy based on agriculture to a pool of cheap Arab labour for its economy, particularly the city of Bir Al Saba'a. My younger cousins, who are struggling to get into Israel legally for work, recount how it is easier to get work permits if one is married with children to support because young unmarried Arabs are presumed to constitute a bigger threat to the Zionist state. It is quite intriguing to contemplate how these everyday sketches reveal the role of sexuality within the settler colony. Furthermore, colonial laws, which are enacted on the basis of the so-called Arab demographic bomb, suggest the always *already* queered position of the indigenous child, thereby challenging some of the mainstream thinking of queer theory. As the burning and killing of the Palestinian child Muhammad Abu Khdeir illuminates (see Chapter 3), the future belongs only to some children; it is 'the stuff of some kids' (Muñoz, 2009: 95). Yet the class dynamics within the settler colony, moving from the structure of *Avodah Ivrit* (see Chapter 2) to the construction of the figure of the legible Arab labourer father, activate hetero-paternal relations within the racial capitalist structure of the settler colony.

Palestinian feminists have long documented the ramifications of such institutional and quotidian management onto indigenous Palestinian bodies, particularly those of women and their everyday life in the settler colony. The

Conclusion 193

Zionist state comes to reside in our bedrooms by inflicting a constant fear of deportation from our families while simultaneously imposing native kinship orientations around the patriarchal modality of the nuclear unit (Shlahoub-Kevorkian, 2015). Decolonial queering builds on such methodological and theoretical contributions. Yet it also invites Palestinian and native feminists more widely to map the necessary linkage between gender and sexuality. In other words, what are the methodological implications of decentring hetero-normative sexualities when confronting patriarchy within the settler colony?

One answer offered through the pages of this book pertains to excavating modalities of homing and kinships that emanate from native queer locations within hetero-conquest paradigms. By historicising hetero-conquest, decolonial queering simultaneously entwines the urge to dig for past and present communal orientations, including—but not exclusive of—women to women forms of support, that could carry the potential for queering the nuclear family unit in the settler colony. In this regard, the labour of care that queer Palestinian work (see Chapter 5) produces animates a sense of native be/longing, where longing for other modalities of kinship—beyond the heteronormative and capitalist nuclear unit—helps reconstruct one's relation *within* the familial home. Decolonial queering invites us to challenge the centrality of the maternal/pregnant body to a Palestinian feminist epistemology. Its epistemological concerns resonate with those offered by queer indigenous feminists regarding the need to problematise heteronormative conceptions of native womanhood (Simpson, 2012). This, however, does not exclude the emancipatory and queering potential that maternal and pregnant women's bodies and intra-women relations offer to native queer/feminist epistemology.

Through analysis of alQaws and the aesthetic examples, I have argued that the injured sexual/gendered native body does not collapse to predominant identity signifiers and the political positioning they hold within the liberal West. Instead, to weave queerness in relation to the native subject position means transcending the subjectless stance of critical Middle East queer analysis. In other words, scholarly investment in decolonial/native queer *subjects* should simultaneously require the employment of queering methodologies as they historicise social formations in the settler colony. This book has done so by providing a queer reading of the Zionist logic of conquest while showing its ongoing erasure and regulation of natives through policies and discourses on LGBT freedom. It has captured the spatio-temporalising mechanisms of hetero-conquest and shed light on the historical location of an 'outside of time' and 'present absentee' *queered* Other (see Chapter 4). In this regard, tracing the journey of alQaws has been emblematic in showing the process of native self-recognition as Palestinian and queer.

Departing from an apolitical and single-issue LGBT organising, which was nonetheless Zionist, alQaws rejected the reality of peaceful violence the Oslo structure propagated. The objective force of a Palestinian Second Intifada interacted with subjects' self-(re)constitution according to the material and

194   *Conclusion*

symbolic terms encapsulating a queer Palestinian identification. Indeed, such an identification inscribes the politics of refusal. It counters sensual/political scripts including legal and socio-economic colonial institutions that mark a Palestinian native Other for disappearance and theft of their pain. Activists' anti-normalisation work challenges the material/hegemonic expansion of the settler colony through the sexual promulgation of settler spaces, i.e., Tel Aviv, and subjects, i.e., Michael Lucas and/or Netta Barzilai. Decolonial queering, therefore, reveals the value of counter-identifications as they capture native queer historical situated-ness within the anti-colonial political project. This refusal to allow 'a wedge between the self and one's wider society' (alQaws in Chapter 3) underpins the urge to push back on humanitarian norms repro-ducing saviour colonial tropes, while maintaining native other entrapment within an unequal exchange system. In countering the colonial ga(y)ze's sym-bolic construction of a victim (gay) Other, decolonial queering engages the material conditions instructing HuManist rescue tropes. Activists' refusal of US aid money along with the grassroots nature of the group's work reveals subjective unseen forces (Simpson, 2014) within Palestine that challenge the internationally backed NGO reality of peace and development. This allows us to re-evaluate leftist perceptions, in Palestine and beyond, of the group's location according to Euro-America's imposed notions of identity politics that are said to reify (neo)liberal and (neo)colonial futures of Palestine.

Second: Queering National Liberation

Palestine's national struggle for liberation takes central focus in queer Pal-estinian identification and work, which emanates from their historical sit-uatedness within the social formations discussed previously. Contrary to previous theses proposing queerness beyond the nation/al, this book pro-poses the productive engagement of queerness from the position of an ongo-ing native struggle for national liberation. Three intertwined implications are borne out of such an engagement. First, Palestine should no longer be approached—whether theoretically or in political praxis—within 'conflict' and 'co-resistance' paradigms, which perpetuate the amnesia of settler colo-nialism. Second, Palestinian queer positionality formulates a political project of liberation that refuses to normalise with the Zionist entity or its imperial-ist and reactionary allies in the region and beyond. Consequently, decolonial queering challenges the epistemic and political assumptions that tend to lock the indigene and her national political affiliations within the unproductive binarism of post/decolonial hybrids versus puritan natives (see discussions on Puar and Atshan in Chapter 3). Third, there is a need to centre anti-imperialist work and analysis vis-à-vis decolonial queering at the regional level. While I have only alluded to this point when discussing the queer Palestinian stance on Iraq's invasion, further inquiry on how decolonial queering is informed by anti-imperialist framework and nodes of solidarity in the region and the global South more broadly remain worthy.

Conclusion   195

By unsettling Zionist sexual/sensual regimes, decolonial queering not only undermines the colonial ga(y)ze, but also reveals epistemologies for national resurgence within that process. Indigene's artistic work can, in fact, redistribute the aesthetic terms suppressing alternative imaginations of the political conditions within the settler colony (i.e., Awad and Abu Asad's visual productions) and the imperial core (i.e., Knorn's performance in the United States). A queering aesthesis, therefore, captures native ghostly hauntings which reconfigure the aesthetic/political fields locking the natives within the psycho-political imperatives of failure and misrecognition. It produces forms of art and/or activism that expand the political value of Palestinian Sumud (steadfastness). By queering established national symbols, such as the olive trees and/or Handala figure, decolonial queer bodies and political productions operate in a twofold manner. They celebrate indigenous sensual ways of knowing and feeling in/of place; yet they reinvigorate a tradition of Sumud beyond the gendered/sexed relations that reify hetero-patriarchy within native communities. That is, rather than collapsing Sumud exclusively to the symbol of the (pregnant) woman that is rooted in the land, decolonial queering articulates it as a way of living, healing, and rebuilding relationships within oneself and the community. Through *hikaya*, the dances and melodies of its land and people, decolonial queering seeks a dialectic between resistance and re-existence to guide liberation, itself seen as a process and not a static event.

Decolonial queering is the labour of activist/artist that counters the violence reproduced within a project of self-determination whose statist epistemology for liberation is part and parcel of hetero-conquest. By challenging the pink-washing logic, activists and artists deconstruct the white saviour narratives towards queer racialised victims, presumed in the need of salvation from homophobic families and communities. At the same time, they reconstruct a native self from within, allowing resurgence beyond the forces reproducing the colonial logic of Manichean delirium (Fanon, 1967). Decolonial queering, therefore, makes room for self-affirmation that is consciously 'disorientated' (Ahmed, 2006) from the Other's colonising ga(y)ze by becoming, first and foremost, invested in recognising oneself. Through this double process of affirmation and critique, alternative modes of being and desiring arise beyond colonially inflicted configurations of emancipation and recognition (Coulthard, 2014). The Palestinian national project has succumbed to the solidification of colonised dismemberment within Nakba substructures. Its imagining of futural state-based recognition on territories captured in 1967 reinstantiated a 'Green line boundary' whose imposition of sub-identities and categories—embedded in colonial power subjectivisation—takes the Israeli presence for granted. Decolonial queering situates violence against queers and women in relation to how the colonised reproduce socio-economic and psycho-political forces reifying Nakba.

Questioning the native path for decolonisation is fundamental when it reproduces the very material and symbolic constituents that inform the

196 *Conclusion*

structure of its dispossession. For these reasons, this book engages those haunting (hi)stories of dancing bodies and queering murals 'rais[ing] spectres, and [it] alter[ing] the experience of being in time' (Gordon, 1997: xvi). Activists disorientations from LGBT happy fantasies haunt the present and futural reality of 'a state of Palestine' wrapped in happy family investments. By rearticulating the present through queering ghosts of the past (i.e., alQaws's re-narration of *auna* and *zajal* songs in Chapter 4) and future (i.e., Omar's futuristic uniform in Chapter 6), decolonial queering invokes a temporal unity that surpasses the linear logic of capitalist modernity. It is here that we can trace time in its becomingness, defined as the capacity to cultivate Otherwise possibilities.

In the follow up to the Palestinian popular uprising against a recent wave of assaults on native's being, from forced expulsion of Palestinians from their homes in Sheikh Jarrah to the latest aggression on the blockaded Gaza strip in May 2021, alQaws organised an online workshop series to think Palestine through the lens of queer politics. In one of the sessions, where I also contributed as a speaker, I asked participants to contemplate how queerness in Palestine can be approached via the idea of 'queering return.' Return has been, and continues to be, the key definition of what the Palestinian plight for liberation is about, capturing the idea of returning to lands and homes for one of the largest and longest-standing unresolved refugee groups in the world today. Return also encapsulates the native's own personal experience of growing up within an occupied land, seeing first-hand the violent mechanisms through which Palestinian dispossession takes place by virtue of stealing our lands/homes and devaluing our lives.

However, for me and other participants, return entails the constant tension between overcoming past defeats and reaching new beginnings. It is the painful and hard work of decolonisation that cannot be reduced solely to a present/futural event, holding the possibility of defeating the enemy and emerging triumphant once and for all. Rather, the very process of seeking return is much more vital, violent, and laborious because it carries the weight of those existential and ethical questions[2] defining the (im)possibility of the native's being. In one of his *I Have Found My Answers* essays, the late[3] engaged Palestinian intellectual, Basel Al-Araj (2018), explains the importance of what he calls the existential depression that defines Palestinian youth *hirak* (movement). Existential depression is a fundamental step for those who are in constant search of answers to the meaning of life at the individual and collective level (Ibid.: 216). It forces the colonised to find the strength and will of the imagination to move beyond the state of resignation that has come to define their (non)being. Participating in alQaws's spaces triggered my own confrontation with those questions (i.e., *what is queering return?*), enfolding the existential crisis from which the writing of this book has also proceeded. To queer return is to problematise certain stories and forms of belonging while excavating others that we can use to reconstruct the past and envision freedom for future returnees. For instance, Omar's

Conclusion 197

usage of queer refugee models (see Chapter 6) mocks the current statist trajectory of Palestine and challenges the current Oslo-impasse. Tarik's performance in the 'La La Land' city of Ramallah seeks to confront passers-by with the ideological and material conditions inscribing 'national loneliness.' Such artistic endeavours bear epistemic and political implications to think queerness in relation to a crisis of exile from oneself, community, and land.

The native dilemma of alienation (*ghurba*) is at the heart of what activist/ artists mostly grapple with. In fact, they all invite the reader to reflect together on their *ghurba* though the production of knowledge and critical pedagogies of healing and homing. Similarly, the narrations of activists' personal experiences with pain, depression, and loss not only serves to preserve a living archive of the bodily and sensorial experiences of native queer subjects, but also underlines that 'what's been concealed is very much alive and present, interfering precisely with those always incomplete forms of containment and repression' (Gordon, 1997: xvi). These interventions in the public sphere capture the indivisibility of a Palestinian decolonial futurity from its queer feminist roots. In their latest rally for liberation that followed the May 2021 uprising, activists' persistence in continuing to organise and take to the streets confirmed the political commitment of building on and expanding the revolutionary openings of a Palestinian Intifada. In distributing the posters of 'Palestine is for all of us,' activists unapologetically affirmed their place within the Intifada and celebrated the haunting presence of bodies and desires carving the way for a homecoming within a queer futurity, one that dares to imagine how to be truly free. Viewed from the lens of queer politics, decolonisation is a complex process which is not simply about a struggle for lands and labour but also for a continuous liberation of minds, practices, desires, and thus ways of being and becoming within oneself and the entire world.

Third: Towards Another International

Decolonial queering carves a directionality towards the yet-to-be inhabited world. Native liberation is an embodied experience, a conscious disorientation from the hetero-colonial forces suppressing the bodies that make them question (Fanon, 1967: 232). It is within colonised openness to divergent 'shades of meanings' that another humanism could be sought, as Fanon warned:

> Humanity is waiting for something other from us than such an imitation, which would be almost an obscene caricature. If we want to turn Africa into a new Europe, then let us leave the destiny of our countries to Europeans. They will know how to do it better than the most gifted among us. But if we want humanity to advance a step further, if we want to bring it up to a different level than that which Europe has shown it, then we must invent and we must make discoveries.
>
> (Fanon, 1963: 254)

198 *Conclusion*

Fanon's words resonate with the concerns voiced by Omar in Chapter 6. His fashion design confronts the PNA elites with their obscene caricaturing of colonial governmentality. At the same time, it unveils the possibility of seeking Other political/material fabrics gesturing towards a decolonial futurity that is yet to come. This book's engagement with artistic productions emanates from the power that art occupies in the process of imagining and inventing that Fanon speaks about. It has taken interest in aesthetic productions that signal for an Otherwise, inscribing the necessity of a queering aesthesis. That is, these performances, video, art, and photography from within decolonially situated aesthetic/political possibilities carry the seeds of delinking from the timeless humanism of the colonial aesthetic regime (Mignolo and Vazquez, 2013).

Queer Palestinian activism also unsettles this sensual regime and its promulgation in global politics. Their call for BDS solidarity targets international aesthetic productions—i.e., Eurovision and film industry, spectacles locking the native within the HuManist rescue frame. Furthermore, their critique of white-streamed narratives of sexuality rights comes hand in hand with building forms of transnational solidarity activism with groups like the DarkMatter collective, where collaborative production of decolonial queer art conjoins the work of political activism and campaigning against settler colonialism, imperialism, and capitalism. While the book discussed the importance of these forms of collaborative and solidarity work (see, for instance, Chapter 3), more research on this dimension could be useful in shedding light on the impact that anti-pinkwashing work carries internationally and within multiple spaces of the Global North and South contexts. For example, through my own experience in decolonising sexuality spaces, I have seen the important intersections with the kind of analysis offered in the context of Kashmir, as well as in the Turtle Island indigeneity context. In my view, these intersections offer a chance to expand analysis of pinkwashing within other forms of washings, such as red- and green-washing policies, widely employed by settler colonial and imperial powers.

This book has shown that Palestinian-led anti-pinkwashing analysis proceeds from a place that challenges the hegemony of the international ga(y)ze with regards to mainstream LGBT rights approaches. Decolonial queering, therefore, contests the liberal LGBT narratives, which seem to reproduce the hegemony of a queer international enfolding the same Euro-Humanism that Fanon opposed. Cynthia Weber (2016) posits a theory of queer international relations through the figure of the Eurovision singer Conchita Wurst that, as the argument goes, destabilises racial, sexual, gendered, and geopolitical binaries within European governance. Contrary to Weber, this book reads Eurovision from the call for boycott of native queers. In doing so, it gestures towards the value of a queering international from within their decolonial positionality and calls for justice. Thus, it challenges the hyper-focus on anti-binarism (beyond *either/or* logic) that queer post-structuralist critique tends to cultivate, watering down the value of the structural and anti-colonial

Conclusion 199

analytical stance. Indeed, much queer International Relations scholarship seems to have followed suit from feminist IR concerns whose famous 'where are the women?' (Enloe, 1990) question then translated into a 'where are the queers?' mantra (Hagen, 2016). While being presented and upheld as fundamental issues for universal agendas, these questions myopically zoom into the category of the women/queer and reveal the limitations found within liberal and state-oriented versions of a feminist/queer international. Their overwhelming investment in the visibility and protection of the woman/queer subject, often located in the Global South (post)conflict and/or state-building contexts, obscures not only the value of historicising 'conflict,' but also fails to capture the political praxis and subject position of those who search for humanity beyond 'the technique and style' of the colonial neoliberal governmentality order (Fanon, 1963: 311).

Decolonial queering posits the value of solidarity work that is committed to taking *pride* in the fight for 'abolishing settler states' and 'liberating indigenous land' (alQaws, 2021: n.p.). Activist/artist commitment to another international informs the disagreements and points of contention they carry with native Femocrats, who became part of the 'new set of policemen, bureaucrats, and merchants' (Fanon in Said, 2000: 450) that has proliferated within the Oslo structure. Recent confrontation between political activists, among them alQaws members, and the PNA regime has brought to the fore (Hammad, 2021) the tensions that decolonial queering bears with those Femocrats who have been employed to serve and work for the PNA security apparatus, whose gender mainstreaming programming is heavily funded by European and American powers (see for example Laub & Daraghmeh, 2014; EUPOL COPPS, 2019). At the same time, decolonial queering does not sit within the 'puritan political stance' that liberal queers articulate against it (Atshan, 2020). Activists, in fact, continue to utilise the very contradictions borne out of the Oslo liberal peace structure to navigate themselves infra-politically. That is, the PNA's framework of law and civil peace—including the signing off on international agendas for human/gender rights—becomes the very base to perform a politics of institutional legitimacy in the face of the PNA's oppressive power. This, however, comes hand in hand with the continued grassroots mobilising that the group initiates, including with other feminist collectives such as Tala'at, for organising beyond the current neo-colonial institutional frameworks. The politics and activism of the two groups are worthy of further exploration particularly in relation to how their mobilising of liberation strives for a decolonial cartography stretching from Palestine's *min al mayya lil mayya* (from the river to the sea) to the rest of the world. This is where queer feminist epistemologies for liberation bear the seeds of another international beyond the sexed/gendered/classed coloniality order of the border security of the modern nation-state.

Activists' anti-pinkwashing work not only maps the value of intersectional analysis in the Palestinian queer struggle but also cautions against the

200   Conclusion

coloniser's utilisation of these very terms (i.e., intersectionality and decolonialisation) to advance its version of humanism. For instance, during this latest round of aggression on Gaza, Eurovision was taking place with Israel contributing the song titled 'Set Me Free' performed by a Jewish Ethiopian woman (Eurovision Song Contest, 2021). If we take it at face value, we can see and almost appreciate the ways in which the fabric of Israeli society emerges as pluralist and democratic, perfectly captured by the figure of the woman of colour singing for freedom. While the colonising entity constructs itself in relation to the diversity it embodies in gendered/sexed/raced terms, Palestinian queers, privileged enough to dismiss the relevance of intersectionality and the anti-colonial framework of alQaws, seem to be increasingly given a central platform within the Zionist media. In a recent *Haaretz* opinion piece titled 'For Queer Palestinians Like Me, Intersectionality Isn't Working' Izat Elamoor (2021) writes that for the sake of promoting diversity and inclusivity, Palestinian queer spaces like alQaws should also enable normalisation and collaboration with LGBT Israelis. Decolonial queering confronts native reproduction of liberal diversity which illustrates native's psycho-social polarisation between homophobia and copy-pasting of the bourgeoise/colonial politics of inclusion (see Chapter 5).

Decolonial queering emanates from indigene's serious engagement with the question of decolonisation not as a metaphor (Tuck and Yang, 2021), but as something that needs constant excavation for hope, along with hard work on psycho-social and socio-political levels. This book has revealed that activists are in constant confrontation with settler colonial violence aimed at alienating the native from who she is first and foremost. The pain and layers of oppression that they deal with also become a site for colonial theft, and this discursive violence becomes materialised in the very policies of dispossession enacted upon the colonised. In other words, there is no such thing as returning Arab Palestinian but only Jewish absentee properties, rightfully restoring their native right to the land, particularly manifested in the settler movement of dispossession in places like Sheikh Jarrah. Similarly, there is no space for queers in Palestine, and so their only way of being is within and in relation to the democracy and humanism that the Zionist state and its imperialist allies embody. In challenging the political and social imperatives of 'my father wants to kill me/Israel is a democracy,' decolonial queering confront a colonial humanistic regime that shames the native and disables her being (see Chapter 5). Activists/artists understand the psychic and material implications of inheriting and reproducing the logics of shame/homophobia and humanism/democracy. And, for these reasons, they call to be and imagine beyond the structures of space, time, and sex that enable the continuity of a global (settler) coloniality order.

In such a context, research can either enable such a continuity or opt to interrupt the analytical frameworks and epistemic tools distributing imperial worldviews. Through the lens of a decolonial ethnography, this book has shown how native queering unsettles the compulsion to produce knowledge

Conclusion 201

within the ontological parameters of the international colonising ga(y)ze. The unsettling of such an ontological system does not merely bespeak a confrontation with concepts and their limitations. It crucially engages activist's/ artists' real and day-to-day struggles to build and construe possibilities within themselves, as Lorde explains:

> These places of possibility within ourselves are dark because they are ancient and hidden; they have survived and grown strong through darkness. Within these deep places, each one of us holds an incredible reserve of creativity and power, of unexamined and unrecorded emotion and feeling.
>
> (1984: 36–37)

Activists' affectual and poetic narratives mirror the incredible reservoir of creativity found within artistic productions that are channelling forms of being, sensing, and narrating oneself and social relations against the material power dynamics constraining queer decolonial futurity. Decolonial queering strives for theoretical and intellectual solidarities aiming to envision new forms of comparative and collaborative works and rethink decolonisation across multiple geographies and spaces, from Palestine to the rest of the world. Indeed, this book is a mere gesture towards future beginnings in relation to how we theorise decolonial queering and engage in decolonial queer politics and practices elsewhere. It is only a small corner in a larger web of activists/academics/ artists who are committed to imagining the value of a transnational decolonial queering world order. As Sandeep Bakshi, Suhraiya Jivraj, and Silvia Posocco elaborate on the value of decolonial queer theorising and praxis:

> Decolonial queerness entails querying the workings of neo-colonial epistemic categories, systems of classification and taxonomies that classify people. Queering coloniality and the epistemic categories that classify people according to their body configurations—skin colour and biological molecular composition for the regeneration of the species—means to disobey and delink from coloniality of knowledge and of being. At this intersection decolonial queerness is necessary not only to resist coloniality but, above all, to re-exist and re-emerge decolonially.
>
> (2016: 1)

To re-emerge decolonially requires the power of transnational collectives, of activists and thinkers whose aim is to unsettle 'entrenched hierarchies of our times' (Ibid.: 2). These hierarchies are found both in the realm of knowledge production, which too often assumes a European origin, and extend to current post/decolonial formations of racialised, gendered, sexed, and classed others. To bring queerness, thus, in conversation with decolonisation remains a necessary task, as well as a challenge from which the past, present, and futurity of our world can be reimagined differently.

202 Conclusion

Notes

1 See Chapter 2, Endnote 8.
2 Alluding to Basil Al Arjaj's engaged intellectual methodology of 'seeking and finding answers.'
3 On 6 March 2017, Basel was ruthlessly killed by Israeli troops in a house in al bireh-Ramallah; prior to that he was arrested and tortured by PNA regime.

Bibliography

Ahmed, S., 2006. *Queer Phenomenology: Orientations, Objects, Others*. Durham, NC: Duke University Press.

Al-Araj, B., 2018. *I Have Found My Answers: Thus Spoke the Martyr Basel Al Araj*. Jerusalem: Ribal Press.

alQaws, 2021. 'Abolish Settler State, Liberate Indigenous Land, Take Back Pride.' *Facebook Post*. Available at: www.facebook.com/AlQawsorg/photos/4374315909291758 (Accessed 22 December 2021).

Atshan, S., 2020. *Queer Palestine and the Empire of Critique*. California: Stanford University Press.

Bakshi, S., Jivraj, S., and Posocco, S. (eds.), 2016. *Decolonizing Sexualities: Transnational Perspectives Critical Interventions*. London: Counterpress.

Coulthard, G. S., 2014. *Red Skin White Masks*. Minneapolis: University of Minnesota Press.

Driskell, Q., Finely, C., Gilley, B., and Morgensen, S. (eds.), 2011. *Queer Indigenous Studies: Critical Interventions in Theory, Politics and Literature*. Arizona: The University of Arizona Press.

Elamoor, I., 2021. 'For Queer Palestinians Like Me, Intersectionality Isn't Working.' *HAARETZ*. Available at: https://www.haaretz.com/israel-news/2021-11-11/ty-article-opinion/for-queer-palestinians-like-me-intersectionality-isnt-working/0000017f-f63c-ddde-abff-fe7d99280000 (Accessed 22 December 2021).

Enloe, C., 1990. *Bananas, Beaches & Bases: Making Feminist Sense of International Politics*. Berkeley: University of California Press.

EUPOL COPPS, 2019. 'Palestinians to Raise Women's Participation in Security Sector to Double Digits.' *EUPOL COPPS News*. Available at: https://eupolcopps.eu/single-news/65/en (Accessed 22 December 2021).

Eurovision Song Contest, 2021. 'Eden Alene – Set Me Free – Live-Israel.' *YouTube*. Available at: www.youtube.com/watch?v=26Gn0Xqk9k4 (Accessed 22 December 2021).

Fanon, F., 1963. *The Wretched of the Earth*. New York: Grove Press.

Fanon, F., 1967. *Black Skin, White Masks*. London: Pluto Press.

Gordon, A., 1997. *Ghostly Matters: Haunting and the Sociological Imagination*. Minneapolis: University of Minnesota Press.

Hagen, J., 2016. 'Queering Women, Peace and Security.' *International Affairs* 92(2): 313–332.

Hammad, S., 2021. 'Nizar Banat Killing: Witnesses Recount Palestinian Authority's Violent Crackdown on Protests.' *Middle East Eye*. Available at: www.middleeasteye.net/news/palestine-nizar-banat-killing-violent-crackdown-protests-women-journalists-target (Accessed 22 December 2021).

Laub, K., and Daraghmeh, M., 2014. 'Palestinian Presidential Guard Unveils Its First Female Fighters—Headscarved Commandos Taking New Ground.' *The Independent.* Available at: www.independent.co.uk/news/world/middle-east/palestinian-presidential-guard-unveils-its-first-female-fighters-headscarved-commandos-taking-new-ground-9244604.html (Accessed 22 December 2021).

Lorde, A., 1984. 'Uses of the Erotic: The Erotic as Power,' in Lorde, A., *Sister Outsider: Essays and Speeches.* Trumansburg, NY: Crossing Press.

Meghani, S. A., and Saeed, H., 2019. 'Postcolonial/Sexuality, or Sexuality in "Other" Contexts: Introductiom.' *Journal of Postcolonial Writing* 55(3): 293–307.

Mignolo, W., and Vazquez, R., 2013. 'Decolonial AestheSis: Colonial Wounds/Decolonial Healings.' *Social Text-Periscope.* Available at: http://socialtextjournal.org/periscope_article/decolonial-aesthesis-colonial-woundsdecolonial-healings/ (Accessed 24 June 2021).

Muñoz, J., 2009. *Cruising Utopia: The Then and There of Queer Futurity.* New York: New York University Press.

Said, W., 2000. *Reflections on Exile and Other Essays.* London: Granta Books.

Shlahoub-Kevorkian, N., 2015. 'Israel in the Bedroom: Citizenship Entry Law,' in *Security Theology, Surveillance and the Politics of Fear,* edited by N. Shlahoub-Kevorkian. Cambridge: Cambridge University Press.

Simpson, L., 2012. 'Queering Resurgence: Taking on Heteropatriarchy in Indigenous Nation-Building.' Available at: https://blogs.cc.umanitoba.ca/mamawipawin/2012/06/01/queering-resurgence-taking-on-heteropatriarchy-in-indigenous-nation-building/ (Accessed 22 December 2021).

Simpson, A., 2014. *Mohawk Interruptus: Political Life Across the Borders of Settler States.* Durham, NC: Duke University Press.

Smith, A., 2005. *Conquest: Sexual Violence and the American Indian Genocide.* South End Press: New York.

Tuck, E., and Yang, K. W., 2021. 'Decolonization Is Not a Metaphor.' *Decolonization: Indigeneity, Education and Society* 1(1): 1–40.

Weber, C., 2016. *Queer International Relations.* Oxford: Oxford University Press.

Index

Note: Page locators in *italics* indicate a figure.

Abu-Rumailah, Muhammad 161
aesthetics: futural imaginaries, role
of 146; as occupying the senses 10;
politics and 16, 42, 87; unsettling
82–83
Aguda (Israeli National Association for
LGBT) 81, 115–116
Ahmadinejad, Mahmoud 88–89
Ahmed, Sara 9, 119–120, 175
Al-Araj, Basel 196
Al-Khatib, Omar 64, 134, *134*, 137,
147, 163
ala dalouna 98–100
alienation, sexual 113–114, 125, 164;
see also ghurba
alQaws for Sexual and Gender Diversity
in Palestinian: comics, release of
(*see tarwiha* comics); *ghanni a'an
al taa'riff* 94–95, 97; homing spaces
122–124, 139; prominent queer
grassroots organisation 2, 11, 51, 54;
reciprocity, establishment of 100, 125
Anani, Yazid 39
anti-normalisation 51, 61, 65, 194
anti-pinkwashing 11, 51, 58–60, 64, 73,
113, 198–199
Arafat, Yasser 36
Asad, Alaa Abu 15, 79, 84, 89, 104
Aswat: Palestinian Feminist Centre for
Gender and Sexual Freedoms 1
Atshan, Sa'ed 71–72
Audre Lorde Project (ALP) 67, 69
Awad, Nadia 80, 89

Bakshi, Sandeep 201
boycott, call for 15, 60, 168–169
boycott, divestment, sanctions (BDS)
51, 64–65, 198

capitalist elites 37
Christian: disdain 22
Christian: meta-narrative 83
colonial wound 9, 15
comics 165, 175; *see also tarwiha*
comics
COVID-19 1, 17n11

dabkeh (dance) 98–99
Dana, Tariq 62
dancers 91, 93
decolonial ethnography 11, 200
decolonial queer spaces 122, 200
decolonisation: politics of 16, 61, 67,
129; significance of 2–3, 7, 16, 72;
struggle, as a 5, 8, 10, 14, 21, 98,
118, 191; work of 15, 55, 72–73, 104
decolonising from within 15
decolonising sexuality 16, 146, 198
delinking 9, 53, 67, 170, 198
Demonstration, A (video) 80, *81*,
81–84, 104
Denetdale, Jennifer Nez 9
dispossession, native 25, 28, 58, 61, 161
divestment 51
duality 63
Duggan, Lisa 3

economic peace 37, 52, 174
Elamoor, Izat 200
ethnographic refusal 12
Eurovision 64, 198, 200

Fanon, Frantz 9, 120, 140, 197–198
fashion design, role of 10, 16, 84, 146,
176
Fatah (political party) 33, 36, 130, 185
femininity 24

Index 205

folk music 97–98
Friedman, Thomas 37
futural imaginaries 16, 146

ga(y)ze: colonial 42, 58, 67, 69–70, 72, 79, 89, 195; international 61, 73, 91, 100, 198; liberal 26, 28
Gay International 15, 71–72
gender: diversity 55–56, 97–98; experiences 146; expression 163; identity 127, 148, 163; orientation 123, 164; sexuality and 11, 14, 21, 68, 111, 126, 132, 138, 149, 188; violence 93, 126–128
ghurba (exile/alienation) 5, 15, 80, 101, 161, 188, 197
Global North 42, 51, 198
Global South 7, 194, 198–199
god trick 12
Goeman, Mishuana 9

Haaretz (Israeli newspaper) 85, 200
halutz (pioneers) 23–24, 28, 42
Handala (national symbol and personification of the Palestinian people) 137, 167–168, 195
happy family 38, 39, 41, 121, 139, 196
Haraway, Donna 12
Hassan-Nahoum, Fleur 112
Hawamesh (margins) 111, 126, 128, 140n1
hetero-conquest: defined as 7–8, 21, 26; peaceful violence 73, 86, 95; re-instantiation 28, 37, 41, 53–54, 112–113, 118, 139, 161, 169, 191; structure of 14–16, 28, 42, 65
heteropatriarchy 8, 31, 156, 170, 182, 186, 195
hikaya (story) 95, 97, 99, 101, 104, 195
Hilal, Ghaith 54, 56, 114
historic Palestine 23, 60, 66–67, 84, 87
Hochberg, Gil 4
Homonationalism 3–4, 6–8, 15; *see also* pinkwashing
homophobia: activism 72, 89, 200; persecution of gays 62–63, 65–66; violence and 113, 116, 118, 120
homophobic 10, 51, 89, 150, 156, 191; violence 54–56, 116; *see also* pinkwashing
HuManist 58, 70, 79, 86, 194, 198
HuManist (Human/Man) 58, 70, 79, 86, 198

illusionary presence 97
imperialism 59, 93–94, 198
indigene's return 122, 126
indigenous: conditions 101; culture 12, 91, 98, 100, 192, 195; feminist 191, 193; queering 7–8, 10, 122; resurgence 9
internalised pinkwashing *see* pinkwashing
international ga(y)ze 61, 73, 91, 100, 198
Intifada (uprising) 28, 133–138; first 14, 31, 98; Second 30, 44n14, 52–53
Iraqi people 63

Jankovic, Collen 83, 89
Jewish-Zionist 25, 57, 84

Kauanui, J Kēhaulani 9
keffiyeh (checkered black/white scarf) 1, 137
Khoury, Omar 55, 84
KKK (Ku Klux Klan) 82
Knorn Art 166
Knorn, Tarik: aesthetic/political framework of liberal colonialism 89–90; artistic dance 91, 92, 93–94, 104; satire 166, *167–168*, 169–171, 188
Kratsman, Miki 85–86, 88

LaBruce, Bruce 88
La La Land 16, 146, 173–175, 188, 197
LGBT: community 55, 80, 89, 94; liberal narratives 164, 169, 198; rights 51, 65, 115, 198
LGBTQ 2–3, 8, 14, 111–112, 115, 132, 169
liberal colonialism 89–91
Lorde, Audre 67, 70, 201
Louise, Louise 126

M.I.A. (artist/singer) 91, 93
Maikey, Haneen 11, 51–52, 60–61, 113–114, 127, 137
male- and state-making 16, 146, 176, 185–186, 188
Man and White 12
masculine (identity) 29–30, 130, 135, 180, 185
masculinity 24, 89, 98, 127, 135, 185
Massad, Joseph 11, 71–72
Masturbate bil Beit 88–89
masturbation, act of 88–89

206 Index

Mignolo, Walter 9, 105n6
Mikdashi, Maya 7, 59
minkom o feekom 97, 100
misrecognition 42, 53, 79, 104, 175, 195
Morgensen, Scott Lauria 6, 116
mourning ritual 91, 93
Muñoz, José Esteban 9, 60, 152

Nakba (Palestinian): as displacement/
destruction 8, 12, 21; structural
reality of 21, 23, 25–26, 54–55, 61,
104, 188, 191
nation-statism 32, 180
national liberation 9, 29, 113, 194
nationalism 3, 30–31, 59, 122, 127
native feminism *see* indigenous
native queer: reality of a 56, 64; refusal
15, 51; voice 51, 65
Ndlovu-Gatsheni, Sabelo 12
neocolonial 166
Neumann, Boaz 23–25, 28
normalisation 15, 33, 51, 61, 64–65,
73, 200

objectificationist 12
Ong, Aihwa 2
oppression: patriarchal 93; shame and
114, 157; structures of 4, 73, 85, 97,
114, 119–120, 164
Oslo Peace accords: establishment of
PNA 14, 21, 33, 35, 37, 52; sexuality
within 146, 168; structure of 38, 41,
100, 193, 199
Other: as barbaric 28; native 57, 65,
79, 104, 192, 194
Otherness 89
Otherwise Imaginings 9–10, 116, 133,
147, 188

Palestine Liberation Organisation
(PLO) 29, 33, 61, 98; clogs 178,
179–180
Palestinian feminist 1, 10, 126, 193
Palestinian National Authority (PNA):
Fatah-controlled government body
33, 36–37, 41; state building, imagery
of 176, 185 (*see also* Talismaic Shirt);
violence, use of 98, 112, 114, 128
Palestinian queer: activism 3, 11, 15,
42; movement 1–2, 63, 72; work 5, 7,
14, 51, 65, 71
Palestinian queer movement 1–2, 63, 72

patriarchy 9, 51, 67, 126, 137, 193;
see also heteropatriarchy
photographer 85–86
photography 79, 84–85
Photowar Project 86
pinkwashing: agenda 112–113;
countering 55–56, 59–60 (*see also*
anti-pinkwashing); internalized 15,
118–121, 169; narratives 3–4, 26,
89–90; policies/practices 14, 58,
61, 63
pinkwatching 51, 55, 59–60
power structures: colonial 2, 8–9, 61;
dominant 59, 120; oppressive 180,
188
Puar, Jasbir 3–4, 7, 59
pusspuss 166, *167*, *168*, 168–170, 175

queer: emotionality 157, 165–166;
failure 151; futurity 197; haunting
95, 97; *hikaya* (story) 95, 97, 99, 101,
104, 195; liberalism 3, 5–6, 8, 26
queering: aesthesis 10, 15, 79, 82, 95,
100, 102, 104, 195; decolonial (*see*
decolonisation)
queer politics: homosexuality and
112; Israeli boycott 168; lack of
engagement 2; native 51, 56, 70,
191–192

Rabin Square 80, 84
Rallying Cry for Queer Liberation, A
1, 16n1
Rancière, Jacques 10
Rawabi (promised city) 38–39, *40*, 119
Razack, Sherene H. 57
recognition: of self (*see self-
recognition*); of sexual identities 14,
116; of statehood (Palestinian) 33,
35, 37–38
refusal: ethnographic 12; native queer
51; politics of 9, 51, 61, 68, 194
Ritchie, Jason 3, 16n7
Roy, Ananya 2

Safiah, Ayman 15, 79, 102–104
sanctions 51
satire 166, 169
Sedgwick, Eve 97
self-determination 28, 112, 139, 185,
191, 195
self-recognition 42, 51, 61, 64, 73,
193

Index   207

selfhood (Palestinian) 16, 146–147, 165, 188
sensual regime 15, 42, 79, 82, 100, 104, 195, 198
settler colonialism: amnesia of 6, 104, 194; history of 5–6, 42
settler rescue-empathy 57–58
settler sovereignty 64, 73
sexual: freedom 118–119; identity 14, 132; oppression 6, 59, 114, 118, 133, 139; orientation 52, 116, 118, 121, 124, 127; pluralism 15, 64, 79, 84, 104; violence 114, 126, 128, 135
Shalhoub-Kevorkian, Nadera 10
Shihade, Magid 65
Simpson, Audra 73
social: change 11, 90, 121, 125; media 57, 95, 111–112, 126, 130, 137; minority 6; violence 111, 114; workers 124–125
sovereignty 9–10, 94, 118
spatio-temporal paradigms 27, 42, 193
strangeness 97

Talismanic Shirt 176, *177*, 178, 180
tarwiha comics 146–147, 188
Tel Aviv Pride 60–61, 64
terror 62
terrorism 3, 37, 39
Tuhiwai Smith, Linda 11–12
turath (heritage) 98–99, 101, 104

Vazquez, Rolondo 105n6
visual representation 148

Weber, Cynthia 198
Weir, Shelagh 183
Wurst, Conchita 198

xenophobia 62

Zaatry, Haya 95
Zionism: sexual representation 30, 53; transformation (Jewish) 22–24, 117
Zionist: configuration of sex and sense 15, 79, 84, 88, 104; settler colonialism 4–6, 25, 98, 104

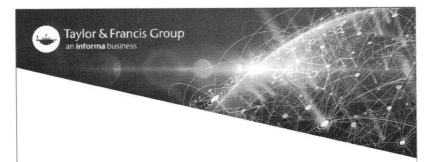

Printed in the United States
by Baker & Taylor Publisher Services